After the Parade

After the Parade

BILL LEHMANN

Copyright © 2015 Bill Lehmann
All rights reserved.
ISBN: 13: 978-1502814005
ISBN-10: 1502814005

ACKNOWLEDGEMENTS

As a newspaperman I have lived an interesting and fulfilling life. Everyone has help along their journey in business and in life and two men were responsible for allowing me the opportunities I have enjoyed.

Ted F. Chase as advertising manager of the Muskogee (OK) *Phoenix-Times Democrat* took a chance on a skinny 19-year old kid who thought he could sell advertising. Turned away several times, persistence finally paid off. Chase relented when told I would wear a hat to make me look older and perhaps more respected by the business clients I would face. I wore the hat and had success, but when I left, Chase said, "Take off the hat. You don't look good in it anyway!"

A tall, distinguished man, with a pencil-line mustache, Chase cut a handsome figure is his gray and black pinstripe suits. His body motion just seemed to flow as he walked. He placed my desk next to his to give me vital sales development.

Jarrell L. Jennings was a vice-president of the Donrey Media Group, a conglomerate of newspapers, television stations and outdoor advertising properties in seven states. There were ten daily newspapers in the Oklahoma division. When our local owner-publisher died, Donrey purchased the Pawhuska (OK) *Daily Journal-Capital* newspaper. I was serving there as business manager. Jennings named me publisher-general manager of the newspaper, opening a whole new world of experience and opportunity. One year later Jennings asked me to transfer to the *Guthrie (OK) Daily Leader*. Guthrie offered new and exciting opportunities that I accepted with enthusiasm.

Standing six feet five inches tall with flaming red hair and mustache, Jennings had a deep, commanding voice. Jennings was the elephant in the room. You couldn't miss him. A good friend and mentor, I will forever be grateful to J.L. Jennings.

Thank you, gentlemen. May you rest in peace.

I also acknowledge with gratitude my niece, Janis Thomas Cramer, who so willingly assisted me in preparing this book for publication.

And to my son Gene Lehmann, and dear friends Kip Stratton and Esther Waner my gratitude for their encouragement to undertake the project and introduce you to a cast of some unforgettable characters.

TABLE OF CONTENTS

Laredo
Crusading Texas Publisher   3
Segura and "Beelee Boy"   7
Pressroom Pinups   11
Washington's Birthday Celebration   12
Viva Village Girls   13

Ponca
Clyde Muchmore and Sons   17
Two Rich Men Build Ponca City   20
Gus McDonald, Fancy Dancer   29
Remarkable T. J. Cuzalina   32
Entertainment Committee   35
The Tallywhackers   36
Wayward Garters   37
The Goose Hunting Farmer   38

Pawhuska
Sally's   43
Unlikely Champions   67
Jim Slick—Jailbird, Guitar Picker, Friend   74
Old Black Joe   77
The Unloaded Gun   80
Klansmen Meets His Match   83

Guthrie
Coffee Clubbers' Bull Meat Dinner   87
Genuine American Success Story   89
Five Shots, Five Birds   91
Elbert Clymer, the Mushroom Man   96
Moonshine or Formaldehyde?   99

Breathtaking Moonshine	101
Best Friends	103
Secret to a Long, Healthy Life	104
"They Will Remember Paul Kroeger"	106
Harvey's Terrapin Pointing Birddog	109
The Blown-Up Toilet	110
The Glocks	111
The Building Collapse	113
Stolen Safe Recovered	115
Stowaway Cat	116
The Vencedora	117
Lost Bird Dog	120
Stolen Bird Dog	122
Cahill's Dairy Maid Drive In	124

Oil Field

POBOCO—Poor Boys Oil Company	129
Croton Oil Company	138
The Thumb Box	143
The Exhibitionist	146
CB Radios	148
The Day the Big Rig Stopped Turning	151
Lunch at the Chinese Restaurant	152

Newspapers

John Lewis Stone-Fighting Editor	155
The Guthrie Daily Leader: News Town!	160
By the Way	169
Raymond Fields, Publisher and Patriot	174
The Great Escape	185
Responsibility	188
Astronaut Balls	189
Secret Stash of Cash	190

History
The Strange Case of Elmer McCurdy	195
Wild Bill Posey	204
Where in the World Are You, Max Lehmann?	228
Max Lehmann's Lament	235

Guthrie History
Bicentennial Outlook—Guthrie Awakens	241
Joseph Foucart, Father of Guthrie's Skyscrapers	251
The Guthrie Restoration Leaders	265
Ralph McCalmont	266
Guthrie Restoration Program	270
Guthrie Saloons Ran Wild in Territory	282

My Parade of Unforgettable Characters
Hilda walked the Mile in Different Shoes	289
Walt Harris, Indian Artist	295
Fred Olds, Artist and Sculptor	300
Paul Parkers' Maverick Champ Steer	306
Duffy Martin's Fart Box	310
Willis Warren, Answering God's Call	314
Rosemary's Pets	317
Roger Van Kyke, Small in Size, Big in Heart	321
Carl Albert Makes a Special Visit	324

Musicians
Becoming a "Musician"	329
The Country Gentlemen	335
My Second "Career" in Music	338
Musician Friends Remembered	343
Bud Smith, Logan County's Music Man	349
Fronting Tommy Collins	353
Booger Red's	357
A Lesson in Dedication and Perseverance	362

FOREWORD

"A full 8 seconds and then some!"

In rodeo jargon I have had a helluva ride! I came out of chute number two aboard a wild-ass bronco named "Life" and rode that sucker for the full eight seconds. I had such a deep seat that I rode him twisting and turning for another two, raked his flanks with my spurs, whooped him across the ears a couple of times with my hat before jumping off, standing up to the cheers of the people who counted most—my friends and family.

My ride on Life began when I entered the newspaper business. It is difficult for me to imagine a more interesting career. I never made much money but realized an abundance of wealth in meeting interesting people and events along the way. The newspaper is a busy and fascinating place. You are among the first to know when things happen—mundane or monstrous! There was never a day in my career that I was not eager to go to work.

While aboard Life, I've sipped fine wine and dined on steak and lobster tail swimming in melted butter atop the ritziest restaurants to drinking Jack Daniel's on the rocks in sleazy barrooms, playing bass in country music bands. Pretty tall cotton for an Okie from Muskogee who doesn't know the difference between an adverb and a proverb! But I guess I faked it pretty well and have been just damn lucky! In any event, I had a high perch atop Life, and the higher I went, the sweeter the breeze!

Successes were many. The dedication of my colleagues at the *Guthrie Daily Leader* allowed me to associate with national and state preservationists, state political leaders and civic affairs. We actively campaigned for museums, school improvements, libraries, airport expansion and fire equipment and worked to provide housing for elderly and low income families. Things a newspaperman is supposed to do.

I was appointed chairman of the museum study committee by the Guthrie City Council and acted as liaison between the City of Guthrie, philanthropist Fred Pfeiffer, and the Oklahoma Historical Society in bringing two museums to Guthrie. Through this connection I worked with national and state preservationists, associated with Oklahoma state governors and U.S. Senators, and became good friends with U.S. Speaker of the House of Representatives, Carl Albert, third in line for the Presidency of the United States. None of this would have been realized outside of my newspaper career.

Along the ride I got to know some other very different, unusual and interesting people. There were cowboys, Indians, drunks, teetotalers, artists, musicians, war heroes, bulldozer operators, oil field roughnecks, bank presidents, bartenders, and barflies. I hope you enjoy reading about some of the interesting personalities.

My ride on Life is over. Interesting people are out there to be enjoyed and written about by others. It is time for Life and me to go to pasture. I'll give him an extra ear of corn and a sugar cube or two, pat him on the nose, and tell him what a wonderful ride we had together.

I have been one lucky son of a gun!

Laredo

International bridge over Rio Grande River between Laredo, Texas, and Nuevo Laredo, Mexico.

CRUSADING TEXAS PUBLISHER

William Prescott Allen was a newspaperman, sometimes reporting the news and sometimes making news headlines himself!

As publisher of the *Laredo, Texas Times*, Allen carried on a crusade for decades to improve relations between the United States and Mexico. He traveled extensively in Mexico becoming close friends with Mexican government officials including several presidents of Mexico. Allen was a close personal friend of Miguel Aleman, one of Mexico's most popular presidents. He was also a friend of U.S. President Dwight D. Eisenhower.

Allen was the first recipient of both the Order Of the Aztec Eagle and the Military Order of Merit awarded him by the Mexican government in October 1942. Officials of both countries attended the ceremonies honoring Allen. Many considered Allen to be the unofficial U.S. ambassador to Mexico and he had the ears of the Mexican government. He also received personal honors from Pope Pius XII and the Knights of Columbus during his career.

Allen released from jail

William Prescott Allen was born in Olympia, Washington in 1896. He left home at age 16, traveling from New Jersey to Florida in newspaper circulation jobs until settling in San Antonio, Texas where he became the circulation director of the San Antonio *Express* and the *Austin American Statesman* in the U.S. and Mexico, working both sides of the border. He bought an interest in the *Laredo Times*, eventually becoming full owner. Newspapers in

Montrose, Colorado, and Juneau, Alaska, were later added to his ownership.

I was in the advertising department of the *Laredo Times* in the early 1950s and had close contact with Allen most every day. He was friendly to all the employees, but especially those in advertising and circulation. He observed me making an advertising layout one day and inquired if it had been sold. I told him the layout was being made to present to the advertiser as an idea for sale and publication. I explained I preferred to have a presentation for the customer to hold in their hand instead of just listening to a sales pitch. "That's great," he told me, "the more of those you tear up the more you will sell." Allen was a businessman in addition to his crusading interests.

Allen always had visitors in his office. Many people from Mexico were frequent visitors as well as businessmen, politicians and many of obviously questionable character. He was a busy man and never was idle. When not in his office he was traveling to Mexico or visiting one of his other newspapers in far flung places. When not in town the newspaper was supervised by a nephew, Allen Tish.

The *Laredo Times* published two inside pages in Spanish daily to attract readers in the sister city across the Rio Grande River in Nuevo Laredo, Mexico. The *Laredo Times* was the voice of South Texas and had a large circulation in both Texas and Mexico. The managing editor was a small man of Irish ancestry named Tim Green. Green was very valuable to the paper because he was fluent in Spanish and wrote in Spanish as well. Few had the abilities of a Tim Green. But Green had an alcohol problem that surfaced about every six months. Green was sober for months but when the alcohol urge struck, he would go to Mexico where he would be drunk for two weeks before sobering up and coming back home. Tim would suddenly appear back to work at the newspaper as if he had just gone home the night before. Allen would come in and find Green at his desk and fire him immediately.

Allen would stand at Green's desk, raising his arm, pointing his finger to the door and in a loud voice shout "Out! Out! I never want to see you again!" Green would leave, but his wife and three small children would be at the paper in minutes begging Allen to reconsider his action of firing Green. "Please, Mr. Allen," she would plead with tears streaming down her eyes, "we have three children who depend on him. Please take him back." Allen would tell her the paper depended on him as well and it was difficult to produce the Spanish edition when he was not there to edit the paper. She would plead again and again telling Allen that Green would mend his ways. Allen would finally relent and hire Green back. The same scenario would be repeated in another six months.

In 1956, Allen began a series of editorials claiming widespread gambling, and "a syndicate" in Tarrant County, Texas, was conducting other illegal activities. Payoffs were being made to city, county and state officials that stretched all the way from Fort Worth to the state capital at Austin. The editorials continued for months and got the attention of the Associated Press and United Press International wire services, which picked up on the allegations and fed them to other Texas state media. Allen never identified the recipients of the payoffs, but the editorials angered public officials in Tarrant County. Finally tiring of the charges Tarrant County officials issued a subpoena to Allen to testify before a grand jury about his knowledge of the syndicate and the payoffs.

Allen appeared before the grand jury and was defiant about his sources, refusing to name names or incidents of payoffs. The jury was dismissed for the day and the judge sentenced Allen to jail for contempt of court. Allen then relented and told the judge he would reveal all to the jury. The judge ruled it was not possible to reconvene the jury that day and sentenced Allen to spend the night in jail and fined him the maximum $100 fine. He was issued striped jail coveralls and lodged in a cell with 15 other prisoners who had committed misdemeanors and were awaiting trial.

Allen's jailing prompted some 45 publishers of daily newspapers in Mexico to protest to the U.S. Embassy in Mexico City Allen's detainment in the Fort Worth jailhouse. The protest deplored the action against "the upright publisher William Prescott Allen, which fills us with sadness because it happened in that great country which is the champion of democracy, freedom of expression and of a free world." The protest by the Mexican publishers had no effect on the judge, who was intent on lodging the contempt charge against Allen.

Appearing before the grand jury the next day, Allen told jurors that the editorials and charges were based on an anonymous letter he had received. He did not know the author of the letter and had no knowledge of the officials taking payoffs or who the syndicate might be. It is possible Allen had sources but refused to identify them since proof could not be produced. The judge returned the $100 dollar fine and released a professionally deflated Allen.

A still defiant Allen told the judge as he left the courtroom that he was on a crusade to "purify" Texas. "I regard the gambling in this area as a sideshow," he said. "The big picture is Austin. I'm interested in cleaning up the state government. But if you let state officers in one area get corrupt, it spreads throughout the state," he concluded.

One lawyer commented that to "purify Texas" would require the return of Jesus Christ on Judgment Day. "And even HE would require a lot of help!" the lawyer said.

SEGURA AND "BEE-LEE BOY"

I liked Segura from the moment I first met him. Two opposites if ever there was a pair!

Segura was all Mexican, short, thin and obviously from ancient Aztec ancestry. He had jet-black hair, bulging eyes and a toothy grin that seemed to always be on his face. Smelled of garlic. He spoke very broken English.

I was a tall, skinny, white gringo, and spoke no Spanish at all. If I did it would have been in an Okie dialect he couldn't understand anyway. We were a couple of opposites for sure. He called me "Bee-lee Boy."

We met in 1951 when I had gone to work for the *Laredo, Texas Times*. Laredo was then a community of 50,000 located on the Rio Grande River. Probably 90 percent of the population was Hispanic. Across the river was Nuevo Laredo, Mexico, a city of 100,000 and perhaps all Mexican nationals. Laredo was mostly modern with a prosperous downtown business district and had nice residential homes. Nuevo Laredo had a nice city section the tourists saw, but had a large section of squalor and poverty.

The *Laredo Times* served both communities and had a large circulation in Mexico. Two inside middle pages were printed in Spanish in every issue. I worked in the advertising department, selling and servicing the advertising accounts. Segura was an artist, doing sketches of personalities featured in the news section of the paper. He also did some editorial cartoons and was a master of creating caricatures, an exaggerated image of their facial features, but unmistakably recognizable as the individual portrayed.

His name was Porfirio Segura Castro. He lived on the Mexican side of the border and did oil painting portraits as well as his cartoon features for the *Times*. He was gifted at oil painting as well and the likeness of his subjects appeared so real they could begin talking to you from the canvas. They called him Segura and that is the name he used to sign his artwork. Oh, how I envied and was in awe of his talent.

Segura was originally from Mexico City and his mother and younger sister still lived there. His father was a conductor on a passenger train and had been shot to death in the late 1920s by a gang of train robbers during a train robbery. Segura faithfully sent his family money with every paycheck.

He had once worked for the Walt Disney Studios in Los Angeles, but spent his entire time with Disney on Donald Duck projects. The pay was minimal but Segura said all artists would almost pay the Disney company to have Walt Disney Studios on their resume. He grew tired of drawing "Pato Pasquel," as Donald was known in Mexico. He finally gave up working for Disney, moved back to Mexico doing freelance and portraits.

Segura was somewhat the Norman Rockwell of Mexico with occasional front cover paintings on *Todo*, a nationally circulated magazine of Mexico. He told me he had to go into hiding following one of the humorous *Todo* covers showing a Mexican policeman brushing his teeth getting ready to put the "bite" on the public, portraying kickbacks.

Segura wanted to show me the sights and sounds of Nuevo Laredo and to treat me to some "genuine" Mexican food instead of the Tex-Mex variety of Texas. We went to a nice restaurant and ordered a quail dinner. The menu also listed a variety of mixed drinks available. Gosh, there must have been two dozen. Growing up in "dry" Oklahoma, I had never drunk anything but moonshine or bootleg whiskey. Rosemary and I had moved to Sherman, Texas and it was even drier than Oklahoma! You couldn't even buy a beer in Grayson County, Texas.

With all the variety of mixed drinks available I thought I should try one of each to determine which one I liked best. I tried a margarita, whiskey sour, martini, a Manhattan, and a tequila sunrise. I was soon drunk on my ass before I realized it. There was no way I could drive us back to the Texas side of the border. Segura decided he would drive us so he took the wheel of my 1948 canary yellow Plymouth convertible. The car had a standard shift transmission that Segura had never driven before. We took off in jerks, jerks and more jerks. The top was already down and I became sick from all that booze. I hung my head over the side of the car every once in a while to puke. Segura had no driver license —Mexico or Texas. It's a wonder we made it out of Mexico and another miracle we made it across the International Bridge to the Texas side without being arrested. But it was a different time. Lesson learned. I quickly knew scotch or bourbon on the rocks was the best drink for me. No more ruining good whiskey with sweet crap!

Summertime can be hot in Laredo, Texas!

Rosemary and Cathy also took up with Segura right away. He visited and had dinner with us often. We made a few trips into Mexico. Once across the Mexican desert from Nuevo Laredo to Monterrey, some 150 miles south. Monterrey was one of the most modern cities in Mexico at the time. We thought it looked like Tulsa back in Oklahoma. In Monterrey we visited a resort called Horsetail Falls in the mountains, a part of the Rockies that stretches north into the United States and Canada. It was another world up there: lush greenery, a forest of trees and the beautiful falls.

After a couple of years in Laredo, Rosemary and I became somewhat homesick to see family and the trees and lakes we were accustomed to in Oklahoma. William Prescott Allen, publisher of the *Times* did not want me to leave the newspaper, but after knowing a change was imminent offered me jobs on newspapers he owned in Montrose, Colorado, and Juneau, Alaska. We relocated to Ponca City, Oklahoma. Segura and I kept in contact by mail from time to time.

One day I received a letter from Segura telling of a trip he would be making from Mexico to Washington, D.C. He was to show some of his paintings in an exhibit. He said he would make a side trip and come to Ponca City where he would visit with us before going on to the nation's capital. His bus arrived early at the Ponca City bus station. I was not there to greet him, so he checked into a hotel above the bus station building. I went up and had to rescue him from a whore that had him cornered in the hallway.

Checking him out we went to our house where he stayed for a couple of days before moving on.

Segura thought Cathy was very pretty and decided to do an oil painting of her while he was visiting. I liked to paint myself and had needed supplies on hand. He painted a likeness of Cathy on an 8x10 canvas that looked so real you would expect her to begin talking to you. Then suddenly he took a rag and wiped off the image before I could stop him. He wasn't satisfied with the result, he said, and would do one another time.

Sadly, another time never came. Segura went on to Washington D.C. and I never heard from him again.

PRESSROOM PINUPS

The *Laredo, Texas Times* pressroom looked like a pinup gallery! Large, double page foldouts of skimpily clad women graced about every square inch of the four walls in the pressroom. All the photos showed the ladies in some bikini attire. The year was 1951, and before the birth of *Playboy* and *Hustler* magazines that took off even the bikini and held nothing back. The display would have been offensive to visitors who might enter the pressroom.

Manuel Rodriguez was the head pressman. He was brought up in the old school of printers who thought it was bad luck for women to enter the back shop of the newspaper. It was okay if they were just pictures of women without any clothes on, however.

Occasionally a Boy Scout or Girl Scout group or adult groups might want to visit the newspaper to observe the operation in action. It was particularly interesting to be present during the press run to hear the noise of the press and see the papers coming off, being folded in the folder and bundled for delivery. These groups had to give the paper a 24-hour notice to allow Rodriguez time to cover all his naked ladies with long sheets of newsprint.

After the press run and exit of visitors, all the newsprint came down and his ladies were exposed again for the pressroom crew to enjoy!

WASHINGTON'S BIRTHDAY CELEBRATION

If you believe the largest Washington's Birthday Celebration would be held in Washington, D.C. you'd be wrong!

It's in, of all places, **_LAREDO, TEXAS!_**

The month-long celebration begins January 23 and concludes February 22 with a giant parade and a large fireworks display. Participants and celebrants come from both sides of the Rio Grande River.

This is nothing new—it was started in 1898!

Several hundred thousand visitors attend the special events during the month. Women dress in beautiful colonial gowns with layered petticoats that Martha Washington never dreamed of. Men wear colonial dress with leggings and stockings and wear white, powdered wigs!

Mexican citizens and Texans of Hispanic ancestry join the Anglos, and are all a part of the festivities as well. There are Mariachi bands and traditional Mexican dress and dance with beautiful embroidery and fancy sombreros, women in lovely gowns and mantillas. And there is a big jalapeno festival and pepper-eating contest for those with iron stomachs. All this mixed in with a big Colonial Ball and dance of George (or Jorge) Washington's time period.

They call it Washington's Birthday Celebration, but it is one big Mardi Gras with plenty of beautiful floats and Mardi Gras type figures to mix in with the colonial theme.

It is just one big party in Laredo, Texas!

VIVA VILLAGE GIRLS!

In 1952 there was big doings happening in Laredo, Texas and surrounding area. Marlon Brando had come to town with a movie production and they were filming *Viva Zapata.* The story line was about a Mexican revolutionary operating between 1909 and 1919. Brando was the star along with Jean Peters, the female lead.

Brando was not well known at the time—his fame would come later. But in the cast was Anthony Quinn, of Mexican ancestry. Quinn was the star of the show to the folks of the area who flocked around him on his visits off camera. He visited the bars in Nuevo Laredo, Mexico, and always had a large entourage of followers. And they partied hardy!

I was working for the *Laredo Times* and curiosity got the better of me, and a couple of us went to location to watch the proceedings. I had no idea who Marlon Brando was at the time, but had seen Anthony Quinn in many movies and liked him. They had several filming locations in and around the area. One location was a river scene and a location had been established on the Rio Grande River near the little town of Roma, Texas, just south of Laredo. Every day at 2 p.m. a group of girls on the Mexican side of the river came down, took off all their clothes and went swimming and wading in their birthday suits. Filming had to stop during this interval because this activity was not a part of the script.

Anthony Quinn and Marlon Brando in "Viva Zapata."

The producer-director of the movie tried to get the girls to leave the area several times, but to no avail. They giggled and kept on swimming and wading in the buff! The director then went to the mayor of the little Mexican town seeking his assistance in curtailing the activities of the naked girls. Everyone on both sides of the river had been very cooperative with the movie crew in providing their wishes. But the Mexican mayor told them it was a tradition that been going on for centuries and the movie company could just go somewhere else if they didn't like it. The movie company then installed a "siesta time," and called off filming until the next day. The tradition continued, this time with a larger audience of onlookers after word spread of the girls and the swimming hole.

Anthony Quinn won an Oscar as best supporting actor in the film. Brando's Oscars were yet to come. The unscripted parade of Mexican girls swimming in the nude lay on the cutting room floor and never made it to the movie.

Ponca City

Pioneer Woman Statue, Ponca City, Oklahoma

BILL LEHMANN

CLYDE MUCHMORE AND SONS

One of Oklahoma's most respected publishers was Clyde Muchmore of the *Ponca City News*. His sons, Allan, who was business manager, and Gareth, who was editor of the paper, assisted him in the management of the newspaper. Gareth had been an Associated Press reporter and correspondent during World War II, but had come back to Ponca City to manage the news operation. It was a good team and the *Ponca City News* was a strong voice in northern Oklahoma with impressive circulation figures.

Clyde Muchmore had come down to Ponca City from Kansas in the 1920s to partner with Lew Wentz, a Ponca City oilman who had made a fortune from the Three Sands oil discovery west of Ponca City. Wentz was a stalwart Republican and was intent on establishing a strong Republican voice in Oklahoma's political affairs by buying several small daily newspapers with his new wealth. Muchmore was a Republican as well but limited his political views to the editorial pages. The paper supported most Republican candidates for state offices but seldom won in a (then) strong Democratic state. County officials were usually Republican because northern Republicans settled the northern half of Oklahoma with the opening of Oklahoma Territory for settlement in 1893.

Clyde Muchmore

Muchmore was not timid in his support of local issues. He once wrote an editorial on the death of an Oklahoma outlaw from neighboring Osage County. Muchmore claimed the death of Henry Grammar was the end of an era of horse and cattle thefts, gambling, bank robberies and other outlaw activities in the area.

Grammar's death would not be grieved by law abiding citizens Muchmore said in his editorial, and Grammar's death was really good riddance. An associate of Grammar's showed up in Muchmore's office one morning following the editorial, closed the door, placed a chair under the knob preventing entry from outside and proceeded to give Muchmore a lashing with a quirt horse whip.

Clyde Muchmore was always available to visit with employees and I enjoyed many sessions with him. The newspaper had a rowboat that was moored at Lake Ponca. The oars to the boat were kept in a locked shed next to the boat. The boat was available for employees to use and Muchmore kept the keys to the oars in his desk. He delighted in handing over the keys saying, "here are the keys to the oar house," and then he would burst out in laughter.

A bond issue the newspaper had supported failed to pass in an election. I asked Mr. Muchmore why he thought the issue failed to pass with the voters. "Well, Bill," he observed, "I have found in all my newspaper career that you will have fifty percent of the people's support on issues all the time, but they will never be the same fifty percent on every issue. Some times you need that extra one percent" I have always remembered his observation and found it to be true even today.

Allan Muchmore ran a tight ship with finances as general manager. He also was business manager for radio station WBBZ, owned by the Muchmore's and Wentz. Gareth was a very solid newsman and directed all the news functions of the paper. He was married to a much younger woman who was a member of the news staff. They had met in New York City when Gareth was with the Associated Press bureau. She had been a personal assistant to Dick Cavet, a network radio and television talk show host before her marriage to Gareth.

Allan Muchmore

Gareth also had a penchant for hunting and went to Colorado every fall on elk hunts. He also loved horses and horseback riding. A riding accident occurred one day when one of the reins dropped. Gareth bent over to retrieve the rein, the horse spooked and jerked its head back abruptly striking Gareth in the face. Several bones in his face were broken in the incident causing him to lose an eye.

Gareth was a good friend of an aging Joe Miller of the famous Miller Brothers 101 Ranch Wild West Show that traveled the world. Miller still lived in the "White House" ranch headquarters west of Ponca City. Muchmore had a strong interest in the history of the Old West and the 101 Ranch. In its heyday of 1890-1929, the Miller Brothers sent their show of cowboys, Indians, rodeos, stagecoach races and exotic animals to worldwide places. They even performed for the king and queen of England. Gareth's visits with Miller were subjects of stories written by Muchmore for the newspaper.

Gareth Muchmore

With the death of Muchmore's partner, Lew Wentz, Muchmore became full owner of the newspaper. The *Ponca City News* is one of very few daily newspapers in Oklahoma remaining in local family ownership. Sadly, most are owned by out of state owners with only the bottom line of interest.

The Ponca City News is now owned and managed by the grandchildren of Clyde Muchmore. The newspaper remains a strong voice on local issues in northern Oklahoma.

TWO RICH MEN BUILD PONCA CITY

Ponca City oilman Lew Wentz was rich. Very, very rich! He was rated with the seven richest men in the world during the 1920s. Many might say he was just lucky at being in the right place at the right time. But in any event Lew Wentz was not stingy with his wealth. Many people are beneficiaries of his generosity today and for generations to come. Some said he was "quirky," but it adds flavor to his personality. Wentz was unusual to say the least.

Lew Wentz

Lew Wentz was born in Iowa in 1877, but grew up in Pennsylvania where he was a better than average baseball player and coach. He crossed paths with J.L. McClaskey who had made a fortune in sauerkraut. McClaskey had invested some of his wealth into wildcatting oil ventures in Oklahoma and asked Wentz to go there as a partner and oversee his interests. McClaskey soon died and Wentz bought the oil interests from his estate. Then, big oil strikes in the Three Sands and Tonkawa oil fields near Ponca City made instant millionaires of Lew Wentz and E.W. Marland, another Ponca City oilman.

Earnest W. Marland was born in Pennsylvania in 1874, where he became a lawyer and an oilman. He made and lost a fortune in Pennsylvania but came to Oklahoma in the early 1900s to explore for oil in the newly opened former Cherokee Strip lands. Marland struck it rich in the Tonkawa and Three Sands oil field west of Ponca City. Marland entertained lavishly, introducing foxhunts and polo to the area. He built the "Palace on the Prairie," costing millions and enjoyed a life of splendor with his wife Virginia. The couple was childless and in 1916 adopted two children of Virginia's sister, George and Lydie Roberts, then 19 and 16. Virginia died in 1924. Marland then stirred a little controversy by revoking the adoption of Lydie and the two were married in 1926. Marland commissioned Jo Davidson, a famous sculptor to do marble statues of him, Lydie and George which adorned the mansion.

E.W. Marland had long thought the role of women settling the West had been overlooked. Men had been given the credit of pioneering the new country, but the women had hardly been recognized and had endured the same hardships while raising the family. Marland wanted a tribute to the pioneering spirit of women and in late 1926 invited 12 leading nationally known sculptors to submit designs in the form of a small 3-foot bronze model depicting women's role in taming the prairie. He paid each $10,000 with the sculptor of the model selected to receive $50,000. The winning model would be cast in a heroic size bronze and displayed in Ponca City.

Earnest W. Marland

Four months later, the models were exhibited across the nation and 750,000 persons cast votes for their preference. Bryant Baker's vision of the pioneer woman was the clear winner. Ironically, Baker was the last to enter with only 30 days before the deadline. He sculpted his model, had it cast and entered the day before deadline.

The Pioneer Woman

Baker's Pioneer Woman was a statue of a young, sun-bonneted pioneer mother, leading her son by the hand, striding confidently, head held high—a woman of sturdy beauty and dignity, whose eyes are fixed on the far southwestern horizon.

The bronze statue was dedicated and presented as gift to the State of Oklahoma on April 22, 1930. The date was 41 years after Oklahoma Territory was opened for settlement on the same date in 1889. A crowd estimated at more than 40,000 people gathered at the unveiling. The event was carried on a nationwide radio broadcast. President Herbert Hoover spoke from the White House by radio, as did Patrick J. Hurley, a native Oklahoman and Secretary of State. Speakers on site were Oklahoma Governor W.J. Holloway, Marland and Oklahoma's favorite son, Movie Star, Humorist and Columnist Will Rogers who acted as master of ceremonies.

An estimated 40,000 attended dedication of the Pioneer Woman statue, presented to the state on April 22, 1930, 41 years after Oklahoma Territory was opened for settlement.

The entire collection of the twelve Pioneer Woman bronze entries is a part of the Woolaroc Museum located between Barnsdall and Pawhuska. When viewed collectively together the Bryant Baker creation is clearly superior and it was the overwhelming favorite of the voters who viewed the tour of models.

Despite his newly-found wealth, Lew Wentz continued to live a very modest life at the Arcade Hotel in downtown Ponca City. The owner of the little more than run down hotel had been generous with Wentz in his poorer days and he rewarded her with his loyalty as a tenant and taking more rooms as his business demanded. Million dollar deals were made in the lobby of the dingy hotel. Wentz' income was estimated to be one million dollars a month. Lew Wentz was the world's richest bachelor at the time.

Ponca City prospered with the oil discovery and the new wealth of Wentz and Marland. Marland established the Marland Oil Company refinery in Ponca City refining oil and gasoline for the northern Oklahoma and southern Kansas markets. The new refinery brought in jobs and Ponca City began a period of strong growth.

Wentz never married and continued to live in the hotel for 39 years until the owner died. With her death Wentz bought the hotel from her estate and completely renovated the structure as his residence. He added an elevator to access the upper and lower floors. Marland built a Mediterranean-style mansion in east Ponca City for his family. He built a large complex nearby also in Mediterranean style to accommodate his many guests and business associates. Marland's oil refinery added jobs and population growth to Ponca City. Wentz gave them a place to play.

Wentz had a strong interest in children. Even before his oil riches, Wentz borrowed money to fund a program to provide a Christmas gift and candy to children of the community. After his first gusher, he built the Wentz Boy Scout and Youth Camp and established a Children's Home for orphan children. He was instrumental in establishing the Crippled Children's Hospital in Oklahoma City and made large annual contributions to the Masonic Shrine's Crippled Children's program.

A lover of nature and wildlife, Wentz established a 2,000-acre ranch and wildlife preserve and stocked it with exotic animals. It is said Wentz enjoyed driving with friends over the preserve in his Pierce-Arrow roadster and watching the animals run. He built a municipal golf course and added an Olympic-size swimming pool for the citizens and children of the camp and Children's Home to enjoy. Wentz established a trust for student loan programs at Oklahoma University and Oklahoma State University that has helped thousands of students obtain a college degree. The programs still thrive at both institutions today with reserves to allow the program to continue far into the future.

Wentz and his Pierce-Arrow Roadster

Wentz was a quiet man, but could be aggressive in achieving what he wanted. Many stories abound about the oilman and some encounters with rivals. It was said during the Depression he attended a movie that impressed him deeply. As he left the theater he remarked to the owner the movie should be enjoyed by the whole community and suggested the owner might offer a free movie night or two to enable all to see it. "I'll tell you what," the owner reportedly told Wentz, "you run your business and I'll run mine." Wentz installed a movie theater, began showing free first run movies with free popcorn and put the operator out of business.

On another occasion Wentz objected to the editorials published in a neighboring Kay County community, the *Blackwell Daily Journal-Tribune*. He offered to buy the paper but the publisher refused his offer. Wentz then sent an associate out in the community saying they were going to start a newspaper with free advertising and circulation. The owner sold quickly and moved on to another town.

Before the depression years and crash of the Stock Market in 1929, Wentz began divesting himself of his oil interests. He began investing in California fruit orchards, timber in Louisiana and real estate in Texas and Oklahoma. Wentz became owner of Oklahoma daily newspapers in Ponca City, Blackwell, Guthrie, Okemah, Weatherford and Wewoka. Good thing, too. Oil prices plummeted to 50-cents a barrel, completely bankrupting many oilmen.

Marland Oil Company was not as fortunate. Marland had offered his company to investors of the Stock Market several years before. The growth of the company had added millions to Marlan's worth as well. The crash of the stock market caused the bankruptcy of Marland's personal fortune and his company. The stockholders booted Marland, elected new officers, and changed the name to Continental Oil Company. They continued in business, but it was a slow recovery until World War II. The company continues under the name Conoco today.

Wentz and Marland were rivals in many ways. Both were heavily involved in politics of rival parties. Marland was a Republican but changed his politics to Democrat following his loss of fortune in the stock market crash. He blamed the economic catastrophe on the J.P. Morgan bankers. Wentz was a staunch Republican using his newspapers as his voice for the Republican cause.

Marland entered politics, ran for public office and served in the Oklahoma House of Representatives for one term from 1930-32. He then ran for governor and was elected Oklahoma's 10th governor, serving a rather lackluster four-year term during the Depression years. Marland continued to lose more of his former personal fortune while serving as governor. He and Lydie moved back to Ponca City after his term ended in 1939. Continuing losses forced him to sell the mansion to the Discalced Carmelite Fathers of Mexico and he and Lydie moved into the chauffeur's cottage. He ran unsuccessfully for the U.S. Senate in 1940.

E.W. Marland died in 1941.

Lydie Marland

Lydie continued to live in the chauffeur's cottage and becoming more and more reclusive. In a strange turn of events, Lydie Marland disappeared in 1953. The former figure of high society and Oklahoma's first lady as wife of the governor was suddenly the subject of wide speculation. Reports in newspapers said she was spotted in a soup line in Chicago. Some said she was seen among the homeless in New York City. Others claimed she was seen in an anti Vietnam War March in Washington, D.C. But no one knew for sure and there was no contact between Lydie and her friends or attorney—or at least no one was talking. She had simply disappeared off the face of the earth.

More than twenty years passed after Lydie's disappearance. The events had largely been forgotten by time. Then as suddenly as she disappeared, Lydie Marland surfaced back in Ponca City in 1975 with little disclosure about her whereabouts during the long interval.

Museum and statue of Lydie Marland

A Ponca City lawyer (and childhood friend) located Marland in Washington, D.C. and financed her return to Ponca City. She moved back into the chauffeur's cottage. She led efforts to have Ponca City purchase the Palace on the Prairie when it came up for sale again. She and other supporters were successful in having the Palace bought and preserved on the National Register of Historic Places. She continued to live in the cottage until her death July 25, 1987.

Marland Statue

Wentz Statue

A marble statue of a seated Marland rests in a small park-like setting at City Hall. Lew Wentz died in 1949. A bronze statue of a standing Lew Wentz also adorns the City Hall Park. Marble statues of Lydie Marland and her brother, George Marland are featured in the entryway of the Marland Mansion and Museum.

Ponca City continues as a thriving community. Continental Oil Company, built and lost by E.W. Marland, continues to grow and prosper. The Marland Mansion and Pioneer Woman statue and museum attracts thousands of visitors each year. Lew Wentz' gifts to the city and his student loan trusts continue to benefit thousands.

Two men who found riches in the Oklahoma oil fields gave lasting treasures to a community and state along with fascinating legacies of their interesting personal lives.

GUS MCDONALD, FANCY DANCER

Gus McDonald was nimble of foot with body motions as graceful as a soaring eagle. He was a Native American fancy dancer. He was good at it too. Gus McDonald was named the World's Champion Straight and Fancy Dancer following competition of dancers at Haskell Institute Indian School in 1926 at Lawrence, Kansas.

McDonald was Ponca Indian, born on the Ponca Indian Reservation in 1898, just a few miles south of Ponca City, then in Oklahoma Territory. He started dancing at an early age and joined with several other Poncas touring with the famous Miller Brothers 101 Ranch Wild West Show also headquartered near Ponca City. The 101 Ranch show toured the United States and the world. They played before royalty in England, France and Belgium with cowboys, Indians, bronc riders, bulldoggers and exotic animals that entertained millions during its heyday.

Gus McDonald and his Ponca Indian dancers were a part of this show exhibiting their fancy steps in full Indian regalia of colorful feathers, beaded moccasins, the incessant beat of the drum and the hey-ya-ya chant of the drummers. McDonald is credited with the creation of the Fancy War Dance steps still in use by Indian dancers today.

The Ponca dancers also participated in mock stagecoach robberies while riding horses bareback at a high gallop, chasing the stagecoach while yelling their blood-curdling screams as they circled the arenas to the delight of the audience. Gus was a part of he Miller Brothers show until it closed in the 1920s.

Fancy dance steps weren't all that was in the ability of McDonald. He is also credited with inventing the "feather-pull" dance that held audiences and fellow dancers in awe of his athletic ability. In this dance, a six-inch feather was stuck in the ground and the dance would begin. Gus would do his fancy steps around the feather to the beat of the drum and the chant of the drummers. The dance would increase in speed and motion while Gus worked himself into an emotional trance-like frenzy. The climax came when Gus suddenly whirled around with his body, plucking the feather in his teeth without touching the ground with any body parts.

Following the years after the closing of the Miller Brothers' Wild West Show, McDonald sponsored annual pow wows at Ponca City where members of many Native American tribes gather to celebrate their heritage. Competitive dances are held with the winner receiving the Gus McDonald Trophy.

Gus McDonald was visiting with friends at the *Ponca City News* when conversation about the feather pull dance became a topic of conversation. Walt Harris asked Gus if he thought he could still do the feather pull dance. Gus was in his fifties but assured everyone he could still perform the dance. A pot of money was quickly raised for McDonald to prove his ability. Walt Harris, a printer at the newspaper and Native American himself, cleared an area in the composing room suffcient for Gus to perform his dance.

A six-inch soda straw was placed between two lead slugs as a challenge for McDonald. Harris started a drumbeat on an empty coffee can and began a chant. Gus danced around the straw for several minutes, suddenly whirled around and plucked the straw between his teeth to the cheers of some 25 employees of the newspaper who witnessed the event.

Gus McDonald died in 1974. It was said he could still do the feather pull dance while in his sixties.

The "Oklahoma Fancy Dance" originated by Gus Mc Donald is one of the most popular styles of Native American dance seen at most modern powwows. The costumes are much more colorful and elaborate than in McDonald's day. Today's dancers are bedecked in costumes featuring feathers from head to toe all dyed in color-coordinated hues. Beadwork in matching colors is also more prominent in the modern costumes.

The McDonald family legacy dates back to the 1850s in their native homeland along the Nebraska-South Dakota border. A McDonald family song is sung in honor of Gus McDonald's tradition to the Ponca tribe and to the pow-wow world. This war dance song is only started by permission of the McDonald family and in their presence. Gus McDonald, Ponca Indian and the first World Champion Straight and Fancy Dancer, is recognized for his contribution to the Native American heritage and its history.

THE REMARKABLE T.J. CUZALINA

I have admired many people among the parade of personalities that passed before me, but T.J. Cuzalina ranks up there at the top. Cuzalina was a fiery little man of Italian ancestry, standing about five foot five inches tall with coal black hair, graying at the tenples, and an olive Mediterranean complexion. He came to Ponca City from the eastern Oklahoma town of Hartshorne as a pharmacist. His father was an Italian immigrant that worked in the coal mines, as did most of the Italian population that settled in the region of Oklahoma near McAlester when it was still Indian Territory. T.J. spent time in the coal mines himself during his early years but found a job as an apprentice pharmacist.

T. J. Cuzalina

Laws in the early years allowed apprentices to become licensed after serving six years under the tutelage of a licensed teacher. Many physicians, lawyers, dentists, pharmacists and other professionals began their practice as an apprentice without ever having attended college. T.J. Cuzalina was one of them. He may not have even graduated high school. T.J. took chances in many things. He loved to gamble. Lady Luck playing craps and poker smiled on T.J. so well that he soon bought the drug store in Ponca City, and it was a thriving business.

As an advertising salesman with the *Ponca City News,* I inherited the Cuzalina account when another salesman left for greener pastures. Cuzalina was a very good advertiser in the newspaper, and I delighted working with him. His advertising program included a daily column published in the newspaper. Since it was paid advertising, servicing his account became my responsibility. I would visit Cuzalina at the drugstore very early each morning about his thoughts for the column that day. The title of Cuzalina's column was "Just Poppin' Off." He had a political mind and would comment on political topics at times, or the subject might touch on thoughts that would improve the community. And there were jokes—lots of jokes.

T.J. would tell me the topic he wanted to write about. I would go to the upstairs office and type out his thoughts on an old Royal typewriter, take it down for his approval, and it would be published in that evening's edition of the *News*. On a number of occasions T.J. would tell me he had nothing in mind and for me to write something. I would go upstairs and write about a subject and bring it down for his approval. I knew his interests so it was not difficult to please him. I never really knew Cuzalina's political party preference as he could, and would, be critical of both parties at times.

Cuzalina was a big fan of General Dwight D. Eisenhower, the World War II hero. Cuzalina began an effort in his column to persuade Eisenhower to run for president when Harry Truman's time in office was finished. In his column Cuzalina offered $1,000 to the best slogan promoting an Eisenhower presidency. Thousands of letters and post cards from all over the country came into Cuzalina's post offce box, which he turned over to a committee he selected to determine the best entry. "I Like Ike" was selected among the entries and the winner was awarded the prize. Cuzalina then ran the "I Like Ike" slogan in his column every day, long before Eisenhower was officially nominated for the presidency. Ike ultimately won the election in landslide voting.

Gambling was one of Cuzalina's passions. Another was golf. The drug store and Cuzalina were very popular and the store did a very brisk business, so brisk it allowed T.J. to participate in his golf passion every afternoon. There he could participate in the other passion by gambling among his golfing partners. Then in the evening it could be a spirited gin or poker game at the Petroleum Club. Life was fun for T.J. Cuzalina and he enjoyed every minute of it.

President Eisenhower heard of Cuzalna's early enthusiastic support, and Cuzalina received communication from Eisenhower at times. President Eisenhower loved golf and played often. He always played in the annual Cherry Hillsdilly golf tournament at the Cherry Hills Country Club in Denver. Knowing Cuzalina enjoyed golf, Eisenhwer invited T.J. to be his partner one year. T.J. was on cloud nine! He thought he had died and gone to Heaven! Cuzalina arranged to get some out-of-service oversized twenty-dollar bills from the Federal Reserve in Kansas City. Taking his bundle of twenties to Denver, Cuzalina autographed and gave a bill to his group of players. He came back with a one-dollar bill autographed by the president, which he framed and hung in his office.

"You lost money on that deal trading a twenty for a measly one spot," I said to T.J. "Not really," T.J. replied, "I took fifty off him on a putt he bet I couldn't make!"

That was typical T.J. Cuzalina. He was proud and sure of himself even in the company of the president of the United States. He paraded around like a bantam rooster, never obnoxious, but bowing to no one. He was always laughing and full of fun. I loved his philosophy: Do it, and see what happens!

People made a mistake if they bet against T.J. Cuzalina!

AFTER THE PARADE

THE ENTERTAINMENT COMMITTEE

Bob Walker and I were assigned to provide the entertainment for the upcoming Ponca City Jaycees Stag Party. The Jaycees had had an active year with great accomplishments. Ours was a club for young men, and not to be confused with the "old men's" clubs like the Rotary and Lions Clubs. We got out and got things done physically. We cleaned the park, provided new benches, and raised money for Polio and a host of other projects to benefit the community. It had been a good year and this was to be a celebration party for things well done. Other young men in the community were invited to attend in hopes they would join the club and boost our numbers.

Walker and I were advertising salesmen for the *Ponca City News*. We were also hunting and fishing companions when not working. Walker had a wife and five daughters. The last daughter he named "Jo" so, he said, he could go to the door and shout "Jo, it's dinner time," and people might think he had a son.

Bob and Bill,
Entertainment Committee

Among our thoughts for entertainment might be a "girlie" show since it was a stag affair. We went to a local hotel known to have "entertainment" available. We were directed to room 320 where the "entertainer" was still asleep. After we explained our mission, she agreed to appear in bikini style attire with long, flowing scarves and mingle among the tables during dinner. The charge would be $50 for thirty minutes. "Let's see what you look like," Walker said as he grabbed the sheet pulling it off her. She was stark naked. She was shapely, big boobs and about twenty-five years of age. No raving beauty, but no beast either.

The night of the big party came and the "entertainer" was skipping along between tables with her long, billowy scarves flowing behind her. All of a sudden she stopped at a table where local veterinarian Sam Wallace was seated. Wallace was a young man of twenty-five or so with a prematurely bald head. The "entertainer" stopped at Sam's table, removed her top and placed her generous boobs on top of Sam's bald head. With that Sam threw up in his plate. Turn out the lights—the party's over!

Walker and I were not kicked out of the Jaycees, but we were never asked to provide entertainment again. We didn't collect any Brownie points at home when word got out about the goings-on!

It was believed that Sam had been "entertained" by the young lady on a previous encounter.

THE TALLYWHACKERS

When our children were very young, we sometimes rook baths together—Rosemary with Cathy and me with Gene. Gene was just a couple of years old and sometimes he would be in the tub with Rosemary and Cathy.

We had built our first house in 1956 and occupied it two weeks before Gene was born. It was a nice, three bedroom, one bath home. The bath had no shower, so we filled the tub for baths. Gene and I had just finished a bath one evening and came into the kitchen. A neighbor lady was having a Coke with Rosemary at the kitchen table.

Gene decided to share an observation with the neighbor lady and announced, "I have a tallywhacker," he told her. "Mommy and Cathy don't have a tallywhacker—but Daddy's got a B-I-G tallywhacker!"

It was time to stop taking baths with the kids!

THE WAYWARD GARTERS

Dora Lee Frohlich owned a popular ladies' shop in Ponca City. She had the latest styles before anyone else in town and an impressive list of clientele. Since Dora Lee was on my advertising account list at the *Ponca City News,* I called on them most every day for their advertising program. Dora Lee was middle aged and very attractive, and she fitted very well into the styles she sold. Two sales clerks assisted her. All the girls were very friendly with me and we enjoyed a little banter with business.

Making the sales call one morning, I noticed Dora Lee was overly friendly with me. She took hold of the lapels on my suit coat and told me I looked very handsome that day. She gushed over my suit, even though it was a couple of years old and she had seen it on several previous occasions. I thought things were a little odd but dismissed it from my mind and went on about my business making sales calls.

Returning to the office a little later, I happened to put my hand in the pocket of my suit coat and felt a strange object in my pocket. It felt like a piece of rope. I pulled it out of my pocket and discovered it was a pair of ladies' garters! So that's why Dora Lee was overly friendly this morning—she planted a pair of garters in my pocket while gushing about how handsome I was that day.

Rushing right back to the dress shop, I went in the door and found Dora Lee with a customer. I went to the sales counter, held up the pair of garters and said, "Dora Lee, you left these in the car last night!"

The sales girls burst into laughter. I left a red-faced Dora Lee to explain the circumstances to her customer.

THE GOOSE HUNTING FARMER

Emil Lauterbach was an elder in the First Lutheran Church where our family was members. Like many of the members, Emil was of German ancestry whose parents had made the Land Run into the Cherokee Strip Outlet on September 16, 1893 to stake a claim of 160 acres when the country was opened for white settlement. Emil was a large man, more than six feet tall. He looked a little out of place in the suit he wore to church on Sunday. It was a little tight on his big frame. Emil had the look of a farmer with heavily tanned face and hands while his brow and forehead where white from the hat shaded his face as he wore in the fields.

Oklahoma and the Southwest were in the midst of a severe drought in the early 1950s. Trying to make conversation with Emil after church one Sunday I asked how his wheat crop was doing. He said it was very dry and needed a good rain or snow to make a crop by harvest in the spring. I said, "Do you think it will ever rain again?" Emil, in his very quiet manner said, "Oh, it always does." That was Emil's way—just wait it out and rains will come again sometime.

I asked if he had seen and ducks or geese on his farm since fall weather was in the air and temperatures were cooling.

"As a matter of fact," Emil said, " I heard a flock of geese on my pond early in the morning last week. They had moved in ahead of a cold front and had stopped to rest at the pond. They were gabbling and honking so loud it woke me up," he said. "I haven't hunted in years, but I remembered an old single shot, 10-guage shotgun my daddy had that was in the closet. I thought I might get that gun and go down to the pond and shoot some of those geese and maybe have a goose dinner for the neighbors and me.

"It was still very dark outside, so I found the old shotgun and slipped a couple of those shells in my pocket and went down to the pond. There was a grouping of willow trees at the edge of the pond, so I sneaked up behind those willows and saw about twenty-five Canada honkers on the pond. I slipped a shell in the gun and thought I'd shoot them sitting on the water and get several.

"I remembered shooting that old gun when I was a kid, and it had kicked like a mule. I parted those willows and started leaning forward to brace myself for the big punch in the shoulder I knew was to come. As I was leaning forward, I pulled the trigger. The son-of-a-bitch snapped, and I fell into the water! The geese all flew away. It seemed they were laughing at me as they flew off.

"I guess those shells were just too old," Emil said.

BILL LEHMANN

Pawhuska

Triangle Building, Pawhuska landmark.

BILL LEHMANN

SALLY'S

The pub in the 1980s television sitcom "Cheers" would come in a distant second behind Sally's Sandwich Shop when it came to characters. The tevee cast was the result of good writer imagination. The cast at Sally's was REAL!

My introduction to Sally's came in April 1959, when I reported for work at the *Pawhuska Daily Journal-Capital* newspaper. Publisher Glen Van Dyke invited me for a cup of coffee before beginning the day's activities. We walked from the newspaper office to Sally's, only a few steps up the street on Kihekah Avenue. As we opened the door I stepped into a cluttered world I could have imagined only in a dream. The tiny place, not more than 20 feet wide, was filled with people. It was abuzz with conversation and the rattle of dishes and the clanking of coffee cups hitting saucers. Behind the door was a man standing with a beer  bottle in his hand. He was engaged in conversation and I heard him say, "...and General Eisenhower told me, 'John, this war's not good!'" I looked to see to whom he was talking. Apparently, he was talking to himself.

The next instant a shrill female scream came from the kitchen and a plate sailed through the room, striking the wall before falling to the floor in shattered pieces. Harry Rairdon had goosed Ethel, the dishwasher, as he passed by. Her reaction was to throw the plate at him, still soapy from the dishwater.

"You sonofabitch," she yelled. The patrons burst into laughter because Harry had struck again!

A man sitting at the counter was drinking beer and laughing. He was laughing to himself because no one was talking with him. He apparently was caught up in his own little world and laughing at who knows what? Another man, Merlin Forney, had out his billfold with the folding photo cards. Instead of photos, the display contained at least 25 membership cards to American Legion posts all over Oklahoma. He was talking about the different posts to disinterested people seated next to him.

This rowdy scene that greeted me on my first day on the job caused me to wonder if I had made a wise decision in moving to Pawhuska, Oklahoma. "Don't worry about it," Van Dyke assured me. "They are all good people and you'll get used to it." It was too late now. I had already rented a cabin on Sand Creek six miles north of town and moved the family in.

Van Dyke was right. I soon embraced Sally's and the reserved and the rowdy but interesting people that frequented this most unique spot in Oklahoma. I adopted as friends the characters that came with it. People like Dorsey McCartney, the friendly undertaker, dressed to the nines because he would be conducting a funeral later in the morning. Seated next to him might be a cowboy smelling like the cow lot he had just left who stopped by for breakfast on his way out of town with his saddled horse waiting in the trailer parked right outside. It might be one of the several beer drinkers who would leave around noon, when the beer joints opened for the day. Or perhaps an Osage Indian wrapped in a colorful blanket waiting for the bank to open. One never knew what to expect when entering Sally's Sandwich Shop.

Osage County had been set aside as the Osage Indian Reservation. The Cherokees sold the land to the Osage in 1870. The Osage Reservation was a vast area in the northern reaches on

Indian Territory, comprising some 2,300 square miles that would become a part of the state of Oklahoma in 1907. Pawhuska is the county seat. Osage County is larger in size than the states of Rhode Island and Delaware.

The eastern half of the reservation was wooded and hilly with Blackjack trees. The western half was rocky prairie with tall Bluestem grasses that was taller than a horse's belly. Texas cattle raisers leased this nutritious grazing land to fatten cattle on their way to the eastern market. Today's feedlots have changed that, but for many years Osage County was thriving with activity of cattle being shipped in by rail and cattle trailer to Osage County pastures to fatten the cattle in the spring and summer months.

Oil was discovered in Osage County in the early 1900s. Not just oil—but LOTS of oil! The oil discoveries would make billionaires out of likes of Frank and Waite Phillips of Phillips 66 Oil Company fame. The Osage Indians had the foresight to reserve ownership of the minerals in the county to the tribe. Surface ownership of the land could be separate, but revenue from minerals all went into the treasury of the Osage Tribe. The revenue was distributed quarterly by "Head right." This made tribal members so wealthy that work was unnecessary. This was a blessing and a curse. The wealth and activity in Osage County created a melting pot of cowboys, Indians, oil workers, businessmen, lawyers, bootleggers and the connivers wanting to separate all of them from their money.

Sally Elias was born in October 22, 1916, in Pawnee City, Nebraska, to Philippe and Luz Elias, Mexican immigrants that came first to Texas, Nebraska, and then to Oklahoma. Philippe was born in Mexico in 1900, and was employed as an adobe maker. He married at age 13, immigrated to the United States and secured employment in construction as a laborer. Sally was one of 10 children. The family moved to Pawhuska in 1918, the parents would live there the rest of their lives.

A man named George James built the sandwich shop in 1922. The building was very small, being tucked in between two larger buildings on a 25-foot lot. Sally went to work for James in 1943 and bought the place from him in 1950. At the front was the griddle for frying eggs, bacon and hamburgers. A pie cabinet displaying the 7 pie varieties made by Sally every morning was at the front counter. Some 12 stools were at the counter to seat the customers. The early morning rush would find many standing between the seated customers clambering for service.

Sally Elias Carroll

One of Sally's specialties was chili. Her chili had a special touch of spices that created a remarkably good flavor and aroma that few chili parlors could equal. Served with oyster crackers, saltine crackers or bread, Sally's chili was a favorite lunchtime treat. Sally also grew cayenne peppers in her home garden that she canned and made available to go with her chili. The peppers also had a special firm texture and flavor that was the envy of all who ate them. Many times I heard customers ask if she boiled her vinegar before canning and if the jars received a hot water bath. "Trade secret," was her always response, with a sly grin.

The menu at Sally's was mostly traditional items, but occasionally she would cook a Mexican dish taught her by her mother. Knowing my interest in Mexican food, she would invite me to come over for a delicacy that was not a normal menu item. Once she prepared a dish including something that resembled green beans. "Do you know what this is?" she asked. "No, but it's good," I replied. "Well, it's cactus," she told me. She had taken the new growth on a prickly pear cactus, stripped the stickers off and cut them into strips and cooked them with special Mexican spices. It was delicious.

Sally's customers were from all walks of life. There were some real characters in both appearance and life. I attempted to put some of these characters to pen and paper by drawing some caricatures, an exaggerated likeness of some of the regulars. Roger Van Dyke, son of the newspaper publisher, became interested in the project and joined me in drawing a couple of characters. Soon we had a "rogues gallery" hanging on the walls of Sally's. They still adorn the walls there, but as they have passed, Sally placed their likeness in a black frame. Unfortunately, not many of the 1960s folks are left. Someday Roger and I may be framed in black.

Some of the "Special" folks that graced the stools at the counter of Sally's Sandwich Shop:

Harry Rairdon, the Clown Prince

Harry Rairdon was the mischief-maker at Sally's. He was descended from a French Trader among the Osages. Harry's ancestor was adopted into the Osage Tribe in the 1800s. With the adoption went head rights. The head rights of oil royalties to the Osages in later years would make it unnecessary for Harry, through inheritance, to ever have to work a day in his life.

Harry Rairdon was alcoholic and lived from one royalty "payment" to the next.

He was always dressed in khaki shirts and pants. He was at Sally's from the time she opened, drinking beer, and visiting with the regular 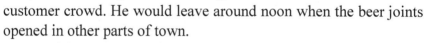 customer crowd. He would leave around noon when the beer joints opened in other parts of town.

He delighted in sneaking up on Ethel, the dishwasher, and goosing her and rolling with laughter at her reaction.

Harry never drove because he always had a snoot full. This was probably a blessing to everybody concerned. Most everywhere he went was by friend or by taxicab.

An Osage tradition was to eat scrambled eggs and wild onions in the springtime. Harry would hire a taxi to take him to the field where he would pull wild onions and bring them to Sally to cook for him. Others would also share in the feast.

Sally would bar him from the cafe from time to time because of his antics. He would always return, hat in hand, and beg forgiveness. Then the whole process would begin again.

Bill Carroll, Sally's Other Half

Bill was Sally's right hand at the sandwich shop, helping with cooking, cleaning chores and serving the customers. A friendly soul with a quick laugh and humor, Bill stayed until the breakfast and noon crowd departed, then he was off to do chores around the home, or to go fishing, which was his favorite activity. He also hunted deer in Colorado in the fall.

Bill was born in 1920 in Joplin, Missouri. He was in the U.S. Army, came to Pawhuska to visit his mother who lived there at the time. He went into Sally's café, decided he wanted to pursue Sally and stayed in Pawhuska. He received his discharge and went to work in the oil field for Osage Mud Company.

When he and Sally were married he left the oil field to help her at the café. They were married 45 years before Bill's death from a heart attack in 1999.

Bill and I were hunting companions during duck season. I raised a litter of Labrador retriever pups and gave Bill a female pup. He named the dog "Belle." We would take the mother dog, "Princess" and one of her pups I was training, along with Belle and we would all pile into Bill's truck and head for Bluestem Lake where we had built a duck blind to hunt. We enjoyed watching our dogs retrieve.

Simeon James, "Four Roses"

Simeon James was fullblood Choctaw Indian who had come to Pawhuska from the Choctaw Nation in southern Oklahoma. Unlike the Osages, James did not receive any royalty payments, and was a poor Indian. He was addicted to alcohol, hence the nickname of "Four Roses," his favorite brand of whiskey.

Roses was the town lush for many years and was well known to the Pawhuska police force because he furnished much of the labor to the city by paying off municipal fines for public drunkenness by painting crosswalks, digging ditches or any other menial physical labor the city needed at the time. Whenever the city needed labor they could always go pick up Roses because he was always drunk.

Roses was a good worker and was mild mannered. Sally hired Roses to do work around her house and garden and always saw that he was not hungry. One day Roses decided to give up booze. Through perseverance and help from Fred Lookout and the Alcoholics Anonymous he kicked the demon whiskey habit. The Pawhuska city budget increased dramatically when Roses sobered up and could no longer be charged with public drunkenness.

Roses rode a Cushman motor scooter around town and between jobs. He could be seen racing down the street with an aviator's helmet on his head with goggles over his eyes and earflaps flapping in the breeze.

Four Roses was a kind and gentle man and his labor was in high demand around town because he was an excellent worker.

"Windy" Garrett

Windy Garrett was a loud and obnoxious white man whose voice could be heard for a mile. He was a cowboy and horseman in earlier years but had been retired for some time.

He was somewhat crippled, perhaps from an injury or arthritis, and walked with a slight limp. He came into Sally's one day and announced in his loud voice that he had just returned from "New Ricky Springs." I asked where that was. "You know--New Ricky

Springs, over in Arkansas," he said. "Oh, you mean Eureka Springs," I said. "Yes," he answered, "New Ricky Springs!"

"Been over there to cheer up my old friend John who is in the hospital. I walked in there and the minute I saw him I said, 'John, you're a dead man!'"

"Boy, that must have cheered him up," I said.

"By God, I was right!" Windy said. "He died Friday."

Windy's son, Orbin Garrett, owned a quarter horse named Vandy whose offspring had been in the winner's circle at quarter horse races all over the southwest. Vandy was standing at stud at a dandy $2,000 a pop, and Orbin kept him busy. All quarter horse raisers were anxious to have Vandy's bloodline in their racing stock.

I hope Orbin saved his money, because his "golden goose" died earlier than expected. Many thought he might have been overworked. But what a way to go!

Sherman Newton, "Groucho"

Sherman Newton was a regular at Sally's for meals, but he was mostly just a coffee drinker. Newton had dark black hair and a thick black mustache that curled on the ends. He always wore a big cowboy hat, and had been a cowboy and horse wrangler before marrying an Osage woman with money. How he came about the Groucho nickname is unknown. He must have married well because he was never known to work.

Kenneth Jump

Kenneth Jump was fullblood Osage and had been addicted to alcohol at one time in his early life. A large, but very quiet man, he stood about six-foot-five, weighed over 300 pounds and was an imposing figure of a man. I thought if he played lineman on the football team he would have been an immovable object. He lived with an unmarried sister in Pawhuska.

Kenneth had a strong interest in sports and particularly youth sports in Pawhuska. *Journal-Capital* editor, Frank Spencer, asked Jump to be a sports writer for the paper, and he accepted.

Kenneth asked me to assist him in coaching a 12-and-under Little League baseball team one summer. That's a story for later.

I can envision Kenneth Jump as a great Osage Warrior dressed in an otter skin hat with a bear claw necklace and a peace pipe holding council among the Osage people.

Abner "Shorty" Selby

Shorty Selby was a carpenter that loved his Stag beer and the Alley Oop comic strip. He never seemed to be busy at carpentering, and perhaps received Social Security to supplement his income to make ends meet.

Shorty was waiting at the newspaper office every afternoon as the presses would roll with the *Journal-Capital* evening edition. He had come to see the latest escapades involving Alley Oop and his dinosaur friends. Said he didn't give a hoot about the rest of the paper—just Alley Oop.

V.T. Hamlin was the creator of Alley Oop, a caveman that lived during the dinosaur period. I wrote Hamlin via the syndicate and told him about Shorty being one of his best fans, and requested an autographed picture of Oop to give to Selby. Hamlin sent two original frames of the Oop strip and signed them to Shorty.

On Shorty's birthday I presented the copies to him when he came to the paper for the evening edition. Shorty cried. Sally framed them and they hang with the other Rogue's gallery pictures at the café.

Glen Van Dyke, Newspaper Publisher

Glen Van Dyke came to Pawhuska shortly after World War II from Keokuk, Iowa, as business manager for the newspaper. The paper was a part of the Giffin Company, who owned several small newspapers in the mid-west.

Van Dyke was small in stature, standing about five foot six or seven. He smoked cigarettes, but placed them in a cigarette holder he held between his teeth.

Van Dyke and I would have coffee every morning at Sally's where we discussed the newspaper activities and upcoming promotions. He then would visit with the bookkeeper and editor, work on his Sunday column, hit the till for twenty bucks and be gone for the day.

He told me one day the newspaper had surpassed $100,000 in advertising revenue for the first time, something Giffin had told him would never be possible. "You're doing a good job," he told me.

There was an extra twenty spot in my paycheck that week.

Jim Hamilton, Cattleman and Sculptor

Jim Hamilton owned a ranch near Foraker where he had a large herd of cattle including the Brahama breed. He had been raised on a ranch and had been a cowboy all his life.

Jim's wife, Dorothy, owned a ladies' dress shop in Pawhuska. Jim would occasionally come to Pawhuska and always stopped off at Sally's for a bowl of chili.

Dorothy had an interest in the arts and Jim would take her, somewhat reluctantly, to plays or art shows and exhibits in the Tulsa area. Seeing a display of sculptures at a show, Jim told himself, "Hell, I can do that."

Consulting with John Free, a local artist and sculptor who established the Turkey Track Foundry at Nelagoney, Jim obtained everything necessary to begin sculpting.

"I have been looking at the backside of horses and cows all my life, Jim said, "so I certainly knew the anatomy of the animals." Jim's pieces were things he was familiar with on the ranch: kids and horses and cowboys and cattle. A talented artist, he won several awards at art shows.

One of Jim's acclaimed pieces was a sculpture of two cowboys on horseback shaking hands. The piece was titled "The Contract."

"A handshake was all that was needed," Jim said. "Their word and a handshake sealed a contract that would not be broken."

A Tulsa bank bought the piece and it sits in the lobby for all to see when they visit the bank.

I wonder if a handshake would be good enough for a loan at the bank?

Roger Van Dyke

After graduating Pawhuska high school, Roger came to work at the paper selling advertising. He had been quarterback for the Pawhuska Huskies football team and was to enter Oklahoma University in the fall, where he was to also play football for the Sooners.

Roger loved the atmosphere at Sally's and contributed a couple of caricatures that are a part of the "gallery."

Among Roger's interests and activities during his high school years was participating in bull riding events at area rodeos.

He came in one day wearing a beat up cowboy hat that had been stomped on and drug through mud and manure of the arenas many times. Boy, that hat had character and Roger knew I coveted it. He gave me the hat.

Roger completed one year at OU and then transferred to Warner State College where he was again playing football. He then joined the U.S. Navy and was accepted into flight training where he became a jet fighter pilot. He flew many combat missions over Vietnam before being accepted into medical school and becoming an eye surgeon.

Retiring from the Navy, Roger opened private practice where he established a clinic near the naval base at Groton, Connecticut. He sold the clinic in 2009 and retired.

Roger Van Dyke had several careers and was very good at them all. An unforgettable character if I ever met one.

Roger and his wife, Sally, are active in the Lions Club and travel New England states on behalf of the Lions International. He is also a gifted artist.

Wanting to wear the hat Roger gave me with all the character I asked my wife if she knew where it was since it wasn't on my hat rack.

"Oh, I threw that old nasty thing away," she told me.

That was about as close as we ever came to divorce.

Jack Buck, Saddle Maker and Calf Roper

Jack Buck was one of a kind. He rented one of Sally's small buildings next to the café where he set up a saddle and leather tool making shop. He was exceptionally talented and made beautiful saddles from the rawhide trees to the finished tooled saddle. His saddle work was in high demand as well as his beautifully tooled leather belts inscribed with the customers name if they wanted. The belts were piped along the top and bottom with rawhide strips that were carefully cut and woven into the belt with hand-tooled punches.

Jack smoked unfiltered cigarettes and kept them in his mouth so long you would think the ashes would get behind his teeth before he discarded it.

Jack was also a calf roper and competed in area rodeo events, but never seemed to be in the money winner's bracket.

He told me once that he was going to write a book titled *The Other 999*.

"You always hear about some cowboy winning several thousand dollars at rodeos, but you never hear about the other 999 who never win any money. My book is going to name them," he said in his unusually slow drawl, "and my name will be at the top of the list."

Jack invited me to come to a goat roping that was to be held at a private roping pen north of Pawhuska one time. I went to watch Jack rope goats to practice for a calf-roping event that would be held the next week. What an experience! Those goats had been roped before and they headed for the fence the instant they were released from the chute. If the roper didn't catch them quickly they were at the fence, hugging it all the way down the arena and making it almost impossible to get a rope on the animal.

Jack caught his goat and got the feet of the animal tied, but the goat's bleating cry spooked the horse and he took off down the arena pulling the tied up goat with the goat bleating even more every time it bounced on the ground.

Jack's mother, Ethel Buck, assisted Jack in the shop at times. Ethel Buck had an interesting past as a young teenager in the 1920s. She was a wing walker at air shows in southern Oklahoma. She took a position on the wing of an old Curtiss bi-wing airplane and dove off the wing and into the water of a lake to the cheers of spectators when the plane made a low pass over the water.

Ethel always was dressed in jeans and a western shirt. Her hair was streaked with gray, braided and pinned over the top of her head. She was rather shy and would not talk about her past life even with my prodding.

"I'll tell you the story sometime," she told me.

Unfortunately, "sometime" never came. Ethel died in 2006 at age 96. Her story died with her.

Louie Nikikas, the Mad Hatter

Louie Nikikas, a Greek immigrant, owned a hat shop directly across the street from Sally's. It was a thriving business in the early years because almost everyone wore a hat, especially the cowboys of Osage County, who wouldn't be caught dead without one.

Louie smoked a thick, large-bowled briar pipe and spoke very broken English with a heavy Greek accent. He always wore a hat, even when working in his shop. He was a regular at Sally's for meals as well as a quick coffee break from his work.

Even though the popularity of hats diminished, Louie kept busy steam cleaning and blocking the hats of customers who still thought they were a necessary part of attire.

A favorite cartoon by famed cowboy cartoonist J.R. Williams hung on the wall at Louie's shop. It showed a cowboy on the bunkhouse porch in the dead of night with a lantern in his hand shining out into the darkness. He had been awakened by a noise and had gone out to check the source. The cowboy was dressed only in his long John underwear, but the old cowboy had on his hat and cowboy boots, even to step out the door.

Frank Spencer, Editor

Frank Spencer and family came to Pawhuska from Nebraska. Frank had served in the armed forces during WWII and had entered the newspaper business after discharge.

Frank smoked a pipe and cigarettes. He had a habit of grinding his teeth to the point the bottom teeth were worn nearly smooth. His favorite line when meeting someone was "Hi, Spencer's my name, I guess you know your own." This was his salutation to friend and strangers alike.

Frank was a popular editor, covering activities in the community very well with the limited staff of a small newspaper.

He and his wife, Isla, had seven children and lived in a large two-story house owned by Lillian Matthews on top of "Agency Hill" near the Osage County courthouse and the Osage Indian

Agency building. Lillian was a sister of John Joseph Matthews, famed Osage author. The Matthews' and Spencer were close friends.

As the Spencer family grew, larger transportation was needed. He bought a used hearse. It was amusing to watch as people unaccustomed to the arrangement saw several children pop out of the old black hearse as they went to school or church.

Devout Catholics, he and Isla were very involved with the activities of the church. Frank was a good friend of a fellow Catholic, Fred Lookout, who was active in Alcoholics Anonymous. Together they counseled many folks addicted to alcohol.

Spencer and Isla separated in the 1970s, and he removed to New Mexico. He returned to Pawhuska from time to time. They would come to Sally's to eat and Sally noted they held hands like newlyweds, but they never reunited. One of their children, Brenda, was for many years a clown in the Barnum & Bailey Circus. Another became a doctor.

Spencer died in New Mexico in 2010. His remains were cremated.

Ed Walker Former 101 Ranch Cowboy

Little is known about Ed Walker, but he visited Sally's often for a bowl of chili and coffee.

He had a colorful past as a cowboy traveling all over the world with the famed Miller Brothers 101 Ranch Wild West Show, headquartered in Ponca City.

He was part Osage and always dressed in his cowboy attire complete with neckerchief. It was said that he owned a small ranch west of Pawhuska where he kept some cattle and horses.

Fred Lookout, "Almost" Chief of the Osages

Fred Lookout was fullblood Osage and would have been the last hereditary chief of the Osages had he not been a hopeless alcoholic.

Fred said he woke up one morning, face-up in the gutter with rain pelting him in the face and water running all around him. He vowed to quit drinking, and did.

Having independent income from his Osage head rights, he devoted the rest of his life to causes of the Alcoholics Anonymous. He visited prisons in the Southwest and reached out especially to Native Americans.

He also conducted Indian Peyote religious ceremonies in Oklahoma, bringing back hallucinogenic peyote from Arizona and New Mexico.

Fred had a wonderful sense of humor and was good friends with Frank Spencer and Sally.

He may have quit drinking, but I always suspected he was chewing a few peyote seeds.

Lefler and McGuire, Constant Companions

Harry Lefler and Paul McGuire were members of the Odd Fellows Lodge and were hardly ever seen apart.

Lefler owned and managed Lefler Lumber Company while McGuire was a section foreman on the railroad. McGuire was away frequently, but when in town, he and Lefler were busy with lodge activities. Lefler always wore a cowboy hat and had only one eye. He had some teeth missing in front that showed when he laughed. He and

McGuire laughed a lot. They were a happy pair, appearing to be as different as night and day, but they were fast friends.

McGuire always wore an engineer's hat and smoked little black cheroot cigars.

Both were regulars at Sally's.

Ben Johnson, Academy Award-Winning Actor

Ben Johnson, Jr. was born at Foraker, Oklahoma, in 1926. His father gained fame as a world champion steer roper. Ben the younger, known in Osage County as "Son Johnson, would follow in his footsteps.

The senior Johnson became foreman of the famous Chapman-Barnard Ranch and Son grew up a cowboy on the ranch, tending cattle and wrangling horses. He was also an accomplished steer roper and followed the circuit during the season.

In 1940, a movie company ordered some horses from the Chapman-Barnard Ranch to be delivered to Hollywood for Howard Hughes' *Outlaw* movie. Son was delegated to accompany the horses. His talents as a wrangler were evident and Hughes wanted him to stay and handle the horses, which he did. He also became a stunt man and appeared in many movies in that role.

Discovered by Director John Ford, Johnson soon was appearing in Ford's movies with John Wayne, and assigned speaking parts. His first big movie was "She Wore A Yellow Ribbon."

Johnson never returned to the ranch, but was a frequent visitor to Pawhuska between movies, and always came back to the annual Ben Johnson Memorial Steer Roping on Father's Day Sunday. The event was named in honor of his father.

The Ben Johnson Memorial Steer Roping brings the World's Series of jerk-down steer roping to Pawhuska. This popular event

draws the best ropers to the competition. Past winners that have been crowned world's champion include many legendaries like Ben Johnson, Sr., Shoat Webster, Ike Rude and Clark McEntire, father of Reba. McEntire won four national championships in the 1950-60 era, riding a most beautiful brown gelding horse named Joe. The steer roping event fills the stands with enthusiastic spectators, all dressed in their finest attire.

Son was a competitor for many years, but later left it to the younger cowboys. When in town, he always stopped by Sally's for a bowl of chili and a hug from Sally.

It was quite a sight to see big, strapping six foot three Son Johnson hugging the barely five foot Sally.

Always unpretentious and friendly, Johnson never let his fame go to his head. He won an academy award for his role in Larry McMurtry's *The Last Picture Show.* He always said he didn't like the role because of the foul language he had to use in the part.

"I'm just glad my mother wasn't around to see the movie," he said. "She would have found it very offensive and want to wash my mouth out with lye soap."

Johnson died in 1996 in Mesa, Arizona.

Willie Carmen, Independent Oil Operator

Willie Carmen liked to hunt. He particularly liked coon hunting and had a kennel of coon dogs at his farm/ranch outside Pawhuska. He was an oil field pumper, servicing pumping units and natural gas connections in the Osage County field. He later bought some leases and became an owner-operator in addition to servicing wells for others.

He came by Sally's one morning and announced that he had seen thousands of ducks on the move ahead of a cold front while making his well servicing rounds, and it was a great day to hunt.

He said to get one of my Labradors and we'd head out to do some "pond jumping" where he had seen so many ducks.

"Only one problem," he said, "It's on Mullendore's Ranch next to Bluestem Lake."

Mullendore never allowed any hunting or fishing on any of his big ranches. If an intruder were caught trespassing he would be subject to a severe beating by E.C. Mullendore III, while being held by his thug bodyguard and former convict, Chub Anderson. This happened on numerous occasions and Mullendore delighted in whipping the helpless victim.

"I ain't ready to die yet," I told Willie, but Willie said he had just returned from the south ranch where he saw all the ducks and learned that E.C. was on the main ranch 40 miles away. So we went to my home to pick up my shotgun and a retriever. We invited Bill to go but he declined, saying Sally would miss him.

I decided to take a dog I had named "Shadow of Bluestem" on his registration papers. Shad had distemper as a little pup and it settled in his feet and tail. Part of Shad's tail had been removed by the vet, and I had been doctoring him for a long time. Shad had not received as much training as my other pups because of his condition, but he was feeling better, and I decided to take him.

Arriving at the ranch we stopped by the ranch house to visit with the foreman so he'd know we were there.

The foreman, named "Doodles" Foreman, told us we would enter at our own risk.

"If Mullendore catches you," he said, "I'm tellin' him I ain't never seen you sonsabitches in my life!"

We went anyway.

Arriving at a pond, we crept up over the dam and saw hundreds of ducks on the water. Seeing us, the ducks arose, and the rush of ducks obliterated the sky as they flew off that pond. Willie got off one shot, and his gun jammed. I picked out three ducks and fired three times, but I could see other ducks dropping in the background because they were all so close together. Four shots fired and a dozen ducks down. This was far more than our limit, and unintentional.

Poor Shad, he had never been trained to retrieve anything but a single dummy, and there on the water lay at least a dozen ducks. He didn't know which to retrieve first.

Finally retrieving all the ducks we loaded up and headed out, hoping Mullendore hadn't heard the shooting from 40 miles away.

When we returned to Sally's, she called a lady that liked duck and she sent for them to be cleaned and dressed for family meals.

Mullendore was later shot to death in his ranch home. His bodyguard, Anderson, was suspected of the killing, but the crime scene was so botched that evidence was never put together for a trial. The subsequent stories revealed a multi-million dollar life insurance policy, bankruptcy, ties to the Mafia for unpaid loans, heavy drinking and drug use, and a bitter divorce from his movie-star-beautiful wife, Linda.

Chub Anderson died in a Kansas nursing home in 2011. With him died the truth of events that happened on the Mullendore ranch that night. No one was ever tried.

When we moved from Pawhuska I gave Shad to Willie. He told me later that he had doctored Shad with crude oil on his feet and tail and he had healed. Willie said Shad was the best coon dog he had in his kennel and he had become the "kill dog."

I couldn't believe my mild-mannered Shad had turned from retriever to coon dog.

Bill Lehmann

I had come to Pawhuska and the *Journal-Capital* intending to stay only about a year. There was only one problem: I had fallen in love with Pawhuska and the people there.

With the death of Publisher Glen Van Dyke in 1964, change was imminent. The paper was up for sale. The paper was sold to the Donrey Media Group and I was selected to be the publisher. With Donrey the resources became available to instantly improve and modernize the paper. Exactly a year to the day Donrey bought the Pawhuska newspaper I was asked to transfer to Guthrie to become publisher of the *Guthrie Daily Leader*. I had mixed emotions about leaving Pawhuska but finally decided to accept the new challenges and problems of a larger operation. A new love affair began between Guthrie and me, but I never lost my love for Pawhuska and the genuine and wonderful friendships we had made there.

Like Walter Mitty, I daydream visions of grandeur in my life. One time I might be slaying dragons while my next dream would find me leading an expedition to outer space. In reality I still am trying to decide what I want to do when I grow up.

Sally Elias Carroll, 98 Years and Still Going Strong

People come and people go, but Sally's has remained the same. The coffee maker perhaps has been replaced a few times, but the rest is intact. The counter and stools are the same. The walls have seen little, if any, new coats of paint. The pictures on the wall have been discolored by age but it has only added to the character of the place.

Sally still arrives early every day, but is now open only Tuesday through Friday. She stopped selling beer in 1970, so now it is just food customers, she says. Sally starts the day by baking the 7 different pies she makes from scratch every morning. None of these crusts from the dairy case—she rolls out the dough every day resulting in homemade crusts that melt in your mouth and complement the flavor of the pie.

Since Bill's death she depends on friends to transport her to and from the café. She never has driven. Recently, she commandeered the kitchen of her son, David, and they made 25 dozen tamales. "The way they do it in Mexico," she says, "the way my mother taught me." That means masa flour stuffed in corn shucks with beef or pork, seasoned and steamed for hours. Tuesday is tamale day at Sally's. Friday is fish. Everyday is her famous chili. "I used to make chili 50 pounds at a time," she says, "but I can't stir that much meat anymore at my age." Bill used to stir the chili for her, but now she makes chili in two 25-pound batches that she can more easily handle. Friends keep her supplied with peppers she still cans in glass jars. Ask if she boils her vinegar.

Sally was assisted in the kitchen by her daughter, Andrea until she graduated high school and left Pawhuska to work at the headquarters of Wal-Mart stores in Bentonville, Arkansas. Son David helps from time to time, but he has his own oil business to run. Andrea recently retired from Wal-Mart, but is on the kidney transplant list. David has a bum leg from a motorcycle

accident. "I'm healthier than my kids," she says. Sally Carroll is truly a Pawhuska and an Oklahoma treasure.

UNLIKELY CHAMPIONS

The late spring and early summer in America brings thoughts of baseball. Pawhuska, Oklahoma, in 1961 was no different. Summer baseball youth programs were being organized, coaches and teams selected and baseball gear was being assembled for the season.

"The Summer Baseball League is seeking a coach for one of the 12-and-under teams," Kenneth Jump said to me. "Let's you and I take it. The teams have been selected but they can't find a coach for the Bobcats," he continued.

Kenneth Jump was sports editor of the *Daily Journal-Capital* newspaper, where I was also in the advertising department: two very unlikely coaches. Reluctantly agreeing to help with the project, we called our first meeting of the team that had been assigned us. About 15 of the 20 kids listed on the roster showed up. The first practice was abysmal. It was obvious the other coaches had picked the best players for their teams. We had the culls.

Kenneth Jump

The next practice we had about ten show up and some of those weren't the same as the ones who came for the first practice. By the time summer vacations and other family activities had prevented further participation by some, we were left with seven players

Bill Lehmann

on the team—two shy of what we needed to even take the field for a game.

Of the seven players only four or five could even catch a ball. One of the best players we had at practice was my daughter Cathy, and we couldn't use her in a game because she was a girl!

Cathy had always been a tomboy-type, never playing with dolls, while preferring balls and boy games. In neighborhood games she was always the one most wanted to play on a team. I had worked with her and had her switch-hitting the baseball and she could knock the ball a mile, right or left handed!

Of all the boys trying out we made a discovery the other coaches had missed: We had two pitchers that could get the ball over the plate! One was Larry Sellers, a right-hander that could throw with authority and get it in the strike zone. Larry was part Osage, Cherokee and Sioux. His father, a good athlete, was an engineer with an Oklahoma City oil company and was on the road most of the time.

The other pitcher was a left-hander named Bobby Melton, whose family had just moved to Pawhuska. His parents never showed up at practice. The boys alternated at shortstop when not pitching.

The practice field we were assigned was near the railroad tracks. There was a large hole in the backstop fence. A foul ball that got by the catcher went through the hole in the backstop and landed up in tall weeds. We kept my Labrador retriever, Princess, at the ready to fetch the ball from the weed patch, which she did.

What in the world had we gotten ourselves into by accepting this group of misfits? The chances of this team ever winning one game was minimal at best.

Our first game was a couple of weeks away. When our team showed up with only seven players we would be two shy of the nine needed to fill all positions. We were told we could "borrow" two players from the other team to fill out the roster. It is not difficult to imagine the two players the other coaches would give us—the two worst ones on their team!

We decided to use the two borrowed players in the outfield, hoping the other team wouldn't be able to hit our pitchers. Cathy acted as bat girl, equipment manager and cheerleader.

At first base we were going to play Chance Whiteman, a boy who had never been exposed to baseball. His father was a Pawhuska drilling superintendent working on rigs drilling wells in Iran. He had married an Iranian woman who spoke very broken English. Chance had played soccer, the national sport of Iran, but had never even caught a baseball.

Chance showed up at practice with his mother. He had a tattered fielders glove that was many years old, having been used by his father when he was a boy. It was limp as a rag. The first ball thrown him went right through the glove and smacked him between the eyes, breaking his glasses and giving him a bloody nose. A small tear was visible in Chance's eye. I knew he wanted to cry but he didn't. We told his mother to buy him a new baseball glove, which she did.

At third base was Jimmy Redcorn, an Osage boy; at second base was David Carroll, an Irish and Hispanic boy whose mother owned a Mexican restaurant. We stationed Figley Salz at left field, hoping a ball was never hit his way, as he had never played baseball before. Salz was a Jewish city boy from New York who was spending the summer with relatives. An older cousin played on the Pawhuska junior varsity team and "Fig" wanted to play also.

Butch Thomas was the catcher. A chunky built boy, he was able to catch and throw a ball with some accuracy and was a good hitter. And he wasn't afraid to get down in the dirt to block a bad pitch.

A couple of weeks of practice had been held, and it was now time to play ball! The 12 and under league consisted of five teams and each team would play a five-inning game twice during the season. Then came the all-star games with the winning team coach and the coach of the second-place team choosing players they wanted from the other teams to play in the all-star match.

Our little group of ragtag misfits played each team twice and won every game. Most were not even close. We started Larry Sellers, the rightie, to start. He would pitch about three innings, time enough for the batters to be able to begin getting a bat on his fastball. Then we would bring in Bobby, the leftie, to pitch the last two innings. This was a big changeup in pitching rhythm, speed and action of the ball. It worked!

Winning the league play, Kenneth and I were selected as coaches for an all-star team. We used the same pitching combination in the all-star games winning the best three of five games without a loss! We had swept the league games and the all-star games! We were 11-0! Who would have ever believed it?

A special promotion each year was a baseball special train passenger car assembled at Bartlesville to carry baseball fans to Kansas City for a double-header game between the New York Yankees and the Kansas City A's.

Kenneth and I decided this would be a special reward for our little team for their outstanding achievement against all odds in winning the championship. We decided to take the team to Kansas City on the train, and asked the parents to go as well. About 25 players and parents went from Pawhuska to join others in the area that made up the special railroad car to see the games. Cathy was included in the group since she had been such a good participant at practice and managing equipment.

We left Bartlesville in the early morning hours, arriving in Kansas City about noon. A shuttle bus took us from the railroad station to the baseball stadium. Inside the stadium the whole world changed. We left the concrete jungle of the big city into a beautifully manicured baseball field and lush, green grass in the outfield.

On our way to our seats, we were suddenly stopped by barriers that folded down on either side of the walkway. This left a path from the visiting team's dressing room to the field. Coming out of the dressing room right before our eyes were members of the Yankees baseball team. They were close enough that you could reach out and touch them. The eyes of our little teams suddenly became as big as silver dollars! They began to shout "Hi, Mickey!" and "Hi Yogi!" The players smiled and nodded as they passed by the delighted crowd. Passing right before us were Mickey Mantle, Yogi Bera, Roger Maris, Whitey Ford, Allie Reynolds and the always gruff looking old manager, Casey Stengel! What a reward. It couldn't have been scripted any better!

Yogi Berra, Whitey Ford, and Mickey Mantle

The Kansas City A's were owned by eccentric owner Charley Finley. Finley was known (and cussed by many other owners) because of his off-the-wall, unconventional promotional methods, and his criticism of major league baseball rules and regulations.

Finley had installed some unique features at the stadium that were fan favorites: A Bugs Bunny statue came up from a cavity behind home plate to hold a new baseball to the umpire whenever needed. His classic question "What's Up, Doc?" blared over the stadium speakers.

The playing field had been sculpted from hilly terrain with a large mound of earth lying beyond the outfield fences. This was too steep for conventional mowers to maintain so Finley had brought in a herd of about a dozen white goats to keep the area grasses and weeds down. Each of the goats was dyed in pastel colors of pink, green, yellow and other bright colors. The skyline of Kansas City lay beyond in the distance.

The Yankees took the first game 7-5. The second game started and went into early evening and the stadium lights came on. The highlight of the game was when Mickey Mantle hit a home run to center field. The ball took off on a straight-line trajectory, but as it went farther it began to gain altitude and easily cleared the centerfield fence. The ball landed on the earthen grassy mound, and bounced into one of the pastel colored goats. The goat jumped and the crowd laughed and cheered. It was the only homer of the double header.

The shuttle bus took us back to the railroad depot and we departed back south to Oklahoma. It had been a long day and the boys, coaches and parents were dog tired. But it had been a memorable experience. Kenneth and I retired as undefeated championship coaches and very proud of our unlikely champions.

Criticism of coaches by some parents because their kid didn't get enough playing time didn't happen with us. With only seven players every kid played every pitch! The parents of the two "borrowed" players also loved us because their kid got to play as well.

Larry Sellers later went to Hollywood as an actor and received many roles in movies involving Indians in the cast. He had a long-running role as the Indian in the "Dr. Quinn, Medicine Woman" television series.

Cathy Lehmann was born thirty years too soon. She possessed great athletic ability in several sports and would have been offered a softball scholarship at a major university had the Title 9 laws affecting women's sports been in effect at that time. Cathy later played in women's softball leagues at Claremore, Oklahoma where she was a catcher and good hitter from either side.

Chance Whiteman, the half-Iranian boy moved to Arizona with his family. With excellent coaching and desire he was named to the Arizona high school All State baseball team and later played at Arizona State University.

David Carrol owns and manages a Mexican restaurant in Bartlesville. **Figley Salz** went back home to New York City after the season. It is not known if he pursued sports any longer. It is said he has earned millions buying and selling stocks on the New York Stock Exchange.

JIM SLICK—
JAILBIRD, BOXER, GUITAR PICKER, FRIEND

His name was James Evitt, but everyone called him "Jim Slick." I don't know why and never asked.

Slick was a thin, wiry black man who worked at Benson Lumber Company in Pawhuska, Oklahoma, in the 1960s. He stood about 6 feet tall and was very friendly and outgoing to all who came in contact with him. Born in 1926, he was two years older than me.

His friendly smile and demeanor would never lead one to suspect that he had served time in Missouri State Penitentiary.

While serving time in the pen, he was the sparring partner for another inmate named Sonny Liston. Liston would later become the Heavyweight Champion of the World after knocking out Floyd Patterson in the first round in the 1962 championship fight. Liston was known for his intimidation, toughness and punching power, and his ties to the boxing underworld. He would later lose his title to Muhammad Ali, and again in a rematch which many called fixed fights.

Slick took many poundings and dodged many punches as Liston's sparring partner, but thanks to protective head and body gear he was "able to survive," he said. Slick's general body movements at work and play would suggest that he was quick as a cat and someone you would not want to mess with. I have an idea he got in a few licks on Liston as well.

I have often been accused of having some "unusual" friends, and I was happy to count Jim Slick as one of them. We became acquainted through my association with the local newspaper in making sales calls to Benson Lumber. We had mutual interest in several topics from sports to music. Segregation was still active in many areas during that period, and Slick helped me to better understand the adverse effects segregation had on the black community.

Slick played guitar. Not just guitar, but get down and dirty "Negro Blues" guitar that would be the envy of legendary icons Chuck Berry, Leadbelly, and John Lee Hooker. His talent for the blues sound came naturally to him. He never had a formal lesson in his life but learned the style as a youth playing with the older men in his neighborhood back in Missouri. The riffs and slides he made on the guitar were some of the best blues guitar I have ever heard.

I was trying to learn to play bass guitar at the time and had just purchased a bass and amp from Sears in Tulsa. I had an appreciation for all music styles, but country music and western swing were my main interests. I was playing with friends and family who were trying to make me fit in to form a band. It was a rocky road at first, but I was gradually coming along.

Occasionally Jim Slick and I would get together. He came to my home many times, and I would try and keep up with Slick as he played those wonderful blues licks of his. He had an old blond fender Telecaster guitar that had been played in many bars during its years before Slick bought it at a pawnshop. Its scars and scratches told a story of its past, but in Slick's hands the old Fender sounded mellow and smooth when he bent those strings.

Many times I also went to play at Slick's house. He lived in the segregated black part of town, next to Bird Creek in Pawhuska. His home was little more than a shack that he shared with his wife and three or four children. The furniture was old and faded and had seen much better days. From the looks in the eyes of his children as I came in the house, I am certain that I was probably the only white person that ever came to visit in their home. I enjoyed our sessions there and was soon embraced by the family.

Slick added a room onto the house which he turned into a bar he called "Slick's Place." It was small and cramped and loud. The clientele was all black and probably the only bar in Pawhuska catering to the black community as far as I knew. Slick invited me down to his bar to play on several occasions.

Prejudice is a two-headed beast, and it exists in the black community as well. The first couple of times I walked in the door I would have been a dead man if looks could have killed. It was obvious I was unwelcome, but Slick had put the word out that I was his friend and was to be left alone. I was merely tolerated there and never really accepted by anyone except Jim Slick, but having the opportunity to play with Slick was rewarding to me.

We had fun playing Slick's blues and the patrons seemed to enjoy it as well. There was just the two of us: guitar and bass. There wasn't room for any other pickers even if they were brave enough to sit in. I always left at a reasonable hour before the "spirits" took effect on barroom behavior. Slick's Place had a reputation of being a rough "joint" and Slick had to calm the atmosphere on many occasions. Not many, if any, white people ever went through the door at Slick's.

Slick's Place met its demise some time after we moved from Pawhuska. I lost contact with Slick but found out later that he had been shot by one of his intoxicated patrons. This event almost cost him his life. A flood on Bird Creek then swept through the house and bar, which sealed its fate. Slick was tough, and dodged many punches in life, but his quickness was no match for the speed of a bullet.

Among my friends, I have counted everyone from the governor to the town drunk. Each one has been interesting to me. My daughter would cringe every time I would stop and offer a ride to some of my "friends." But she accepted Jim Slick into our home without reluctance.

Jim Slick was one of those I have enjoyed knowing and counting among my perhaps "unusual" friends. He died in 2007 at age 80. With him died a unique feel and natural ability to play the blues. There was a difference between us as broad as night and day, but also a trust and respect that made our friendship special.

OLD BLACK JOE

Our little family lived in Pawhuska, Oklahoma, in the 1960s. Our children, Cathy and Gene, were still small, and Rosemary would take them to Sunset Lake to swim occasionally. The park allowed pets, so Rosemary would allow our Labrador retriever to accompany them. I named him "Old Black Joe of Bluestem" on the registration papers, and called him "Joe." Joe was a large dog and still in training. I liked his spirit and enthusiasm in retrieving   We had taken Joe and a couple of other dogs from the litter to Kansas City to sell at a retriever field trail meet. I entered Joe in the Puppy Stakes at the meet sponsored by the Kansas City Retriever Club. Joe performed brilliantly with his usual determination and enthusiasm. Joe won the event hands down, but we weren't allowed the trophy because we were from out of state. There was no entry fee but I wondered why they allowed me to enter in the first place.

Rosemary would take a fetching dummy with them to Sunset Lake and throw it for Joe to retrieve. She told me several times about teasing Joe by holding the dummy under water and Joe would go down to get it. I dismissed it from my mind believing it was just play. But one day I decided to take Joe and go pond jumping north of Pawhuska to see if we could find some ducks to further his training. Sure enough, as we came over the dam at a pond there were several ducks that took flight at seeing us. I knocked down three birds. Two were dead and Joe retrieved them in short order.

The third duck was a Bluebill diving duck and every time Joe reached the duck it would dive under water and come up twenty feet or so away from the dog. Joe would swim after the duck again with the same result. This went on for several minutes with the dog chasing the duck and the duck diving below water. Finally tiring of the chase Joe went after the duck following it under water. The dog and the duck both disappeared for what to me was a long time. I became worried that the dog might drown. Finally Joe appeared again snorting and blowing but with the duck firmly in his mouth.

Rosemary had become the trainer of a diving Labrador retriever.

Old Black Joe was one of seven pups born to Princess, the mother dog I had bought for fifty dollars as a puppy from a breeder in Kansas. Princess was a sweet dog and so good with the children. I had bought her to be my retrieving hunting dog as well and she came from hunter breeding stock. After training she became an excellent hunting companion. She retrieved ducks from water and dove from the field. The first time she retrieved a dove she picked up the bird in her mouth. Dove feathers shed easily and they stuck to her mouth. She had had a terrible time trying to rid them from he mouth. From that first encounter she learned to pick up the dove by the tip of its wing to avoid all those loose feathers in her mouth.

For some unknown reason I decided I wanted to have Princess bred and raise a litter of puppies. I found a stud dog in Tulsa and they decided on the pick of the litter as the stud fee. We prepared the back porch for the event to take place. I built a whelping box and placed it on the back porch. The dogs did their thing and the blessed event was nearing. Princess usually slept near me at night but accepted the whelping box as a place to sleep. But the night she whelped I put her to bed in her box. Soon I heard her come across the kitchen floor and felt her head resting on the bed by me. I got up, put her back in her bed and returned to my bed. Soon I felt her head resting on my side of the bed and I could tell she was probably staring at me in the dark and telling me that the time was here. Princess wanted me to be with her when the puppies arrived. I put her back in her box and soon the delivery started. I stayed with her until all the pups were born. She was happy and content then and took over her new duties as mother of seven coal-black Labrador puppies.

I selected Joe as a keeper and kept another dog I named Shadow of Bluestem. Shadow had a bout with distemper as a puppy, losing part of his tail. His feet were also affected and were very slow to heal. I could not train him as well as the others because of his condition but kept him, treating his wounds daily. I grew fond of Shad as well and loved his temperament and attitude even though he was limited physically. As he healed he became and excellent retriever. When we moved from Pawhuska to Guthrie I gave Shad to Willie Carmen, a hunting friend. Willie put Shad in with his coonhounds and reported that Shad became an excellent coon dog as well as a retriever.

THE UNLOADED GUN

Don Edwards was a friendly soul: always smiling when he wasn't laughing, outgoing personality that would engage you in conversation whether you wanted to or not. Don was manager of Benson Lumber yard in Pawhuska. Everybody loved him and enjoyed being around him.

Born and raised in the Osage, he knew every little nook and cranny of the county and knew practically everybody in it. I went hunting and fishing with him to many out of the way locations. He knew the places you could hunt and he knew the places where hunting was prohibited. One of those places was the Chapman-Barnard Ranch, containing several thousand acres of pristine Bluestem grass, rolling hills, Blackjack trees and hundreds of beautiful ponds and lakes. The ranch was established by a couple of Tulsa oilmen who found riches in Osage County with oil wells developed in the 1920s. The ranch manager was a gruff old bastard named Clyde.

Prairie chicken season was opening in Osage County for the first time in many years. We regularly carried items in the newspaper where hunters had paid fines of $100 for shooting prairie chickens out of season. I had not ever hunted the bird but if people were paying fines for killing them then they must be mighty tasty. The prairie chicken had been on the endangered species list for a long time but had made a comeback sufficiently that they had been placed back in season. The bag limit was two birds per hunter. Don and I had made plans to hunt the chicken on opening day.

Don drove us to a spot on the Chapman-Barnard Ranch before daybreak and we sat in his pickup truck waiting for the sun to come up over the horizon. He had brought a sack of apples and we each had an apple for breakfast. "I hope no one saw us come in here," Don said, "because old Clyde will nail our hides to the barn door!" He no sooner got the words out of his mouth than an old rattling pickup truck rumbled up the rocky trail beside us. It was Clyde!

"Don't you sumbitches know this is posted property and you are trespassing on private land?" Clyde yelled to us as he got out of his old truck. "Is there a reason I shouldn't call the sheriff and have you arrested?" he said.

"Hey, you like apples?" Don said as Clyde approached our truck with a scowl on his face. That scowl told of bad things to come for being caught on the posted ranch. I envisioned us in jail or paying heavy fines for trespassing. The scowl on Clyde's face left as Don handed him an apple. "What do you guys think you are doing?" Clyde asked as he took a bite out of the apple. "Well, chicken season opened today and we thought we might get one for Thanksgiving," Don replied. Clyde took another bite out of the apple and reached in the sack for another, then said, "There's a roost down by the pond, and you can probably get a couple there," Clyde said, and then left still munching on the second apple. Whew, what a relief!

We went down by the pond, and sure enough we had our limit of two birds each and went back to town. I cleaned my two birds and told Rosemary to cook one of them for dinner. I put the other bird in the freezer to have at a different time. I came home for dinner that evening anxiously awaiting the first bite of a tasty prairie chicken. Rosemary had made a cornbread dressing to go with it, and this was going to be a feast. I imagined us eating the other bird for Thanksgiving dinner, still a couple of weeks away. That prairie chicken was the foulest tasting bird I believe I ever had! It tasted exactly like the weeds and sage brush seeds in its diet. The dressing was just as bad because she had cooked the bird with the dressing. We wound up eating hot dogs for supper!

I was visiting Don at the lumber yard one day when a friend dropped by to show him a shotgun he had recently purchased. We were standing on the driveway at the lumber yard as Don took the shotgun in his hands to examine it. Placing the gun to his shoulder, he began leveling it off and following passing cars in its sights. He raised the gun up and pointed it at a billboard sign located on the corner across the street. He pulled the trigger, and it went off with a loud boom, spraying buckshot all over the billboard! We could only ponder what could have happened if he had pulled the trigger while following the passing cars. Still trembling, Don handed the gun back to the owner with a valuable lesson learned: Never point and pull the trigger of an "unloaded" gun.

With the deaths of Chapman and Barnard, much of the ranch was given the National Park Service who established the National Tall Grass Prairie Preserve located between Pawhuska and Bartlesville. This beautiful land has been untouched for centuries. The lovely wildflowers and Bluestem grasses are awash in the countryside. Large herds of buffalo and Longhorn cattle populate the preserve where they graze the native grasses. The wildlife therein have no reason to fear hunters.

This should be on your bucket list of beauty spots to visit in Oklahoma.

KLANSMAN MEETS HIS MATCH

The Ku Klux Klan was staging a rally in Pawhuska in the 1920s that included the hooded clansmen participating in a downtown parade. Pawhuska insurance man Joe McGuire said when he was a youngster a neighbor had come to their house wanting to borrow a pair of Joe's father's boots to attend a funeral, he said. The neighbor left with boots in hand.

Joe and his father were downtown when the Klan parade started and were watching as the hooded Klansmen went by. The Klansmen hated all Jews, Catholics, Irish, Indians, Mexicans and Blacks. They still liked apple pie, motherhood and the flag as long as it was white. The Klan had lost favor over the years but a tiny group held on and still were staging rallies and burning crosses on lawns of their hated targets. The McGuires, being both Irish and Catholic, watched in disgust the procession that passed before them.

All of a sudden the senior McGuire saw his boots in the stirrups of a saddle of the hooded rider that passed in front of him. An incensed McGuire shouted "You sonofabitch, you are wearing MY boots!" whereupon he pulled the man off the horse, unhooded him, and beat the stuffings out of the man right there on the street. The parade continued. No Klansman bothered to intervene. McGuire took his boots off the Klansman, who left barefoot.

McGuire's neighbor moved the next day.

BILL LEHMANN

Guthrie

Apothecary Garden, downtown Guthrie

COFFEE CLUBBERS' BULL MEAT DINNER

The Guthrie social event of the week in May 1972 was the Coffee Clubbers Bull Meat dinner (or is that bull MEET?) at the Parker House Restaurant. Cattleman George Chiga hosted the event and provided the nice, large bull meat steaks.

Every community has its coffee club gatherings each morning, but the Guthrie coffee clubbers were a rare and diverse gathering of characters. There was Ray Smith, the friendly undertaker; Harvey Donnell, the casket maker; Kenneth Mitchell and Keith Camerer, abstracters; Harold Glock, stock market player; Clyde Teuscher, Coca-Cola bottler and farmer; Ted Wille, retired tire shop owner; Cliff Burkett, mechanic; Dr. James Petty, physician; Dale Himes, newspaper editor; me and John Krittenbrink, pharmacist and owner of the drug store where the gathering took place.

The two most prominent members of the club were George Chiga and Frank Crews. The two held the floor most mornings with their banter back and forth, taking opposite stances on most topics of conversation. Crews was a very tight conservative, never giving the appearance of being happy. He never seemed to agree with anything done by the federal government, local city council or Chamber of Commerce activities.

Frank and Vera Crews listen to George Chiga's bull meat story.

Chiga was a very outgoing optimist with a hearty laugh that could be heard a half block away. Being a lawyer with a good command of vocabulary, Chiga usually got the better of Crews, but Crews verbal challenges continued.

George had been telling coffee clubbers how tender and delicious bull meat steaks were and how they added to the vim, vigor and vitality of those who were fortunate enough to dine on the delicacy. Frank Crews took immediate exception to the remark saying, "Bull meat steaks are tender—that's bullshit and you know it!" Crews challenged. "Everybody knows that bull meat is tough, stringy and gets bigger as you chew it." Some of the other members scoffed at the claim and told George they were "from Missouri and had to be "showed."

"Not so," said George. To prove it he would host a steak dinner and furnish the steaks from a large Charolais bull in his herd that had recently been butchered. Coffee Clubbers and their wives gathered in a reserved room at the steakhouse dressed in their finery for the special occasion. Steak house owner Wayne Parker charcoaled the steaks in his own special technique that was a closely guarded secret. The steaks were very tender and delicious, believe it or not. Chiga had topped Crews again!

George gave a long dissertation on the many benefits of choosing bull meat over the regular beef cuts. A couple of the points I remember, such as bull meat is very lean and contains very little cholesterol compared to regular beef. Other points he made I forgot because he talked faster than I could listen.

This was the second big social event for coffee clubbers and their wives. Dr. James Petty earlier in the year hosted a wine and cheese tasting party. Not many coffee clubs can boast about such fancy social goings on!

The Coffee Club was the only club in town that had no objectives, no dues and no responsibilities. World and national problems were discussed but never solved. All could coach football and baseball teams better than the coach the universities hired at millions of dollars a year!

Several of the wives gave George a kiss saying it was the first time their husband had taken them out in years!

GENUINE AMERICAN SUCCESS STORY

All was not frivolity with George Chiga. The George Chiga story will reaffirm any doubts you ever had about the American Dream and the opportunity to succeed. Born in Regina, Saskatchewan, Canada, in 1913 to Hungarian emigrants, fate would take him from extremely poor beginnings to the world stage and success as an athlete, cattleman and acclaimed cattle breeder.

Chiga left home at an early age to fend for himself. He worked as a cook for coal miners and even as a bouncer for a nightclub. He became interested in wrestling and became the Canadian National Champion in the heavyweight division. Chiga represented Canada in the 1936 Olympics held in Berlin, Germany. He did not win any medals, but caught the eye of Ed 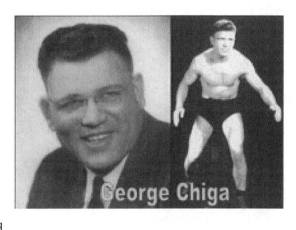 Gallagher, wrestling coach at Oklahoma State University who saw potential and offered him a scholarship.

Arriving at Stillwater, Oklahoma, with 25 cents to his name, he became an OSU Cowboy athlete, participating in football and wrestling. Chiga was more than a handful on the wrestling mat or on the football field. He stood no more than five foot seven inches tall but was built like a Sherman tank. If you ever tried to wrestle a hog, you would have to approach Chiga about the same way.

Chiga had never finished high school in Canada, but quickly passed all exams and excelled as a student as well as an excellent athlete. He placed second in the 1940 NCAA wrestling championships and was named to the All American team. Chiga earned a bachelor's degree in 1940 and his master's degree from the university in 1942. He then entered the U.S. Army, where he attained the rank of T-Sergeant before discharge. Chiga became an American citizen following discharge. He then attained a law degree, later becoming a judge.

Chiga met and married his sweetheart and life companion, Berniece while at OSU. The couple moved to Guthrie where Chiga became a teacher in the agriculture department and practiced law. The couple then began building their dream of becoming cattle raisers and selected the Red Angus breed to build on. In time they accumulated several hundred acres near Guthrie, and their herd of Red Angus cattle grew from a seed of ten cows to hundreds of cattle. They added a few Charolais breed cattle to their operation but concentrated on the Red Angus. Chiga and Berniece led efforts to establish the Red Angus Association and were charter and founding members of the organization. Chiga received international attention in cattle breeding and worked closely with OSU agriculture programs to provide cattle breeders the latest technology.

George Chica

Chiga was given the Pioneer Award by the Beef Improvement Federation in 2002, recognizing his efforts to better the beef industry. In 2006 he was named to the Regina Sports Hall of Fame in his native country as a national champion wrestler and football player.

George Chiga died in Tulsa in 2007 at the age of 94. He left a legacy of $250,000 to the university to chair an additional professorship devoted to bettering the cattle breeding programs. George Chiga never forgot the country or the university that gave him the opportunity to succeed.

FIVE SHOTS, FIVE BIRDS

With great anticipation I was preparing my hunting gear to go pheasant hunting. It was a trek I had made for many years at the invitation of Brady and Jackie Hood, whose large grain farm was located near the southwest Kansas town of Bucklin. I awaited the arrival of son Gene and his friend Rick Tate, students at Oklahoma State University who were to accompany me on the weekend hunt.

During the four-hour drive to Bucklin, the boys were relentless in their challenge about how they were going to kill all the birds. I was getting so old and slow, they said, that I wouldn't even get off a shot. Even turning up the radio in the pickup truck couldn't drown out the banter about how they were going to beat me in the numbers of birds in the bag. I just let them rant while silently thinking, "we'll see."

Brady and Jackie Hood met when Brady was stationed at McConnell Air Force Base at Wichita, Kansas. They married and continued an Air Force career until Brady retired. They then began living a civilian life working with Jackie's father, Everett Copeland, in his several-thousand-acre farm operation raising wheat, corn and cattle. Copeland Farms was very successful, but it had not come easy. Copeland survived the great Dust Bowl that hit Kansas and Oklahoma with a devastating drought that lasted 10 years. With his wife, Bea, they had raised three children and held on to the farms. In addition to the grain crops, they also had a feedlot where they raised cattle and hogs, feeding them the grain grown on the farm. Bea always had a bounty of freshly baked cookies from the oven waiting for Everett

Gandy and Brady

when the farm chores were done for the day. Everett loved his cookies.

During their air force life in Wichita, Brady invited many of his Air Force buddies to hunt pheasant during the hunting season. They continued the tradition following retirement, inviting other friends as well.

Jackie was a slender woman, perhaps from her farming activities as a child. She was always busy as a worm in hot ashes, doing something. She ran the household, got Butch, Leigh, Ralph and Beverly off to school, cooked and cleaned, was active in the PTA and church, but could also run any unit of farm equipment she was called on to do.

Brady, a native Alabaman, was a University of Alabama football fan, always dreaming of 'Bama's return to glory on the gridiron. He loved grits.

Arriving at the farm Friday evening, we were met by many of the guests that were already there, coming from all parts of the country. There was "Cap'n Bob," Brady Hood's old quail hunting buddy from Florida, who had arrived pulling an open top Jeep. There was A.P. Gandy and his wife, Theda, from Ft. Worth, Texas. Gandy was an air force buddy but had retired and worked for Boeing, building fighter planes at Ft. Worth. A rabid Texas A&M Aggie fan, Gandy always chided me about "all those Texans" on Oklahoma University's football team that always seemed to beat his Aggies.

Harry Drake

Then there was Colonel Harry Drake, who had flown in from Germany to join the party. When I first met Harry, he told me his name and added that it didn't matter because I would never remember it. I thought, *Why you bastard, I'll remember it if it's the last thing I do.* I used word association and thought of a Hairy Mallard drake duck. We became fast friends, hunting together often.

Harry was a West Point graduate and had a son that was also a student at West Point. His son was a world-class target pistol champion competing in events all over the world representing the U.S. Military Academy. Tragically, the son was killed in an off-campus motorcycle accident. Harry never completely recovered from the loss. The hunting trips and companionship helped ease his grief, if only briefly. Harry was an excellent shot, and hunting was the activity he enjoyed most in life.

We spent the evening visiting. Some of the guys started a little penny-ante poker game and broke out a bottle. I was trying to keep Beverly and Ralphie entertained by drawing some comic strip characters like Popeye, Olive Oyl, Wimpy and others they knew nothing about. Big generation gap, don't you know? Beverly wanted me to draw Big Bird, that I knew nothing about. I drew Big Bird from a passing memory of a few glimpses on TV. Everyone agreed it was a pretty good likeness under the circumstances.

Arising early Saturday morning, I stepped out on the front porch and felt a sharp north wind blowing some very frigid air. We had arrived the night before in 70-degree shirt-sleeve weather, but a Kansas "Blue Norther" had raced in during the night. Kansas is so flat the only thing between there and the North Pole is barbed wire fences, and they sure couldn't hold the wind in check. "The birds are gonna be sitting tight today," Brady said as we headed for the wheat stubble field that was to be our first hunting destination.

At daybreak the hunters formed a semi-circle that bowed in the middle and we began walking the distance of the former large wheat field. I was stationed on the far left at the end of the line. Suddenly, the early morning silence was broken by the loud cackling of a large cock pheasant as he was flushed by the march of the hunters. The bird was headed my direction. My 20 gauge over and under gave a loud "pop," and the bird fell to the ground. No one else had even had an opportunity to shoot.

"Lucky shot, you old fart," my young adversaries said as I picked up the beautiful, brightly colored bird and placed him in my hunting coat. "That will be your last shot for the day," they taunted.

We walked a little farther, and another bird suddenly jumped up from the stubble in front of me. I fired one shot, and the bird fell. Same result. No one else in the line had a chance to fire a shot. My taunters grumbled that it was just another lucky shot and that one would certainly be my last.

On we marched in the same field when another bird flushed in front of me. Third shot—third bird. No one else had fired a shot and no other birds had been flushed from the field. "Okay, you lucky old bastard, three birds is the limit, so you can go back to the house," they mumbled.

Five birds, five shots!

We continued walking the field, and two more pheasants had flushed in front of me. Two more shots and two more birds fell. No other birds had been killed, and no other shots had been fired in the group. Many times a bird would drop from multiple shots fired in the line by the hunters with each one yelling, "I got him." Not this time. I had fired five shots and killed five birds. No one else had an opportunity to even fire a shot or claim a downed bird. What a good feeling! It was oh, so good to silence the yammering of Gene and Rick.

We continued the hunt that day and harvested a total of 111 pheasants. We gathered at the barn and began cleaning the birds and packing them in the freezer. Each hunter left with his limit of birds and pleasant memories of a successful hunt and friendships.

Gene and Rick had a great time and were successful in their hunting, but they sure didn't outshoot the "old man." They were silent on the trip back home, pretending to be sleeping. The quiet was beautiful!

The years have passed, and many changes come in people's lives. I have not hunted in 30 years. As I grew older I found more compassion for all living creatures. My guns are cased and sit silently in the closet. We feed the birds at several stations in the backyard and enjoy watching them and their beauty. We also have feeding stations for other nocturnal creatures that come out of Deer Creek that runs behind our house.

Grandy, Rick, and Gene

Should a bird jump up in front of me today, I might raise a stick and say, "Boom" as I follow him along. But at least I have memories of the day I shot five times and downed five pheasants while no one else got off a shot. And I gave a couple of kids a shooting lesson.

Brady, Harry and Gandy are gone. Harry is reunited with his beloved son. And somewhere up there, Brady is celebrating with a big bowl of grits the return to Alabama's glory on the football field. His "Crimson Tide" has won three national football championships since 2010.

Brady wouldn't have liked Oklahoma's two-touchdown win over Alabama in the 2013 Sugar Bowl. But I can hear Gandy say, "It's all because of the Texans on OU's football team!"

ELBERT CLYMER, THE MUSHROOM MAN

Elbert Clymer was a mountain of a man. Huge. Weighing probably 400 pounds. 200 pounds of it might have been belly, but he was strong as an ox. Hands the size of hams. Elbert was a gentle giant with a wide smile and a hearty laugh. But don't make him mad; he could clean your plow in a New York minute. Hung out at the Hilltop Café with the other coffeeheads, then left for the woods where he was a woodcutter.

Clymer and his dad, Unie, operated a wood yard at the west end of the viaduct that separated east from west Guthrie. He and his dad cut wood all year long and stacked it neatly in cord and rick sizes. They split the logs the old fashioned way with an axe and a splitting maul. It wasn't until years later they bought a mechanical log splitter. When the weather turned cold and fireplaces were again popular in heating homes the Clymer's did a very brisk business, delivering the wood to the homes where it was stacked for use. The wood yard was located in the Cottonwod Creek bottom and was subject to flooding. Some of the wood would float away when the floods came, but that happened infrequently. The lot would have been valuable if it weren't for flooding, but no permanent structures could be built on the property.

In the very early spring as temperatures barely start to climb; wild mushrooms would begin their annual growth in the woods. Some wild mushrooms are deadly poison.

Some are delicious when sautéed in a little butter and flour. Mushrooms are a fungus that grow in damp areas around old rotted trees in the woodlands. Some are wrinkly, resembling the human brain, and about the size of a silver dollar. Selecting mushrooms and other edibles from the woods is a lost art. The Indians, pioneers, and early settlers knew what mushrooms or greens you could eat safely without making you sick or giving you the shits.

Elbert Clymer knew the difference between the good wild mushroom variety and the poisonous kind that could kill you. He would always pick the mushrooms at just the right time while he was out cutting wood. He never sold them but furnished his friends and family with wild mushrooms when in season. Rosemary and I were fortunate to feast on Elbert's wild mushrooms every spring.

Clymer drove an old black and white '60s model Crown Victoria ex-police cruiser with the insignias painted over. The car was very high mileage after years of law enforcement service, but it got him around. It was about the only size car that he could fit his large frame into. Elbert had several siblings, all large like him and rough as a dried out corncob; even the girls. If you crossed one of the Clymer's you crossed them all. But they were a good family that helped others when needed.

Elbert's younger brother, David, was pressman at the *Guthrie Daily Leader.* David had an opinion on everything and was quick to give it to you. "I'll tell you what," David always began, and he'd tell you "what." But despite a runny mouth, David did a good job as the pressroom supervisor and was very conscientious and dependable. We ordered newsprint by the boxcar load. David had contracted with Elbert to unload the boxcar at the railroad depot, load it on his flatbed wood truck and place it in the newsprint storage room at the newspaper.

The newsprint rolls weighed an average of a thousand pounds each. Most of us would use a rolled up newspaper to place under the roll that made it maneuverable. The unbalance would allow the roll to be turned more easily. Not Elbert. He'd grab onto the side and horse it around effortlessly, rolling it straight where he wanted it to go. He could almost lift one of the half-size dinky rolls and put it anywhere he wanted.

The elder Clymer died and Elbert continued operating the wood yard himself but failing health caused him to stop cutting and stacking wood. David later took on the activity and moved the wood yard to his home in east Guthrie.

Elbert's youngest brother, Jimmy Clymer says hunting mushrooms in the spring is a family tradition. All the Clymer children inherited the art from Unie. They all went to the woods at a young age to help gather wood for the wood yard. "But 2014 was the worst year I have ever seen for wild mushrooms," Jimmy said. "The moisture just isn't there, and when you don't have moisture to go with the decomposing trees and leaves, you don't have mushrooms." Jimmy credits Elbert with teaching him to hunt and fish. "Brother was the best hunter and fisherman I ever knew," he said. "He loved the woods and nature."

Elbert could still be seen around town driving the old police cruiser, smiling and waving. Each spring Elbert would be back in the woods, turning over rotting fallen trees and gathering wild mushrooms for his friends.

I miss Elbert and the wild mushrooms. Haven't had any since he died.

MOONSHINE OR FORMALDEHYDE?

Ray Smith came into my office at the *Guthrie Daily Leader* one morning, sat a fruit jar of clear liquid on my desk. In his deep, very slow drawl said, "I thought you guys might like to taste some of the best moonshine whiskey to come out of a still."

Smith, the friendly undertaker of Guthrie still owned the 160-acre farm his ancestors had settled in the Land Run of 1889. He lived in town but made daily trips to the old homestead in Meridian to check on his cattle. The rolling, wooded hills around Meridian were dotted with moonshine stills cared for by area residents. Some did it just to keep tradition alive, while some still preferred the taste of moonshine.

"Call the sheriff!" Ralph McCalmont joked. "Moonshining is still illegal in Oklahoma!" Ray said, "The guy who made it is the nephew of the sheriff!"

"Smells like drip gas off one of those oil wells to me," Tommy Maker said as he unscrewed the lid and took a long sniff of the contents.

"Don't strike a match!" Fred Olds said as he backed away from Clyde Teuscher, who was getting ready to light a little cheroot cigar.

"Awwwww, I can't believe you sumbitches don't recognize good moonshine whiskey," Smith drawled.

"How old is that 'shine?" Kip Stratton asked as he came by with camera in hand.

"Vintage yesterday," Smith replied.

"Aw, hell, it's just water," Glenn Shirley said as he picked up the jar and held it up to the light.

Ray had me convinced it was good moonshine from Meridian. I tool off the lid, lifted the jar to my lips, and was getting ready to take a little sip. Putting the jar back down, I told son Gene to go get Clyde Graves, our pressman. Clyde was in his 60s and had been a roughneck, moonshiner and bootlegger in his younger days. "Clyde is our resident expert on moonshine," I said, "and he'll be able to identify what this stuff is."

Clyde came in the office and examined the jar, lifted it up to the light, took the lid off, and took a long sniff. He coughed a little and was about ready to announce a decision when Harvey Donnell burst into the office and shouted, "Don't anybody drink that stuff! It's embalming fluid!" Harvey was a local casket maker and best friends with Ray, the friendly undertaker. They were always pulling pranks on one another, and his announcement added more questions about the contents of that fruit jar.

Finally, I decided to give it my own test. "If this stuff is moonshine, it will burn from the alcohol content." I took it to the sink in the break room of the newspaper, soaked some of the liquid in a paper napkin. Placing the napkin in the sink, I struck a match to the napkin. It burned.

"Formaldehyde will burn, too," Harvey said, dashing my own litmus test.

After all the tests and speculation, there was not enough evidence to allow any of us the bravery to take a drink of the stuff Ray had brought in. Ray and Harvey left together with Ray muttering; "Sumbitches don't know good moonshine when they see it!"

We never did know what was in that fruit jar!

BREATHTAKING MOONSHINE

Dr. Don Green entered my office at Cimarron Valley Exploration one afternoon for an always-enjoyable visit. Dr. Green was head of the history department at Central State University. We shared a deep interest in Oklahoma and Texas history and became friends when the restoration movement began in Guthrie. He had invested in some wells that our little company had drilled, but our visits included many topics while we sipped a little Chevis Regal scotch whiskey.

This day Don had brought a friend from New York City with National Public Radio network. During our visit, the conversation turned from history and oil to to a crock jug of moonshine whiskey a friend had brought me from eastern Oklahoma that very day. "Vintage yesterday," I told them, "fresh off the still and strained through an old felt hat." Nothing to do but we try it. Don's friend had never had moonshine whiskey before.

Dr. Don Green

I prepared three little glasses and poured out some moonshine in each glass. Lifting them up, we offered a toast to good health and good fortune. Don's friend threw back his head and downed it instantly. My God! We forgot to tell him to only sip on moonshine. That stuff had a kick like a mule and would probably throw all the rods out of a car if you put it in the gas tank! In an instant, the friend lost his breath. He was gasping for air, turning green and purple, and flailing his arms. His lips began to turn blue. Don and I seated him, beat him on the back, and raised his arms, trying to return air to his troubled lungs.

We were both concerned and worried that he wasn't going to come around. I was just about to lift the telephone and place a distress call to 911 when the man finally responded, drawing in air that returned him to life and very labored breathing for a time.

Don's friend returned to New York City and reported on historical restoration events occurring in Guthrie, Oklahoma. But the moonshine incident failed to make the report on National Public Radio.

BEST FRIENDS

Ray Smith and Harvey Donnell were best friends and had been for years. You could say they were "somewhat" business partners. Harvey manufactured caskets at Central Casket Company and Ray put people in them. Smith had established Smith Funeral Home back in the 1930s and was known as Guthrie's friendly undertaker.

Ray Smith was thin and wiry, standing about 5 foot 8 inches tall and weighing perhaps 150 pounds. Smith had a very deep, though soft voice and seldom smiled, perhaps because of the solemn business he operated. Harvey Donnell was a large man, standing more than six feet and weighing 250 pounds. Harvey was not loud, but when he spoke, you knew he was around.

Both men loved quail hunting, and both had dogs. Smith had a family farm at Meridian handed down from his ancestors who had made the Land Run into Oklahoma Territory in 1889, establishing a 160-acre homestead claim. Harvey kept his birddog, Joker, in an enclosed chain link pen at his home in Guthrie. Smith's dog stayed on the farm until he was fetched to go hunting. The two hunters constantly bantered over which one was the best shot and whose birddog was the better pointer in finding quail.

They often invited me to go with them. It was a fun time listening to the two go at one another. The dogs came down on point, and we rushed up to flush them to flight. They flushed on Ray's side, and he fired three quick shots at the departing birds and missed them all. "Sumbitches flying with their hearts shot out and don't know it," he protested.

Harvey's turn came, and he missed all his shots too. Old Joker took out after the birds to fetch the fallen ones, but there were none to retrieve. "Look at poor old Joker," Ray said. "He's hiding his head in shame because you are such a poor shot! And the birds are sitting up in the tress laughing and pointing fingers at you!"

SECRET TO A LONG, HEALTHY LIFE

Lonnie Jefferson was 95 years old and still going strong! He got up at 5 o'clock every morning and still prepared his own breakfast. He was alone after outliving three wives. He retired when the Guthrie Furniture Factory shut down fifteen years earlier. Lonnie had a total of twelve children born to the three wives over a period of his marriages. A couple of the children lived nearby and looked in on Lonnie every day.

One of Lonnie's daughters called and told me about Lonnie. She thought he would be the subject of a story about reaching the ripe old age of 95. I agreed and went to see Lonnie for a little squib in my weekly newspaper column, "By the Way."

Lonnie lived in a small frame house on Vilas Street in east Guthrie. It needed paint and a few repairs, as did most of the homes in the neighborhood. But Lonnie did the best he could at keeping up with the needs of the house. When I arrived he had a screen door off and was making repairs to the screen that had come loose in a few places. "Lets the flies in too easy," he said to me as I came up, "and ah hates flies."

Lonnie Jefferson was a small black man weighing no more than 110 pounds. His overalls were thin from long years of wear, but they were clean. His thin arms had put together many chairs and tables at the furniture factory where he had worked for more than 35 years. His hair was mostly white, peppered with a few curly black hairs in between. I took a photo of Lonnie working on the screen door and asked if he had time to visit with me. We talked a few minutes about his earlier life and then I said, "You've hit a big milestone in reaching 95 years of age. Would you share the secret of reaching 95 and being in good health as you obviously are?"

"Well, I does something most folks probly don't do, but ah've done it since ah was about 20 years old. Ever' morning before breakfast, ah sips a little moonshine whiskey."

"Lord. You need to get a patent on the recipe for that moonshine," I said to Lonnie.

"Well, they's mo' to it than that," he said. "When ah gits a new jar, ah puts it in mah crock jug and drops in two pieces of hard rock candy. Ah believes that does the trick," he said. "Mah, ol grandaddy taught me that an' he lived to 101 years old."

Lonnnie Jefferson died in 1997. He was 105 years of age.

"THEY WILL REMEMBER PAUL KROEGER"

Every town has a "Town Crazy"—someone who marches to a different beat of the drum than we "sane" folk. When I was growing up in Muskogee, a young black man would pass by our house frequently in all sorts of different dress and costumes. Sometimes he would be dressed as a cowboy complete with wooly chaps, boots, spurs and a big cowboy hat. He also carried a six-shooter in a holster.

Other times he might be dressed to the nines in a pinstripe suit, Homburg hat, spats covering his shoes and leading a goat. Other times I saw him dressed as an aviator with goggles over his eyes, arms outspread dipping like wings while he made sounds like and airplane engine. Everybody gave him a wide berth as he walked down the sidewalk. His attire was not a cheap variety either. It was said he was the son of an affluent black family and had suffered a brain injury at birth.

Paul Kroeger was considered the town crazy in Guthrie, Oklahoma. He might appear downtown in the dead heat of summer dressed in a Cossack fur hat, a heavy coat in short shorts and bare legs. Most times he wore a Jungle Jim pith helmet, sometimes pushing a old reel type push mower and carrying a leaf rake. He was known to do lawn work and a few odd jobs around town. If Paul liked the lady that hired him to mow the lawn, he would mow a pattern in the grass leaving the shape of a heart. But whatever his source of income, he led a meager existence and was considered a recluse. Some said a sister, Katherine, helped support him.

A glove hanging on a stick in front of his house had its middle finger upright while the other fingers drooped. That was Paul, giving the middle finger to the world as it passed by his house.

Kroeger was downtown often in his shorter than short shorts that exposed his manly body parts. The shorts were so short that when he placed his foot on a windowsill or car bumper one or both testicles might drop down and be exposed. Paul's dress, or lack thereof, disturbed some of the little town's ladies so much that many lodged complaints with Dale Orndorff, Guthrie's police chief.

The complaints were so numerous that Orndoff was compelled to address Kroeger about his behavior. The chief hauled him into police headquarters one day and told him about the many complaints and told him he needed to wear pants that would cover his genitals. Ordndorff went on to tell Paul that they had known each other for many years. "You want people to think you are crazy, but you are not and I know you aren't. But people don't understand why you live the way you do."

Paul looked Orndorff squarely in the eye and said, "Dale, we will both die one of these days, but I guarantee the people will remember me long after the memory of Dale Orndorff has faded." Hardly the comment of a "crazy" man.

As a teenager, Kip Stratton played pick up tennis at Highland Park during the summer. Though much younger, Stratton played with Kroeger occasionally. Kroeger always dressed in a black pin-striped double-breasted suit, white sneakers without socks, and a broad-brimmed white Panama hat. But Kroeger never wore a shirt under the jacket, just the jacket. He wasn't very mobile, Stratton said, but he had a way of getting to the ball, and then he'd hit enormous lobs, high, high in the air, and while you were waiting for it to come back to earth, he'd position himself at the net for the return.

Paul once came down with pneumonia and nearly died. Mary Agnes Ferris went to his house every day and nursed him back to health, literally spoon-feeding him soup while sitting beside his bed. One day, after he'd recovered, there was a knock at the door of the Ferris home. Paul was at the door and asked for Mary Agnes. So Mary Agnes went to the door and followed Paul out to the yard. He had a wagon of some sort that he had pulled by hand over to their house. In the back of the wagon was an old-fashioned pump organ. Paul had found it in a chicken yard and had painstakingly restored it, fixing the bellows and everything so that it worked like new. And he refinished the wood so that it looked like it had just come out of the factory. He gave it to Mary Agnes for taking care of him.

Actually, little seems to be known about Kroeger. Always reclusive, he related to were very few friends. Known as a man of unusual talent, he was Poet Laureate for the state of Oklahoma from 1931-40. His appointment at age 23 came by way of Governor "Alfalfa Bill" Murray. It was said that Kroeger campaigned hard for Murray, and the appointment came as payback. No published poems by Kroeger are known to exist, but some say he did have a small booklet of poems that resulted in his appointment. Many say Murray was "crazy" himself, so the appointment was fitting. But to his credit, Kroeger remained Oklahoma's Poet Laureate through the terms of two other governors.

Kroeger at one time was organist for the Catholic Church and played beautifully without being able to read a note of music. He would also sit on a park bench in Highland Park and without notes play beautiful classical music on a violin. Somewhere this training was in his youth, but it remains a mystery, as does Kroeger himself.

Some say there is a fine line between madman and genius. Perhaps Kroeger was smack dab on that line. Perhaps he was leading the life he wanted as a misfit dropout from a society he didn't particularly care for—an early-day hippie, so to speak, without the marijuana and LSD.

I had conversation with Kroeger many times. He was always alert, well-spoken, articulate, with excellent vocabulary and knowledgeable about the topic being discussed. He was well-educated, but a well-educated odd wad to say the least.

Paul Kroeger was born in 1907 and died in 1977. He is buried in Seward Cemetery. A small tombstone is inscribed, "Brother of Katherine."

Paul Kroeger did it his way.

HARVEY'S TERRAPIN POINTING BIRDDOG

Harvey Donnell's birddog, Joker, was more than a quail dog—he pointed terrapins. This was a good thing at times. At other times it was bad, particularly if they were hunting quail. Old Joker might come down on a strong, steady point, and when the hunters got there ready to flush a covey of birds, it would be a terrapin at the end of Joker's nose. Fortunately, the terrapins were mostly in hibernation by quail hunting season.

At other times this was good because Harvey and old Joker furnished the terrapins for the annual turtle races for Guthrie's '89er Day celebration every year. Harvey would take Joker to the field, and they would accumulate enough terrapins over a course of a week or so to stage the turtle races. They would put the terrapins in a big circle and each would have a number painted on its shell. The terrapin that crossed the outer line of the circle won the race. The child holding the number of the winning terrapin won a prize.

The terrapin races could be very spirited with the kids yelling encouragement to their numbered terrapin to get the lead out and get across that line! The shouting sometimes made the terrapins go back into their shells and balk. It might take thirty minutes or more for a terrapin to cross the line. A first, second and third prize would make the races even longer.

I had told Harvey I wanted to do a story on Joker and the terrapins, so the next time they went to give me a call. When the call came, I picked up a camera and joined Harvey and his best friend, Ray Smith, to scout out the quail population and pick up some terrapins for the races. Harvey released Joker from his pen in the back of the pickup, and Joker bounded off at a fast pace, but stopping to pee on every bush and tree, as most bird dogs do until they settle down. Joker soon came down on a strong point, and Harvey and Ray ran over to see what the dog had pointed. I was right behind them with my camera. Suddenly both men turned abruptly and headed back toward me at a dead run. Joker had pointed a skunk!

The skunk and Joker were holding each other at bay until Harvey and Ray rushed in. The activity spooked the skunk, and he let Joker have it right in the snoot! Poor old Joker was coughing and gagging, frothing at the mouth, and rolling in the grass to try to wipe the terrible skunk odor off himself.

Harvey and Ray had been spared, but Joker rode back to town in his pen, where both were left at the veterinarian's to be fumigated! I got a story for my column, but of a different twist—and no pictures.

THE BLOWN-UP TOILET

Donnell Roach was a Guthrie police officer. He came into headquarters one day with a case of diarrhea and had to go to the bathroom. In a hurry to get to the pot before an eruption, he shucked his trousers and started to sit down. With no time to set aside his belt, holstered gun, and ammunition, Roach's service revolver hit the floor of the men's room and exploded with a thunderous report. The .357 magnum bullet shattered the toilet stool, blowing it to smithereens and sitting Roach down on top of it!.

Fellow officers rushed in to find Roach standing in toilet water, diarrhea and several gashes in his butt where he had sat on the jagged remains of the toilet stool. A few stitches in his butt at the hospital emergency room along with a couple of anti-diarrhea pills had Roach back on the job in a few days.

THE GLOCKS

Harold and Madelin Glock were as opposite as day and night. But they had one thing in common: They liked money! And they had plenty of it.

Harold Glock's money hadn't come easy. He skimped and saved every penny and nickel he could. He denied himself meals in order to accumulate money. He bought stock with his savings—mostly General Motors stock. As his wealth accumulated he would loan money to individuals in building homes the lending institutions had denied. Harold was albino with a chalk white complexion and very light blue eyes. His hair was not gray, it was white as cotton and had been all his life.

Harold was very conservative. A group of businessmen met daily at Murray Drug to have coffee. The group would then match coins and the loser would have to pay. Harold never participated, always paying for his own coffee. He said he would just as soon throw his money into the street as to match for the coffee. He would take a gamble though. When he learned I was going to drill a well for oil and gas in Logan County, Glock was one of the first to come forward to buy and interest in the well. It paid big dividends and added a sizable chunk to his banking account.

Madelin Glock had inherited her wealth initially from her family, who owned Gerlach Motors in the early days as a Studebaker and Packard dealer. But Madelin was a very smart businesswoman as well, making wise investments over the years that had paid big dividends to her portfolio. Harold was a salesman for Gerlach Motors and then had a lengthy career selling Buicks with B.K. Daniels Motor Company in Guthrie.

Harold and Madelin married. They were as different as night and day in personality, but both were as tight as bark on a tree when it came to money. Madelin was active in city affairs, some saying she was a nuisance with her ultra-conservative political philosophy. But Madelin got the attention of the women voters in Guthrie who propelled her into two terms as mayor.

The conservative values of the couple in their personal life went so far as to split household expenses right down the middle. Harold paid half from his account and Madelin paid half from her separate account. This practice was well known by the people who knew the Glocks.

Being a newspaperman, and brash as well, causes me to ask questions others may wonder about but be reluctant to ask. But one day I was visiting with Harold and asked teasingly how they handled their sex life since every part of their life seemed to be divided separately. Instead of telling me their sex life wasn't any of my damn business, which he should have, Harold said, "Oh, we don't have any trouble at all when it comes to sex. Madelin tells me, 'Harold, you are quite a man!'"

THE BUILDING COLLAPSE

In the early morning hours of Memorial Day 1967 the Lyon Building on the northeast corner of Harrison and Division collapsed out into Division Street of Guthrie, Oklahoma. Fallen bricks covered more than half the street causing closure until the debris could be hauled away. Thankfully, it was a holiday and in the early morning hours, so there was little effect other than the destruction of the building. There were no injuries even though the second floor of the building contained several apartments.

One of the apartment dwellers was a little lady of about seventy years of age. She was still in her gown and robe when I saw her about 8 a.m. I asked her reaction to the event that took the whole east wall off her apartment. "Oh, Lord, the noise was awful!" she said. "I thought it was a tornado! I went and grabbed my bottle of wine and hid under the bed," she said, shaking her head in disbelief.

The collapse of the Lyon Building caused concern about the safety of other buildings in Guthrie that had been constructed in the 1889-1907 period. Engineers had warned the Guthrie city council that many of the buildings were unsafe and could collapse at any time. Several historic buildings had been demolished during the 1950s, including old City Hall where the Constitutional Convention was held in 1906 to hammer out the state's Constitution that was adopted at Statehood, November 16, 1907.

Demolition of the old City Hall was very unpopular with the citizens. And it was so difficult to bring down that it quelled the cry for further historic building demolishment in the city. The collapse of the Lyon Building renewed warnings of unsafe buildings in Guthrie. This caused the Council vote demolishment of the Brooks Hotel and Opera House and the Ione Hotel, all very important buildings where many historical events occurred in the history of Guthrie and the state.

The razing of these buildings was the springboard in organizing an effort to preserve Guthrie's history and historical buildings. It was a wake up call to Guthrie and the citizens responded.

STOLEN SAFE RECOVERED

"Well, we got the mystery of the stolen safe solved," Logan County Sheriff Nolan Welch told me on the phone. "Get your camera and I'll be by to pick you up and take you to the location."

Two days before, the entire safe had been stolen from the office at Langston University, just 10 miles east of Guthrie. The safe was large and weighed more than 100 pounds, so it must have taken more than one man to pull off this heist. University officials reported they kept no money in the safe and were puzzled by why the safe was taken in the first place. The safe had been spotted lying face up in the Cimarron River, some 15 miles west of Guthrie. The safe door was open and papers were lying around the riverbed, according to the report made by a citizen crossing the bridge that morning. The Cimarron River is notoriously shallow during dry periods. The riverbed is a half-mile wide and the water about an inch deep in a very narrow stream. The safe was clearly visible and had no chance of being submerged.

Sitting in the back seat of Welch's car was Elmer Hogg, chief of security at the university. Hogg had been a member of the Guthrie police force for several years before taking the head security position at Langston. It was quite natural for him to accompany the sheriff to the location. I began quizzing Hogg about the heist that happened on his watch. "You don't understand, Bill," Sheriff Welch interrupted, saying "Elmer done it!"

Hogg and a fellow security officer had loaded the safe on a dolly and wheeled it out to Hogg's pickup truck and hauled it to his garage. They worked most of the night breaking into the safe only to discover it did not contain cash as they expected. They loaded the safe on the truck and pitched it over the bridge railing in the dead of the night and returned to Langston. Welch suspected an inside job from the start since there was no forced entry. The sheriff also suspected Hogg from Hogg's shady past with the law. Welch interrogated Hogg most of the following day and got him to confess to the crime. Hogg and the assistant were sentenced to five years in the state penitentiary, served their time and were released.

Hogg later was operator of a "joint" on South Wentz Street in Guthrie where loud music, whiskey, beer and women were the principal attractions. Hogg was shot to death in a dispute with a patron. The "joint" was closed much to the relief of the neighborhood residents.

STOWAWAY CAT

Don Bretz was on his way to work at his sign shop in Guthrie one morning when he stopped to visit with a neighbor down the street. Parking his car on the wrong side of the street, Don and the neighbor visited while Don sat in the car seat with the door open, his feet resting on the curb.

Don's little Rat Terrier that accompanied him everywhere got out of the car with the open door, went about the yard sniffing and doing what dogs do. Unbeknownst to Don, a cat had climbed in the open door and into the back of his car. After finishing his visit, Don whistled for the dog, and the dog ran to the car and jumped in. Don closed the door of the car and started off down the street to town.

It took only a couple of seconds for the dog to find the stowaway cat! The chase began with the dog and cat going round and round in the car and all over a startled Don. He stopped the car as quickly as he could. He opened the car door and the cat sped out with the dog right on its heels. The cat scampered up a nearby tree allowing Don to be able the catch his dog and proceed to town.

THE VENCEDORA

The movie *The Last Picture Show* could have been filmed in Guthrie, Oklahoma. The Vencedora pool hall and domino parlor was already there and in vintage condition. It had not changed since the early 1900s.

Entering the Vencedora was like a trip back in time. Sawdust, peanut hulls and floor sweep covered the wooden floors. It was seldom cleaned. Several pool tables and a snooker table were available to patrons along with several domino tables that were usually occupied by older men playing the ancient game. Several brass spittoons dotted the floors. Some tobacco chewers hit them from time to time but the misses were soaked up in the sawdust and peanut hulls

Merv Gray, who bought it from Jack Cahill, owned the Vencedora. Merv had living quarters in an apartment upstairs in the two-story building. Merv was a big man, standing more than six feet tall with sandy-colored graying hair. Merv had a very white complexion indicating he seldom left the pool hall to seek the sun. You could call Merv's complexion a "pool hall pallor." Soft drinks, snacking crackers and pickled eggs in a two-gallon jar were the only food and drink available. Cigars, cigarettes and chewing tobacco were also available.

High-stakes poker games were played in a room upstairs. Nig Eaton was a regular patron of the poker games, and a regular loser. Nig owned a feed store in Guthrie that was run by his wife. He was a second cousin of Frank Eaton, an early Oklahoma character known for tracking down and shooting to death the killer of his father when Frank was but a teenager. The Oklahoma State University mascot "Pistol Pete" was created from images of Eaton.

Nig Eaton was an easy target of the card sharks. He would make foolish bets with no hope of winning possibilities. He loved to gamble. On the golf course he might be 50 feet from the cup and bet you fifty dollars he could make it. Friends would tell Nig that he was an easy patsy and say, "Nig, don't you know those guys are screwing you like a tied-up goat?"

"Yeah, I know," Nig would reply, "but it's the only game in town."

Most of the high-stakes poker players entered the Vencedora from an entrance in the back alley to conceal their identity. But one other patron I knew about was my own pressman at the *Guthrie Daily Leader*, Clyde Graves. Graves had been the pressman for many years starting when the *Leader* was printed on an old flatbed Goss Duplex press that only printed eight pages at a time. While publisher of the Pawhuska newspaper, I had gone down to Guthrie with Donrey vice president J.L. Jennings to observe their transition to offset printing in April 1965. We were to get a brand new 3-unit Goss Community Press like the one installed at Guthrie. I was transferred to Guthrie in 1966 and inherited Clyde. Clyde adapted very well to the new equipment even though he was getting to an advanced age. He had been a roughneck in the oil field many years before becoming the pressman. He bore the marks of injury in rig activity by losing partial fingers on his left hand. Clyde had also been a bootlegger before whiskey became legal in Oklahoma again.

Lehmann and Clyde Graves

My office at the *Leader* was located directly across the street from the Vencedora. From my office window I observed Clyde on many occasions leave the pressroom after the last press run of the day and enter the Vencedora. As I came to work early each morning I could observe Clyde coming out of the Vencedora. He had been upstairs all night playing poker. He would go to the sink in the pressroom, remove his false teeth, rinse them off, put them back in place and go about duties of the day. He always had a smelly cigar clenched between his false teeth. Sometimes it was lit, sometimes it wasn't. Clyde seldom lost on the poker table. He might have been one of the players taking money from Nig Easton.

When I was a teenager I enjoyed playing snooker rather than pool. It seemed more challenging to me because the balls were smaller and the pockets you shot them into were smaller as well. The snooker table had numbered balls but also some red balls you had to make before shooting a numbered ball. When son Gene was a carrier boy at the *Leader*, I would take him on occasions to play snooker after he finished his paper route. We had a lot of fun at the Vencedora.

Sadly, the Vencedora is no more. When Merv Gray died, the pool hall with all the character became another antique store. Gone are the pool tables, wafting tobacco smoke, spittoons, dominoes, and the sawdust and peanut hull carpeting. Guthrie lost another treasure.

LOST BIRD DOG

Harvey Donnell invited me to go quail hunting with him one day and I eagerly accepted. I had hunted with Harvey before and always had a good time. Harvey had a fine birddog named "Joker." Old Joker was getting on up in years for a bird dog but was still very dependable on finding and pointing quail. We were hunting on land adjacent to the municipal airport. We had bagged a few birds and were preparing to leave when Harvey decided to check out a small field next to a road. We noticed a group of hunters with a couple of bird dogs hunting on land across the road.

We started to leave and Harvey whistled for old Joker, but the dog didn't respond to the whistle so we started looking for him. After searching for several minutes I said to Harvey, "maybe he went across the road and joined those other hunters."

"No way in hell that would happen," Harvey said. "That dog would not leave me and go with another bunch!" We backtracked all the places we had been and still no Joker. Finally I told Harvey, "Let's go see Soc Nelson and get him to take us up in a plane and check out the countryside." Harvey was still protesting that old Joker wouldn't leave him.

We went to the office at the airport. Soc Nelson was manager of the municipal airport and we were good friends. I used Soc to take me up to shoot pictures of news events that could be enhanced by a view from the air. Soc would call every once in a while and say, "Let's go to the City and have a cup of coffee." I'd go out and we would fly to Wiley Post airport, have coffee, visit with other pilots and return to Guthrie. We had even flown to Kansas to hunt pheasant a couple of times. That was a time when gasoline was not expensive.

Soc fired up one of his planes, Harvey and I boarded and we took off to look for old Joker. We flew over the area where we had seen the other hunters. Sure enough, there was old Joker with that group seemingly happy as a lark and not missing Harvey at all. "I never would have believed it!" Harvey said.

We went back to the airport, got in my truck and found the hunters and retrieved old Joker. One of the hunters even wanted to buy Joker because he had outperformed his other two dogs. Harvey politely declined, but I saw a button pop off his shirt when the hunter bragged on Joker.

Joker probably wondered what all the fuss was about!

STOLEN BIRD DOG

The door to the *Guthrie Daily Leader* office burst open one morning and a loud voice proclaimed, "I want to see Bill! Some dirty son of a bitch stole my bird dog last night, and I want to run an ad in the paper!"

There was no mistaking that voice. It belonged to Jack Cahill.

Cahill's voice could be heard a half block away when he talked normally, but today he was so enraged his voice could be heard in the next town. The commotion got the attention of everyone in the office. Even pressman David Clymer had come from the back of the building to see what the excitement was all about.

Cahill handed the advertising clerk a sheet of paper on which he had written the message he wanted to place in the ad. After looking at the note Cahill had written, she said, "Mr. Lehmann, I believe you had better look at this."

I took a still-shaking and loudly cussing Cahill back into my office and closed the door, hoping to cool his emotions down to an acceptable level. It did no good. He was still raving mad and shouting curse-words that would make a roughneck blush, and spitting tobacco juice into the wastebasket between words! I opened the paper and the written words were the very same profane words he used in describing the fate that awaited the dirty son of a bitch who had stolen his bird dog the night before.

After reading the message I said, "Jack, I can't run this ad using the words you have written."

"Well, by God, why not!" he raved. "It's my money and I want it worded exactly as I have it there. I'll have that son of a bitch's balls hanging on my front porch," he continued.

"This is a family newspaper," I said to Jack. "We have women and children that read the paper and have a policy to not publish profane words. Quite frankly," I continued, "most people would find it highly offensive, and I do as well. I can't run this in my newspaper," I told him.

"Well, I'll take the damned thing to the *Daily Oklahoman* and I'll bet they'll run it," he said.

"No, they'll not publish it either," I told him. "You never see profane words published in the *Oklahoman*, but I would suggest a solution that might be satisfactory," I said. "What do you think of this idea: the comic pages use symbols that suggest the comic character is using cuss words. How about something like this," I said to Cahill, while sketching out the ad on another sheet of paper.

"To the dirty @#%!& that stole my bird dog yesterday:

If I catch you I will cut your (^%$#$ out, stuff them in your #@!^^%^ mouth, run a hot poker up your %*&$ and hang your dirty ^%&$#@ from the light on my front porch! Signed Jack Cahill."

"Well, I don't like it as well as mine, but if that is the best you can do I guess we'll run it," Cahill said. He paid for the ad and left much to the relief of everyone in the *Leader* office. Cahill wasn't satisfied but somewhat pacified.

After Cahill left the office society editor Mamie Oliver stuck her head in my office door and said, "You should have been a diplomat, Mr. Lehmann."

CAHILL'S DAIRY MAID DRIVE IN

Jack Cahill and his wife Lois were owners and operators of Cahill's Dairy Maid on South Division Street in Guthrie. They say opposites attract. Theirs must have been a cosmic collision because I never saw such opposites in all my years. Lois was a very soft-spoken, refined, beautiful lady while Jack was a loud, tobacco-chewing, whiskey-drinking man whose actions and vocabulary provoked attention wherever he was.

Jack and Lois worked side by side at the tiny eatery. There was no room inside for seats, so customers ordered at the window and took the food, drinks, and Dairy Maid ice cream to their cars or to a picnic table outside. The Cahills did a brisk business and had lots of take-away trade. Jack operated the smoker, where he prepared brisket and other meats that went into the sandwiches. Lois handled the grill, where she grilled hamburgers and managed the French fry potato unit.

The specialty at Cahill's was the "Shirley Special," a dripping beef sandwich named for their daughter. It was made from brisket Jack smoked all night in their barbecue oven. The brisket was chopped fine and the meat loaded with a special recipe broth. This was placed between two thick slices of dark rye bread and wrapped in wax paper. Add a little mustard or horseradish and you'd think you had died and gone to Heaven, it was so tasty!

Jack kept a hidden pint of whiskey he nipped on from time to time. Actually it was more than a nip. He'd take several gulps straight out of the bottle blended with the tobacco chew he always had in his mouth. Obviously, he had a cast iron stomach. He kept Lois busier trying to find his stashed bottle, but she seldom found it. She would fuss at him from time to time, but they had been married for many years and raised three children very successfully. Jack was also an avid hunter who cared little about season times or bag limits.

One night a customer complained about something he had been given. Jack, being a little tipsy, left the building and confronted the customer outside. The man happened to be black. Waving a pistol he had retrieved from the business, Jack began dressing him down verbally using a few racial terms. The black man promptly took the pistol away from Jack and whipped him about the head with it before throwing it on the gravel drive and parking lot at the business. Lois quickly called for police assistance, but the customer had disappeared into the night. Jack was a bloody mess but not seriously hurt.

Jack Cahill had been a roughneck on drilling rigs in his early days. He later operated Cahill's Recreation Parlor in downtown Guthrie. The business, catering to men, was furnished with several domino tables, pool tables, and an upstairs room where high-stakes poker games sometimes lasted all night. He and Lois then opened the Cahill Dairy Maid that they operated for many years until the chain operations began building in Guthrie locations.

Despite his gruff outside appearance, Jack Cahill was very well liked by all who knew him. They accepted him at face value, being Jack Cahill, one of a kind. Lois had him cleaned up pretty good when they went to church.

BILL LEHMANN

Oil Field

*Cimarron Valley Exploration rig
on location in Logan County, Oklahoma, 1978.*

POBOCO—POOR BOYS OIL COMPANY

What do you do if you have spent forty years in the newspaper business and never have any hope of owning your own newspaper?

How about starting an oil business? Are ye daft? Drilling rigs and associated hardware cost millions of dollars, much more than even a small newspaper! True, but there is a way of doing it without owning any of all that iron.

Having grown up in Oklahoma and having friends in the oil business, I knew how competitive oil well service companies are. Need a well drilled? Call a drilling company. They'll come out and provide all the equipment and personnel you need to drill the well from start to finish. And there are dozens of companies to select from and competition keeps the price down. It's the same with other companies in the oil field. Need a geologist, engineer, drilling mud, electric logging unit, or the well cemented or fracked? They are as near as your telephone. Lift up the phone and call whatever service you need. They will provide the service and personnel and they provide their own liability insurance and payroll. All you need is a telephone. No Inventory, no building, no office hours.

After our children were grown and gone, Rosemary and I had a little "play" money for a change and we invested in a well or two. I liked the excitement of watching a well go down and decided I would like to start my own company. She was agreeable so our local attorney drew up incorporation papers and registered them with the state of Oklahoma in July 1976. We named the company Cimarron Valley Exploration, Incorporated. For $500 we were in the oil business! Oklahoma oil company directories listed little bitty Cimarron Valley Exploration right in there with Halliburton, Phillips, Conoco, Kerr-McGee and all the biggies!

We were in the oil business, but what next? We needed a lease. We didn't have money to lease a drilling location. We didn't have a pot to piss in or a window to throw it out of. All we had was a dream and we needed some help from a lot of other folks who might want to gamble and become dreamers with us. We had three friends that owned rural property that had not been leased for years. I told them if they would give me a one-year lease we would drill a well. Since we didn't have bonus money for the lease we would give them an additional 32nd royalty interest instead of the usual 1/8th royalty of the oil and gas production. Each bought into the plan and now we had a place to drill.

Oil prices had dropped to a low of $3 per barrel in the 1950s. The price went to $5 per barrel a little later and that spurred some new drilling activity. In 1974 the price had risen to $12 per barrel so there was beginning to be a renewed interest and incentive in drilling. I thought we were getting into the business at an opportune time. I liked the thought of having an oil well pumping oil 24 hours a day. It would be making money while you ate, slept or while you played golf. If we hit a good well, we could grow on it. After all, Frank Phillips, J. Paul Getty and Robert S. Kerr started with just one well. I wasn't about to quit my day job though!

We had jumped the first hurdle. We had a lease; now all we needed was money! I had visited with several family and friends who indicated an interest in participating in drilling for oil and gas. All I needed was 32 people willing to gamble about $2,500 each to drill a well to see if we could find oil or gas. The money was gathered up in a couple of weeks.

Family, friends and business acquaintances from all walks of life: a druggist, an insurance agent, a banker, a stock market player, a Coca-Cola bottler, a casket maker, a college student, and a county treasurer. Rendal Hamby, *Guthrie Leader* advertising manager, had a few friends in Texas familiar with the oil business, and, eager to "roll the dice," they joined us. Oh, there were a couple or three millionaires in this bunch, but by and large it was a "poor boy" oil company if there ever was one!

Sandy King, an Ardmore geologist, agreed to be our consultant and work our first well. He selected the drill site after studying the electric logs on wells that had been drilled in the area. A location was selected, and the No. 1 Helen was spudded in. After two weeks of drilling with no show of oil or gas in the drilling samples or electric log, our No.1 Helen well was declared a dry hole. Disappointed, but undaunted, the group decided quickly to try again at a location on the 160-acre Schneider farm a half-mile away.

The money was anteed up, and we were ready to go again. Sandy selected a location a few miles east of some drilling activity that had found pay in the Bartlesville sand. We named the well the No.1 Alma after the lease owner's wife, Alma Schneider.

Rosemary, Bill, and driller Archie Dexter

Our No. 1 Alma was spudded in February 2, 1977 and we were off and running again trying to find oil and gas riches 5,000 feet below the surface. A lot of prayers went up and fingers crossed when the drill bit hit the ground! It would be another two weeks of drilling twenty-four hours a day before reaching our intended depth.

I had rented a travel trailer to park on location to stay overnight if needed and to use for evaluating samples. It was also a place for local participants to visit the location and observe the activities. It was a grand experience for most, who knew nothing about the mechanics of drilling a well.

Early indications of finding oil or gas were dismal as we drilled. Sandy came up every day or two to check samples of limestone, shale and sand as the well was drilled. Sandy was expecting to possibly have a well in the Skinner sand, but the formation had been reached, and there was no show in the Skinner. We were nearing our intended drilling depth and Sandy had now rented a motel room and was staying there until the well was finished. He checked 10-foot drilling samples with his microscope and black light where drilling samples would glow a gold color if oil or gas were present in the cuttings as they were circulated up in the drilling mud. Checking the latest samples and finding no shows of pay, Sandy left to go back to his motel room. "Call me if anything happens, but it don't look good, son," he said to me as he left.

Drilling underway on No. 1 Alma

Checking drilling samples on location.

I was sitting at the table in the trailer looking at the drilling samples again and seeing the same thing Sandy saw—nothing! I was about ready to break into tears at the prospect of hitting another dry hole. This would probably put an end to any hopes I had of finding a commercial well for Cimarron Valley Exploration and all the friends that had chosen to throw the dice and invest in the venture.

I wondered how many dry holes Frank Phillips or J. Paul Getty had before they hit the wells that made them rich!

Oh, well, I still had my day job!

Suddenly the door to the trailer opened and a young roughneck said, "Bill, we're getting a good drilling break, and Archie says you might want to come and see it." That was the best news we had had in two weeks! I climbed the stairs to the doghouse on the rig and went inside. The geolograph that measured the time taken to drill one foot was going crazy. Instead of drilling in hard limestone, we had suddenly hit some obvious softer sand that caused the drill bit to go through it more rapidly. I instructed Archie to drill seven feet and pull up and circulate samples of the formation for evaluation. When the first samples reached the surface, the odor of oil and gas was overpowering.

Taking the samples to the trailer, I crushed some of the cuttings together in my hand and sniffed. There was an overwhelming odor of hydrocarbons. I placed some in a tray and put it under the black light that would show fluorescence—the whole tray glowed a brilliant golden color. All the evidence to indicate oil or gas was there. My excitement was on cloud nine! I quickly drove to the Schneider residence and phoned Sandy at the motel. I told him we had a helluva show and he needed to get back as quickly as possible to evaluate the situation. Though only ten miles away, it seemed an eternity had passed before Sandy finally showed up.

Sandy took some of the cuttings and crunched them in his hand and sniffed. He sniffed some more. Finally he put some cutting in a tray and placed them in the black light. That brilliant glow returned. Sandy then placed a tray of cuttings under the microscope for evaluation. He sorted through the cuttings, separating a grain at a time. I was on pins and needles. Sandy had never said a word or showed any expression while evaluating all the evidence: the rapid drilling break, the odor and the brilliance under the black light. Finally, Sandy sat back in his chair, placed his glasses on top of his gray hair and said, "Son, I believe you can call for pipe!"

After total depth was reached, an electric log was run. The log revealed the show of oil and gas had been in the Bartlesville sand formation. Analysis by the logging engineer and Sandy indicated the need for production pipe to be run, which was done and the well readied for possible production.

Excitement was rampant among the participants in the venture. Many were local and were gathered at the well for the perforation of the pipe that would reveal the results. Butterflies were churning in my stomach, and I could hardly hide my emotions. Petroleum engineer George Ramsey and Sandy had determined where the perforations should be made, and the perforating tool with an explosive was run in the hole. After reaching the desired depth, the explosive was detonated that shot a bullet-size projectile into the pipe to permit the gas or fluid from the formation to enter the pipe and reach the surface.

No. 1 Alma Tank Battery

The explosive was detonated, and there was an instant screaming flow of oil and natural gas to the surface. It was allowed to flow and scream like a jet engine for the benefit of the spectators until being diverted to a waiting portable test tank. Cheers rang out among the gathered crowd with my cheers being perhaps the loudest. The well was free flowing and gushing with a thunderous roar to a test tank! The fluid was gauged and the rate of flow was calculated at 1,000 barrels of oil per day. My God—we had hit a gusher!

The No. 1 Alma was one of the best wells to be found in Oklahoma in many years. Three 360-barrel production tanks were set in place, and Oklahoma Corporation Commission allowable of 200 barrels of oil per day was going to the tanks. The well had cost slightly less than $100,000 to drill and complete. Our "poor boy" investors got their investment back, plus the cost of the dry hole, with two weeks' production. Land and mineral owner John Schneider went to town and bought a brand new 4-wheel drive Ford pickup truck, paying cash!

I was on cloud nine! And everybody thought I had hung the moon! But with success came dilemma. Now I had other people calling wanting to invest in the next well, and our Alma investors were anxious to drill the offset wells, of which we had three other locations to drill on the 160-acre Schneider farm. This was no eenie, meenie, minee, moe situation. A serious decision needed to be made, and soon. I loved my job at the *Guthrie Daily Leader* and had a wonderful staff. But half the calls I was getting related to the oil business, and it was not fair to the owners or the staff for me to have such divided interests. Rosemary and I decided we liked the adventure and rewards of the oil business and were anxious to explore an unknown future. We decided to pursue the oil business.

Cimarron Valley Exploration moved out of my upstairs home office and rented office space in downtown Guthrie. Rosemary resigned her job at the bank to be bookkeeper at Cimarron Valley at no pay. A CPA set up operational bookkeeping procedures. Now we were in the oil business for sure! We secured additional leases, one near production in Payne County. This prospect looked so promising I named the well the No. 1 Rosemary. It was a dry hole! We drilled an offset to the Alma well. The Alma No. 2 was a dry hole! The dreams of having four good wells like the No. 1 Alma were shattered. We had measured success with some other wells, but they were marginal. *Welcome to the oil business, you dreamer!*

Securing leases on some shallow well prospects in Muskogee County, we began a drilling program there. We drilled a good gas well near Haskell. We drilled two more wells in the area, and they were gas wells and no oil. There was no pipeline to sell gas, but Phillips Gas Pipeline agreed to buy the gas and build a pipeline. We drilled a total of ten wells in the area but waited nearly a year before the pipeline was completed. We hit a flowing oil well with the No. 1 Qualls that was producing 30 barrels of oil per day. Cimarron Valley Exploration joined the list of other oil companies with a mixture of successes and failures. But there were indications of economic troubles on the horizon.

Unlike most fairy tales, this story does not have a happy ending. Bank and real estate failures in 1980 caused a recession in the economy of the nation and the Oklahoma oil industry was hit hard. Rosemary suffered two heart attacks in December 1978. The last well I drilled in Muskogee County was a dry hole, and I put all future prospects on hold to care for Rosemary. Economic conditions discouraged me in future drilling prospects, but I had an offer to be field superintendent for OFS Tulsa in overseeing their program that was beginning in adjacent Kingfisher County. I accepted the job and put Cimarron activities on hold, but we still had some producing wells.

OFS Tulsa had a multitude of foreign investors from England, Israel and Germany. I supervised drilling and completion of more than 35 wells for OFS before the economic downturn caused them to drop future drilling plans. Cimarron had some wells that needed attention. Some marginal wells needed to be plugged and others needed to be stimulated to improve production. Finally in time, they were all gone. A well has only so much to give. But Rosemary and I had a wonderful, adventurous run. And we provided some excitement to participants in the wells.

What if? What if the Sneider lease had provided four good wells like the No.1 Alma? And the leases we held to the east had been good? The result might have been the beginning of a new Frank Phillips or the modern day oilman from Enid, Oklahoma,

Harold Hamm who discovered the Bakken formation field in the Dakotas. Reserves there are larger than Saudi Arabia they say. New horizontal drilling and fracturing techniques have allowed production from hard shale such as the Bakken and Woodford in large amounts never thought of before. But it wasn't to be for Cimarron Valley Exploration. The "poor boy oil company" went down like thousands of other oilfield wildcatters with big dreams.

Regrets? Absolutely none! I am buoyed by my favorite quotation by Teddy Roosevelt that I have had framed and hanging on my wall for years: "Far better it be to dare mighty things to win glorious triumphs, even though checkered by failure, than to rank with those poor spirits who neither enjoy nor suffer much, because they live in a gray twilight that knows not victory or defeat."

CROTON OIL COMPANY

With some success of Cimarron Valley Exploration and increased oil play in the late 1970s, some of my friends decided we should buy an old cable tool rig and expand operations. I didn't want to buy any "iron," but let them talk me into it. They found an old Waukesha rig at Stroud, just east of Guthrie. The ancient unit probably dated to 1900 and had been idle for many, many years. We bought the old thing for $6,500 and set about finding a few accessories it needed to be operational.

Rendal Hamby, Bobby Ferguson and Bobby Edens were going to run the operation. Hamby suggested we call the company Croton Oil Company. The name came from croton oil, a liquid many watermelon farmers used to inject into watermelons with a hypodermic needle that would give thieves the shits if they consumed a melon injected with the oil. Hamby was advertising manager for the *Guthrie Daily Leader*, but had worked as a roughneck in West Texas in earlier years. Ferguson was a roughneck on rigs for many years and knew the mechanics of the operation.

Rendal Hamby

Bobby Edens had been a roughneck as well, but had returned to Guthrie from service in Vietnam as a helicopter pilot. The cable tool rig was the rig used to drill wells before the rotary table and drilling bits were invented.

The cable tool had a big 6,000 foot spool of steel cable with a bit on the end that was lowered into the hole and it pounded and pulverized the underground rock formations making cutting that had to be cleaned out of the hole periodically with a "bailer." The bit was pulled out of the hole and the bailer attached that was lowered to capture the cuttings and bring them to the surface to be dumped. The drill bit would be reattached and drilling would resume. This process was obviously long and laborious. The drilling method had been abandoned many years before in favor of the rotary rigs. The rotaries could knock out a 6,000-foot well in a couple of weeks. The old cable tool would be there six months drilling to the same depth.

Bobby Ferguson decided we needed an old "jar head" driller for help and consultation. Ferguson and Edens had both worked rotary rigs but knew little about cable tool rigs. Ferguson found an old German living in Crescent that had operated the old cable tool operations. Max Viefhaus decided he would go to work for them at a pay of ten dollars per hour and a "jar of Whitaker's" once a week. None of us knew what Whitaker's was, but learned it was a wine made in Arkansas. With that a deal was struck and Max Viefhaus became drilling superintendent for Croton Oil Company.

Spudding well in Payne County, OK with cable tool rig, 1979
Bobby Edens, Bobby Ferguson, Rosemary Lehmann, Max LaRue and John Viefhaus. No. 1 Christy was a dry hole.

I secured a lease on land in Noble County. Hamby found participants to invest in the well. Rosemary was going to keep books for Croton Oil, so Cimarron Valley Exploration contracted with Croton to drill a well to a proposed total depth of 1,200 feet. The rig was moved and spotted on location, the wellhead spudded in and drilling commenced on the No.1 Christy, named for Edens' daughter. 300 feet of surface casing was cemented in place to protect fresh water sources from possible contamination. From there it was "full speed ahead" at about 20 feet per day from daylight until dark. At least the cable tool operation could be shut in at night unlike the rotary rigs that run twenty four hours a day with three shifts of manpower.

Lots of bad things can happen in the oil field and it happened to Croton Oil. We had reached a depth of about 600 feet when the drill bit separated from the cable and the tool was lost in the hole. A rental tool designed to latch onto the tool and "fish" it out of the hole proved futile so the project was abandoned, the rig moved off and the well plugged as a dry hole. Not to worry: Cimarron Valley's geologist, Sandy King, had a prospect near Guthrie he thought would make natural gas at 1,000 feet. We would re enter a well he had drilled a year before that had been abandoned as dry at a depth of 6,000 feet. He thought we could go in a "wash down" the hole and produce natural gas in commercial quantities. So we were off and running again. The old hole was re-entered, casing run and perforated at the point the geologist felt the pay zone was located. The well was perforated with shots that penetrate the casing opening up a hole for the liquids or gas to enter the casing pipe and be produced at the surface.

The well was given a treatment of acid to open up the formation and swabbing operations began. The "swab" was a rubber cup designed to fit tightly against the inside pipe and draw up by the cable the liquids and gases to the surface. After the water in the pipe was drawn out it was obvious there was no oil but a gas began to give off a hydrocarbon odor but it would not burn when a flame was introduced to the gas coming out of the well. You win some and lose some. We had lost again! The well was abandoned and plugged.

Cimarron Valley had drilled a couple of shallow wells in Muskogee County to a depth of 1,200 feet that tested for natural gas. The test results on the Damme No. 1 and Kirk No.1 were sufficient to cause Phillips Petroleum gas pipeline to commit to lay a gas line to our wells. The wells were shut in to await construction of the pipeline. With this commitment we decided to move the cable tool to Muskogee County to expand the gas wells encountered in the Dutcher formation. The 1,200 foot depth would be just about right for the cable tool to drill a well more economically that the rotary rigs. The rig was moved and the Kirk No. 2 well was spudded in. It took a couple of months, but total depth was reached in the Dutcher sand. The drilling cuttings showed fluorescence and hydrocarbon odor. An electric log was run showing presence of oil or gas. Pipe was run and completion activities begun. The wellhead screamed gas when opened. It was so strong it made all the nesting egrets in the area take flight when the well was opened.

Lady Luck and good fortune seemed to smile on our activities near Haskell in Muskogee County. We drilled a total of seven wells in the new field we had discovered. We awaited Phillips pipeline to reach the wells so payday could begin. The day arrived and the wells entered the Phillips system.

The cable tool rig was unwieldy and had to be loaded on a flatbed truck to be moved and spotted on location each time the rig was moved. The trio invested in mounting the rig on a wheelbase making it more mobile. That worked for a time, but a depression hit the oil industry in the '80s. The price of oil and gas went into a free fall and incentive to drill new prospects died. They decided to sell the rig. Hamby relocated back to his native Texas. Bobby Ferguson bought a used portable work-over rig and is still active in Okmulgee County. Edens is deceased.

Riches come and go in the oil field. It can be feast or famine. One day you can be on top of the world and the next day you might be dead broke. The depression of the oil field in the 80s brought bad economic times and caused many oil companies like

Cimarron Valley Exploration to call it quits. No fortunes were made, so none were lost. But we had a helluva good time playing a rich man's game.

Today. fortunes are being made with oil selling for $100 per barrel. Bobby Ferguson is thriving in the new oil boom. He hopes it will last a little longer this time.

THE THUMB BOX

Gene Pierce was one tough hombre. Practically raised on an oil drilling rig owned by his older brother, G.R. Pierce. Gene worked every job on the rig since he was old enough to hold a pipe wrench, and long before OSHA was a dream of the politicians. He became a tool pusher for Pierce Drilling Company, overseeing all the activity of the rig including the hiring and firing of the roughneck rig hands.

A roughneck on a drilling rig is demanding physically, and one is susceptible to bodily injury in a flash by shoving around all that iron associated with drilling a hole in the ground. Loss of limbs is not uncommon, especially fingers when making a connection of a joint of pipe going in or coming out of the hole. And since a well site is usually in very remote rural areas, immediate medical attention is not readily available to treat severe injuries.

The Pierce rig was drilling a well in far northwest Logan County. All was going well until one of the floor hands didn't get his hand out of the way quickly enough while making a drill pipe connection, and he caught his thumb between the two joints of pipe. The weight of the drill string came down on his gloved hand and he knew instantly he was hurt.

Removing the glove from his right hand, the roughneck realized his thumb was severed when it fell out on the floor. An old rig dog that lived with the crews ran out, grabbed up the severed thumb, and trotted off with it in his mouth. A couple of the rig hands chased the dog down and retrieved the thumb. Work on the rig continued, and the wounded roughneck was rightfully concerned about his injury.

"Hey, Pierce, I'm hurt bad, dammit! Get me to town and the hospital!"

"Aw, hell, you're all right," Pierce told him. "Just throw the sumbitch in the thumb box and we'll get you to town after we finish this trip!"

And that's about the way it was on a drilling rig. Unless you were dying, work went on until a critical part of the drilling operation permitted a stopping point. They put the thumb on ice and eventually got the roughneck to a hospital in Oklahoma City where they were able to successfully reattach the thumb, but he suffered much agony in the meantime.

One thing dependable about Pierce: He would be drunk when the rig reached total depth, or TD. He would be at a beer joint in the nearest town soaking up the suds. Most of the time everything went smoothly with the driller in charge of the operation. But one occasion at a location just north of Guthrie, the rig had reached intended depth. Drill pipe had been pulled and standing in the derrick. The well logged, and presence of oil and gas showed on the electric log.

Pierce left the location leaving the driller to go back in the hole with drill pipe and come out laying it down before running a production string of pipe in the hole to be cemented in place. The driller had run the production pipe in the hole and Halliburton's cement crew was on the floor getting ready to rig up to cement the pipe in place. The pipe lacked about six feet of reaching the total depth of the hole due to some down-hole cave in at the bottom. The driller was attempting to wash the pipe down to TD by circulating the drilling fluids in the hole. Repeated attempts failed, and the driller sent for Pierce, who showed up with the usual snoot full.

"Here, let me show you how to do it," Pierce said as he took control of the pipe string. He pulled the pipe up a few feet and let it drop on top of the fill, trying to break it up and circulate it out so the pipe could reach intended depth. Two or three attempts at this maneuver failed, and he pulled it up a little higher and let it drop heavily. This plugged up the bottom of the pipe, stopped circulation with the result the circulation pressure erupted at its weakest point, the flexible Kelly hose on the floor, where the drilling crew was working and the cement crew waiting to rig up.

The pressure caused the Kelly hose to blow out right in the face of one of the Halliburton crew members. The injured worker had his eye blown out of the socket, and it was left dangling on his cheek. Not having an "eye box," the Halliburton crew rushed him to the hospital in Guthrie where the eye was reinserted without permanent damage. The driller then took over again and was finally able to wash the pipe down, where it was cemented in place.

Such was life on a drilling rig. It is an extremely dangerous occupation. Many improvements have come to modern rigs that make it less hazardous, but the job pays very well.

THE EXHIBITIONIST

"Hey, you wanna see my dick?" the rig hand said to me as I was going up the steps to the drilling platform and rig doghouse.

Before I could answer, "Not no, but HELL NO!" he had it out in his hand. It was small, wrinkly, ugly, and nothing to write home about as far as differences in dicks go.

"Carl, get your ass back on that mud pit and don't come around this rig until you are called!" the driller yelled down from above.

Carl left and went back to work on the dozens of sacks of dry mud mix stacked on the surface waiting to be mixed with water into a mud slurry. This would be pumped into the hole to prevent the hole from caving in and also to contain by weight any pockets of natural gas that might migrate up from the well and appear on the surface.

"Don't mind Carl," the driller said as I entered the doghouse. "Help on drilling rigs is hard to find, and we just have to put up with it whether we like it or not," he said.

Carl Yablonski was a victim of the recession in the auto assembly plant industry, the driller explained. He had been on the assembly line at General Motors in Detroit where he was born and raised, but was a victim of layoffs that hit during the 1970s economic recession. Carl had a relative living in Oklahoma that urged him to come down from Michigan to seek work on a drilling rig where the oil industry was thriving at the time. Carl found work on one of B.K. Davis' rigs out of Muskogee. I had contracted with Davis to drill a well between Muskogee and Okmulgee and was there to supervise the operation.

Despite having no experience in the oil patch, Carl was assigned the duty of mixing drilling mud and fluids used in the down hole drilling operation. He also was assigned duty in the derrick's "crow's nest" to catch stands of drill pipe as they were brought out of the hole to change drillings bits and other operations of the rig. Carl stood about five foot seven inches tall and had a stocky build. About 28 years old, he was learning well and was making a good hand, the driller told me, but he has this "quirk with his privates," the driller said.

Carl was so obsessed with his dick that he carried a set of Polaroid pictures in his shirt pocket that he would display to any newcomer that would look. The other rig roughnecks were obsessed with their collection of *Playboy* and *Hustler* girlie magazines they would look at between drilling activities. They sure didn't want to look at Carl's dick! They would throw things and hoot at Carl in unsavory rig language that would embarrass a parrot. Undaunted, Carl continued his antics despite being married with two kids, it was said.

CB RADIOS

Citizen Band radios were a popular fixture on autos and trucks in the 1970s and '80s. They were the predecessor of the cell phone. I had Rosemary's car and my pickup truck equipped with a CB radio in each. I was active drilling wells in Muskogee County, and Rosemary drove from Guthrie to visit me on occasions. There was constant chatter on the CB radios, particularly among over the road truck drivers who had their own vocabulary and phrases. Sometimes it was entertaining to listen to them talking back and forth.

Rosemary and I were driving to Muskogee one day, and she was going to spend a day or two before returning home. The CB radios made it nice to communicate with one another at times during trips. As we drove through Drumright, Oklahoma, I noticed a steak house restaurant was ablaze as I passed by. Thick, black smoke was boiling from burning structure. Fire trucks with flashing red lights surrounded the building and water was spraying all around.

Rosemary was a short distance behind me in her car. I flipped on the radio and said, "Heh, heh. It looks like they burned their steaks," I said, trying to be funny.

"What are you talking about?" she replied.

"It looks like they burned their steaks at the steak house back there. Didn't you see it?"

"No, I missed it I guess," she said.

Rosemary was an intent driver and kept her eyes on the road. I couldn't believe she missed all that activity only a few yards off the highway on the steak house parking lot.

The CB radio came in very handy for me in the early morning hours one winter day. One of our wells east of Guthrie was flowing oil to the tank and it was nearing capacity. The tanker truck was scheduled to pick up the oil the next day, but I was concerned the tank might overflow and I didn't want to shut the well in for fear it would be difficult to get it flowing again. I went to the location about 2:00 a.m. to monitor the situation.

There had been a heavy snowfall the day before. The well location was about a quarter mile off the county road but I didn't expect any problems. Everything seemed to be operating smoothly and I was heading back to town and my warm bed. The snowfall had drifted over a ditch that had been dug beside the lease road to bury the transport lines that took the oil from the well to the tank battery. The fill in the ditch was still soft but covered with snow and both front and rear wheels on one side of my truck became stuck in the soft fill. Repeated efforts of rocking the truck failed to get me out of the ditch. I was stuck fast!

Turning on the CB radio, I called for anyone on highway 33 going into Guthrie to give me a call back. Chatter on the radio was not very heavy at that hour in the morning, so I repeated the call from time to time but I got no answer. While sitting in my truck, I could hear some chatter between long haul truck drivers on the radio, but they were not near Guthrie. I listened to one trucker near Stillwater talking to a young lady who was a student at Oklahoma State University. She was on her way home to Dallas for the weekend and had left the campus at an early hour to avoid traffic.

"I pulled onto Interstate 35 at the Stillwater exit," she told the trucker. "The road was very icy and my car slid sideways before I got it straightened out. It liked to have scared the pants off me," she said.

"Heh, heh, heh, I would like to have seen that!" the trucker replied. *Typical trucker,* I thought to myself. *Typical man.*

Another appeal on the radio finally brought a reply.

"I'm on 33 near Coyle right now," the voice in the night said. "Can I help you?"

Oh, thank goodness, finally a response! I told him my situation and asked him to call my wife when he got to Guthrie and tell her I was stuck and to call a wrecker. I told him she could relate the location for the wrecker driver. He assured me he would call when he arrived in town.

A few minutes later the wrecker arrived and pulled me out of the ditch, and I made it home to my warm bed.

The CB radio was a handy addition to my vehicle.

THE DAY THE RIG STOPPED TURNING

The roughnecks on the Curt Brown drilling rigs loved to see Harvey Donnell coming up the stairs to the doghouse. It always meant donuts!

Harvey was a retired casket maker who had turned the business over to his daughter and son-in-law and looked forward to quail season and baseball games. Harvey liked to gamble and was one of the first ones to step forward to invest in wells I had started drilling in search of oil and gas. The well sites were located near Guthrie, and Harvey liked to visit the rigs and bullshit with the crew. He always brought a couple of dozen donuts.

The drilling rigs are noisy affairs with all the clanking iron and deafening diesel engines that power everything. Harvey was on the rig one day and was sitting on the steel bench in the doghouse that held a multitude of spare parts, wrenches and other assorted items used on the rig. Things were humming along just fine, so the guys were visiting and eating donuts. All of a sudden Harvey let out a humongous fart that rattled the doghouse to its very foundation. It drowned out all the noise on the rig!

Everything on the rig stopped. The diesel engines quit their incessant whine. All the iron stopped clanking. Complete silence enveloped the rig. It seemed the world had quit turning. You could have heard a pin drop on that formerly noisy drilling rig. Finally Harvey broke the silence. "It don't smell bad, but it kinda burns your eyes, don't it?"

All of a sudden the world started turning again. The diesel engines cranked up and the iron started clanking again. Back to work and finishing off the donuts!

LUNCH AT THE CHINESE RESTAURANT

A drilling rig on location always draws salesmen of services associated with the oil industry. One morning on location in far north Logan County there happened to be four salesmen that came to the OFS Tulsa rig about the same time. As noontime approached, one of the salesmen decided we should all go to lunch together. The nearest restaurant from this location was at least thirty miles away in Crescent, Enid, or Hennessey.

"Do you guys like Chinese?" I asked. Everyone to a man said he loved Chinese food. I told them about a new Chinese restaurant in Hennessey that had great Chinese food. "I have eaten there myself and it is as authentic as you can get." The restaurant was owned by a Chinese family who had only been in the United States a few months. "In fact," I told them "only one member of the family speaks English. It is really authentic Chinese made from old Chinese recipes."

Everyone agreed they wanted Chinese, so off to Hennessey we went for lunch. I was the only one to order a Chinese dish. The others all ordered chicken friend steak.

Only in Oklahoma—or Texas!

Newspapers

Newsboys on the muddy streets peddling their papers.

THE "FIGHTING EDITOR," JOHN LEWIS STONE

John Lewis Stone was a mountain of a man. He had a booming voice that was as loud as he was big! He commanded attention whether he wanted it or not. He stood six foot five inches tall and weighed about 300 pounds. He carried a big stick and a big voice as editor of the *Muskogee Daily Phoenix-Times Democrat* in Muskogee. He also had tons of newsprint and several 55-gallon drums of ink to make that big voice seen and heard even louder!

Stone was born in Okemah, Oklahoma, in 1917. He worked for the Okemah paper as a young man, went to larger papers and later to the Scripps-Howard worldwide syndicate before coming to Muskogee in 1947 as managing editor of the Muskogee newspapers. Stoney, as he was known, was termed "The Fighting Editor" because of the numerous brawls he had on the streets of Muskogee. Many challenged him on editorial issues he had written in the newspaper. Some wanting to take issue with Stone physically and accosted him on the street. None ever won.

John Lewis Stone

Tams Bixby had established the Muskogee newspaper back in the 1870s. Bixby was a powerful voice in eastern Oklahoma affairs and was appointed chairman of the Dawes Commission by Republican President Grover Cleveland in 1892. The Dawes Commission was a typical government maneuver to separate the American Indian from his land. Treaties had been made with the Five Civilized Tribes before their removal from their native lands in the east to Oklahoma Territory. The treaty would be binding "as long as grass grows and water flows." This treaty would be broken like all the others before it.

But now coal, oil, timber and natural gas had been discovered on these Indian lands, and the Republican Congress passed a law to take away tribal ownership of the land and allot each member of the five tribes a 160-acre plot. This replaced tribal ownership and placed it in the hands of individual owners who had little knowledge of what was transpiring. They registered with the Dawes Commission and were given their allotments. It wasn't long before lawyers and politicians "bought" many of the allotments for a pittance of its value. Most Indians did not speak English or understand the consequences. Another rape of the Native American!

Tams Bixby's son, Tams Bixby, Jr., succeeded his father as publisher, and then by Tams Bixby III, who was editor and publisher when Stone came as managing editor. With Stone's interest and leadership, the newspaper took on a whole new perspective and personality. It became more than a paper reporting on bridge club parties and social events. Stone began taking on political leadership and civic needs. Stone was producing a voice in the wilderness, pointing out corruption and ineptness in public servants.

Not long after hitting the ground in Muskogee, Stone suspected wrongdoing in the sheriff's office with bootlegging and illegal liquor activities. Prohibition ended in the nation in 1933, but Oklahoma remained dry by vote of the people. Bootlegging operated freely in Muskogee. People passed out cards on the street with nothing but a phone number. You knew you could call that number and a bottle of whiskey would be delivered right to your door. Stone suspected local authorities were on the take and assigned his cub reporters to ferret out evidence. An editorial campaign was launched in the newspaper concerning the activities. The heat from the fire caused by the publicity began to burn at the feet of Muskogee County Sheriff Eddie Brings.

At a news conference, Briggs took umbrage to a question from one of the young reporters and Briggs slapped him. That straw broke the camel's back! An all-out campaign began to oust the sheriff because of the evidence gathered by the paper and the federal tax agents who had started their own investigation. The sheriff, two deputies, and two officials in the county attorney's office and a judge were indicted by the grand jury, and the indicted were brought to trial.

Evidence during the trial revealed the sheriff himself was the kingpin of liquor activities in the county. He was the wholesale distributor to all the local bootleggers. If they didn't buy from him and his associates, they were subject to raid and harassment. It was revealed that Stone enjoyed a drink at his local country club from time to time. Briggs wanted to know when Stone would be there so they could stage a raid and kill Stone. Briggs said he wanted to "take him out myself" on charges of resisting arrest.

The sheriff, two deputies, and two in the county attorney's office, and the judge were convicted. The sheriff drew only a three-month jail term. When he got out, he ran for reelection and damn near won! Two bootleggers ran against him to split the vote to keep Briggs from winning reelection. But, after all, it was eastern Oklahoma. People expected the sheriff to take kickbacks and county commissioners to receive big kickbacks on tinhorn and equipment sales. It was just all a part of the job. Kinda like a football coach that makes $500,000 a year from a university, but gets four million from "other" sources.

Stoney had a long and bitter battle with the International Typographical Union from 1949 to 1954. The printers were on strike and picketed at the newspaper building attempting to disrupt normal activities of the paper. Non-union printers (scabs) came in to take the place of the union printers, and mayhem ensued when they crossed the picket lines to go to work. Police were called in many times to quell uprisings, and Stone himself brawled with the strikers when they made the mistake of attacking him. Stoney's "The Fighting Editor" title took on a realistic meaning.

But Stone was a kind and gentle giant. Loved his family dearly. Taught his wife, LaRue, to fish and she accompanied him on most trips but left the deer and elk hunts to Stoney alone. They raised two daughters, Beth and Joan. Beth was a state champion golfer and played professionally for many years.

Stoney was very active in Muskogee's civic affairs. His "crusades" also influenced manufacturers, such as Fort Howard Paper Company to locate to Muskogee. He was also one of the leaders and a charter member of the Five Civilized Tribes Museum in Muskogee. Stone and LaRue retired to New Mexico and Arizona in 1981 but returned to Muskogee where Stoney died in 2001.

Fate, or a predestined life is mysterious. "What ifs" come to the surface of the mind? The events in Muskogee of 1948 changed my life forever. I had applied for a printer's job at the *Phoenix*. I could have had the job but they would not recognize any of my time in commercial printing shops toward my journeyman's certificate. I did not want to spend another six years before becoming a journeyman, so I refused the offer and went straight to the front office and made application for a job in the advertising department.

A young, 19-year-old stood before Ted Chase, the advertising manager, who told me I was too young for a sales job. I returned many times over the next few weeks telling Chase I could do the job and to give me a chance. Perhaps, in order to eliminate my persistence, he gave me the job. Though I did not work for Stone, he was always very kind to me and gave me encouragement. I learned well and was successful in making layouts and selling ads. I had a chance at a better job in Texas in 1949 and left the paper before the strike began.

"What if" I had taken the job as an apprentice printer? I would have been on that picket line in all probability. I would have had better sense that to think I could whip John L. Stone's ass, I guarantee. It was not known at the time, but the "hot type" printing profession of using molten lead would be obsolete in 15 years and replaced by computers.

"What if" Ted Chase hadn't given that skinny 19-year-old a chance? I do not believe I would be sitting at my computer today writing about the interesting characters I have met along my path in life. I love you, Ted Chase. R.I.P.

I am reminded of a passage in the movie *Field of Dreams* when "Moonlight" Graham explaining to Kevin Costner why his one inning in the major leagues was a blessing because he left pro baseball to become a doctor:

"You know we just don't recognize the most significant moments of our lives while they're happening. Back then I thought, *Well, there'll be other days*. I didn't realize that that was the only day. If I'd only gotten to be a doctor for five minutes...now that would have been a tragedy."

My life has been blessed because Ted Chase gave me the chance I wanted and I left the printing shop behind.

I saw Stoney each year at the Oklahoma Press Association meetings. He would always come up to me visiting with others, put his big arm around my shoulder and say, "This boy is doing a helluva job up there in Guthrie. Giving them folks a damn good paper. He's a Muskogee boy, don't you know?"

THE *GUTHRIE DAILY LEADER*: NEWS TOWN!

Part of the Guthrie Daily Leader *newspaper staff gather for a group photo after winning the Oklahoma Press Association Better Newspaper contest Sweepstakes Award in 1973. The newspaper won the award five times between 1966-77 for superiority in news coverage, advertising, column writing, features and overall design.*

I did not know it at the time, but I was blessed when my parent company, the Donrey Media Group, asked me to transfer to Guthrie, Oklahoma, as publisher-general manager of the *Guthrie Daily Leader*. I fell in love with Guthrie in one short day. A beautiful, unique and historic city with Victorian buildings unlike anything I had ever seen before. And Guthrie was a hotbed of news. Two days after I arrived, a man with a shotgun cut down five people at a motel south of town, a crime never solved. The city council was in a big fuss with the city manager, and there were a couple of weeks-old murders still unsolved. This paper would thrive on local news!

The editor soon resigned, and we were fortunate to find Jim Wright as editor. Wright had recently been discharged from the U.S. Navy in the public information division and was ready to tackle civilian newspapering. Wright was a dandy newsman and we won our first of five Sweepstakes awards as best newspaper in its class. Wright left for Texas and I began a long association with some outstanding colleagues. I would like to introduce you to some of them who made my job easier and most enjoyable:

Dale Himes, Editor:

Dale Himes was the complete editor. Had served Donrey Media Group as Washington, D.C. bureau chief. Knew politics. He was an avid sports fan and kept accurate statistics on all players. Thorough courthouse and city news beat reporter. Knew how to assign reporters to get the information he wanted. Himes wrote editorials pointing out problems and offering possible solutions. Consistently produced interesting local articles as lead stories. The *Guthrie Daily Leader* won four more Sweepstakes awards under Himes' direction, an honor never achieved before or since by the newspaper. Dale was named publisher-general manager after my departure in 1977. He finished his career with his hometown *Stillwater (OK) News-Press* newspaper and is now retired.

Virginia Mock, City Editor:

Yes, Virginia, there was a Santa Claus with you as city editor. Virginia knew most everybody in Guthrie and had sources that kept her busy reporting their activities. She was always on time at her desk, rain or shine. A telephone was constantly in her ear calling or receiving calls about news events, be it a pie supper or a banquet. Hundreds of local names appeared in the news pages from

Virginia's typewriter. She and her husband, Merle, were avid golfers and she was good at that, too.

Mamie Oliver, Society Editor:

A member of Guthrie's old society, Mamie Oliver was born on the original 160-acre homestead built by her parents in 1889 and lived there until she died. She never married, but was known as "Flaming Mamie" by some who talked of a somewhat flamboyant past when her hair was flaming red. Mamie was a retired English teacher and never learned to type. Wrote all her stories in longhand on a yellow legal pad and turned it in for the composition operators to put in type. Didn't matter. She knew everyone in town and knew where the bodies were buried. Her columns had very high readership.

Mamie Oliver knew Guthrie history. She was there when much of it happened. She was excited when the restoration movement began and personally escorted me on tours of Guthrie's historic sites. She pointed out the box seating of Guthrie's elite at the Brooks Opera House. Told of the wife of publisher Frank Greer who loved to lie naked on a bearskin rug in their palatial home. She also told of a rumored affair between Greer's wife and Leslie Niblack, publisher of the rival *Guthrie Daily Leader*. She was full of stories and told them with an elfish grin.

Her passion was the arts. She loved live Chautauqua plays and classical writings. She attended and participated in the Bread Loaf Writers Conference in Vermont for two weeks every summer, filling her yellow legal pad with longhand writing. Standing less than 5 feet tall, she braided her gray hair with an intertwined red ribbon. Mamie Oliver was one of a kind.

Rendal Hamby, Advertising Manager:

Hamby was perhaps one of the most interesting, yet mysterious, men I ever knew. He grew up in Big Spring, Texas, and attended Texas Tech University where he was a member of the football team. Deathly afraid of snakes, he burned a bunk house to the ground on his father's ranch when he lifted up a floorboard and found a nest of rattlers lurking there. Hamby was probably the best read man I ever knew. Always had a book with him. Could quote you the Bible. I don't know that he believed it, but he knew it. He could also quote Chaucer, Shakespeare and Greek mythology. And he could sell advertising with his winning personality! Hamby, very smart and talented, was also an excellent writer.

Having all his work done by 4 p.m., Hamby could be found at a local bar entertaining many friends who flocked to him to hear his stories and share fun and laughter from his always jovial personality. Later he would drive home in a pickup truck so littered with papers, beer cans, fast food boxes, he hardly had a place to sit. He later organized Croton Oil Company and moved to eastern Oklahoma until getting caught up in the oil bust of the 1980s. He then relocated back to his native Texas. Rendal Hamby is easily one of my most unforgettable characters.

David Clymer, Production Superintendent

David Clymer "got 'er done." Very dependable in everything he did. A Guthrie native, Clymer was a freight manager and delivered rolls of newsprint to the newspaper. The pressman was retiring and I asked David to fill the position. With training, he became supervisor of the production department from the production camera to the pressrun. David trained many assistants including a young lady, Gloria Mondine, who operated the camera and helped on the press.

The Cozby Team:

Louis and Frances Cozby met during Word War II when Cozby was a reporter for *Stars & Stripes* newspaper traveling with Patton's army across Germany. Frances was in the medical corps. Louis Cozby was a native of the east Texas piney woods and took jobs as a tramp printer during the Great Depression years finding temporary jobs where he could. He later graduated from Oklahoma University school of journalism as a top student. The Cozbys settled in Enid where they both worked and retired to Guthrie from Philips University.

Both had an intense interest in history and were active in contributing articles to the *Leader* and were later named as co-editors of the annual '89er edition of the paper published each April. Researchers will find very interesting articles of Oklahoma history in their editions published in the 1970s.

Interns Going To Better Things:

Gene Lehmann

The *Guthrie Daily Leader* was a good training ground for some schoolboys who went to better things in journalism. Gene Lehmann and Kip Stratton were schoolmates and friends who interned at the *Leader* during summers and weekends. Both worked in most every department of the newspaper from catching papers off the press to doing whatever needed to be done. Both eventually learned camera and photo developing and were given assignments covering the news and taking photos. After graduating Guthrie High School, Gene studied English at Oklahoma State University. He then worked for *the Bartlesville (OK) Examiner-Enterprise*, the *Tulsa*

(OK) Tribune and the *Oklahoma City Journal*. He became editor of newspapers in Oklahoma, Texas and Kansas producing prize-winning papers he had learned under the tutelage of Dale Himes. He is now Senior Writer for the Chickasaw Nation in Ada, Oklahoma.

Kip Stratton soaked up training under Himes, Louis Cozby and his school mentor, Kenneth Walter. He asked questions and listened. He graduated Central State University in Edmond and spent some years as reporter for the *Ponca City (OK) News and Tulsa World*. Stratton has an interest in the arena of life and has penned articles for *Sports Illustrated, Oklahoma Today* magazine, *Texas Monthly* magazine among others; everything from bull riding to ballet. He has written four books, a book of poetry and is currently writing a book about the life of movie director Sam Peckinpaw. He currently resides in Austin, Texas. You may expect many other well-written books by Stratton in future years.

Kip Stratton

Stratton is a newsman's newsman. There is not a topic of discussion Stratton would be at a loss to discuss and debate with anyone. He is a boxer which is a salute to his unending love of sports and his dedication to stay in shape and active. His love of music—from hard rock 'n' roll to down home country and bluegrass—has made him an expert. Stratton is a walking book of facts on musicians, what albums they played on, what songs they've written, how they got started, and who their musical influences include. Most amazingly is Stratton's ability to give you a rundown on any musician, from Willie Nelson to the most obscure session picker. No need to "Google" them. Merely ask Kip.

Joe Hight, Circulation and Mailroom

Joe Hight worked in circulation and the mailroom during his high school years developing an interest in journalism. He graduated Oklahoma University School of Journalism and spent many years in the editorial department of the *Daily Oklahoman* newspaper. Hight was later named editor of the *Colorado Springs (CO) Gazette* newspaper. In 2013, the newspaper was awarded a Pulitzer Prize for National Reporting. Under Joe's steady management style and insistence of top-notch integrity in reporting, the paper's series concerning how the federal government targeted U.S. veterans to deny them everything for medical care to retirement won journalism's most coveted award. Before bringing a Pulitzer home to the Colorado newspaper, Joe's contribution to news reporting, training of journalists, and national involvement in organizations dedicated to quality news reporting and integrity, earned him inclusion into the prestigious Oklahoma Journalism Hall of Fame. Hight retired from journalism and purchased, Best of Books, a book store in Edmond, Oklahoma. His "Oklahoma Joe" column is published each Monday by the *Oklahoma City Journal Record*.

Joe Hight

Laurence Parker, Circulation Manager:

Keeping circulation routes filled by schoolboys and having them delivered to customers is a daunting task. Laurence Parker did the job and did it well. A Guthrie native, Parker had a hardware store but the entrance of Walmart to the Guthrie marketplace was devastating. Parker's two sons were carriers and when the circulation manager's job opened I sought Parker to fill it. He had been a leader for his own children in Boy Scouting and would make a good leader for the carriers.

The *Guthrie Daily Leader* "Village:"

The old adage that it takes a village to raise a child could not be truer than in the daily production of a newspaper. It was teamwork from start to finish. *The Leader* staff adapted to change from the ancient "hot type" technology to "cold type" production of photography and computers. All of a sudden the old composing room printers were replaced with young women on new equipment and building pages in paper rather than heavy metal type. I recall with appreciation young ladies that helped us make this transition so easily, Connie and Marsha Taylor, Cathy Oswald, Sharon Biggs and Sandra Nelson; the Johnston brothers Norman, Tommy and Timmy. Also advertising salesmen Audra Wilbanks, Earl Latchaw. June Reihs and John Strong, along with office manager Carolyn McCaslin who kept business affairs flawlessly. Wonderful people, all.

Ruth Mina and the Trice Family:

A very important link to smooth operations in the circulation department was provided by the Trice family youths. The parents of the youngsters had died one month apart in 1966. Their grandmother, Ruth Mina, took in the five siblings, along with three of her own and two nephews. There were a total of 10 children in the Mina home. No split up would occur in this family. Ruth Mina provided them with a loving, yet structured home. She never let them become idle. "Idle hands are the devil's workshop," she would say. A couple of the Trice boys became carriers and eventually all five became an important part of the circulation department in preparing routes and inserting advertisements. They were all hard working and loyal.

Mina's rules were strict for Maurice, LaVonne, Rhonda, Michael and Anthony, ages three to 10 when they came to live with Mina: If they weren't in school, they were working at the *Leader* or filling flats of nursery pots with soil at a nearby greenhouse to grow plants, or in church. Each of Mina's family members became valuable citizens with strong values. Rhonda retired from Walmart after more than 30 years service. She smartly invested in Walmart stock when it was an infant company. They all cared for Ruth Mina in her golden years. It's what good families do.

The Small Daily Newspaper: A Lost Newspaper Era

Sadly, the newspaper era I entered is gone. Like Norman Rockwell, Bob Hope, Johnny Carson, and Frank Sinatra, perhaps gone forever. Today's technology of television and the internet has caused the demise. The presses are gone, now being printed in larger towns. Carrier boys have been replaced by mail service or contract laborers. Staffs have been reduced from dozens to a handful. Publication of small town newspapers dropped from daily to once or twice a week. People die and are buried before you get the news. The newspapers charge for obituaries, weddings. and the other events we published free of charge as news of the community.

How fortunate I was to be a newspaperman in the bygone era! It was a busy place with the noise and clatter of the old Linotype machines with their long swinging arms carrying the brass mats of letters to be squirted with molten lead and placed in pages to print; reporters rushing out with cameras to record events and meet deadlines. Or the laughter, noise and chatter of dozens of carriers folding their papers as they came off the loud roar of the press, then the deafening silence of when they left to throw their papers to the waiting faithful customers. Millions of successful business leaders were developed by lessons learned as newspaper carriers. Lessons not learned on an iPad.

There will still be a need for the small newspaper to report events of the community but in a much lesser role. I feel so fortunate to have lived during a period of very colorful and exciting newspaper journalism.

BY THE WAY

By The Way...

By Bill Lehmann
Guthrie Daily Leader   November 22, 1973

The re-enactment of the wedding between Miss Indian Territory and Mr. Oklahoma Territory was an impressive ceremony and gave everyone attending an idea of the original ceremony that took place November 16, 1907.

But wouldn't you know it? The public address system malfunctioned and those participating in the ceremony could not be heard by the crowd.

One fellow on the street was heard to say, "I was here in 1907 and I couldn't hear it then, either!"

By The Way....

The Statehood Day Celebration held at the Carnegie Library last Friday drew some 2,000 visitors to the museum. This is only a token of the potential the future holds for visitors to Guthre when the museum is finished and opened permanently.

Displays are still being built and arranged. Much work remains, but it gets better each day. Regular art shows, lectures and seminars on Oklahoma history are planned for the future in addition to regular museum features. The ultimate result will be as important to the Guthrie area as the location of an industry as far as the retail trade development of the area through increased tourism dollars.

Many groups and individuals helped in the open house Friday. Mrs. Dick James and her 9th grade Oklahoma history class assisted in handing out programs, manning refreshment tables and acting as guides to the many museum visitors.

Don Odom, Mr. Oklahoma History, was his old dependable self in handling a multitude of duties for the event. Several individuals also helped at the reception desk and taking visitors on tours.

By The Way....

Governor David Hall made a good speech. He related that at the inaugural of Governor Haskell in 1907, Haskell told of the wealth of natural gas in Oklahoma and that great pressure was being applied to move this state resource to the eastern part of the country. Haskell said if others wanted our natural gas they could just locate an industry in Oklahoma to get it.

The same topic is an issue the governor faces today, he said, and the current crisis in natural gas and gasoline is being discussed in Washington: moving Oklahoma's natural gas to other areas of the country.

By The Way...

Some ornery critter stole the Oklahoma State Seal from the special display at the museum during open house Friday. He came by the *Leader* office with the Seal and we captured a photo of the thief.

For those of you who have never seen the Seal before, the photo shows what was removed from Guthrie in 1910 when the state capital was removed from Guthrie and relocated in Oklahoma City. The state brought the seal back for a special display during open house at the museum, and it was stolen back by the bandit pictured here. The culprit refused to be identified but allowed us to take his picture in disguise.

He is strictly an amateur. He says he is proclaiming Guthrie as the state capital once again on the strength that the Seal is in his possession. He's a squirrelly looking rascal, ain't he?

From what I could determine from the muffled sounds from behind the bandana, he was trying to find someone to take the governor's job in the new administration. He had asked 15 people and they all turned him down. He said he didn't want to be governor himself he wanted the state treasurer's job.

According to museum officials Celia Shafer and Flo Olds, two robbers were involved in the heist. They took Museum Director Fred Olds' gun away and made him lift off the lid of the display case containing the State Seal. One of the bandits could be identified. He left his name badge pinned on himself. The girls said it was Ross Carr, Guthrie Chamber of Commerce manager. Ross refuses to identify his accomplice but said he is prettier with the bandana covering his face than he is with it off.

By The Way...

Some mighty strange sounds drift over the water on the lake where I have a duck blind. The sounds come from a duck blind on the other side of the lake occupied surely by the Keystone Cops comedy team.

The peaceful serenity of the landscape is broken up by the sound of radio football games, duck and goose calls that sound like Halloween whistles and shouts of "Hey, where's the toilet paper?"

A flight of ducks came sailing into our decoys the other morning and just as we were shooting we were greeted by the blast of a bugle from the blind across the way playing "charge." Then as the boat was brought out to retrieve the ducks we heard the soft strains of "taps" being played by the bugler. It is my understanding that the bugle player was Jim Willbanks practicing for the Salvation Army band.

The looks on the faces of son Gene, and our Brazilian foreign exchange student, Joe Pipoli, was just incredible as the bugle music broke the crisp morning air. Joe summed it all up by saying, "You Americans are all crazy!"

By The Way…

Jim Willbanks has been chairman of the Logan County Lung Disease Association for many years. He was even chairman when it was called the Tuberculosis Foundation. It goes back that far.

Jim has done a good job over the years in promoting the foundation through the sale of Christmas Seals and other activities associated with the group.

The organization is now promoting "Cold Turkey Day" November 27 and asking everyone who smokes to give it up for one day. A fine and noble cause, you bet! The association is trying to point out that smoking is hazardous to your health and if they get you to quit for one day you might just decide to give it up forever.

Jim chickened out as chairman on this project. He was successful in getting his mother, Wilma Willbanks, as chairman for Cold Turkey Day. Wilma is making a great chairman. She is going around getting signatures on pledge cards from people who pledge not to smoke on Cold Turkey Day. There's only one catch. Jim smokes and Wilma doesn't. The husband and father in the family, Aud, smoked for many years. He quit seven years ago and hasn't smoked since.

Now I ask you, wouldn't it appear that Jim is being a little chicken in not making the sacrifice being promoted by the organization he heads? It's easy to quit smoking, Jim. I've quit a hundred times myself. I'm going to quit again on Cold Turkey Day. I signed Wilma's pledge card and I challenge other smokers to do the same. That's Cold Turkey Day, not "Cold Chicken Day."

By The Way…

Game Warden: "What's the idea of trying to hunt with last year's license. You know better than that, don't you?"

Quail hunter: "Nothing wrong as far as I can see. I'm only shooting at the birds I missed last year!

End Note:

Warranted or not, this column published in the Guthrie Daily Leader, Thursday, November 22, 1973, won a national award from the National Newspaper Association as the Best Humorous Column of the Year. The column also won the Best Humorous Column of the Year by Oklahoma Press Association.

NNA Judge's comment: "Lehmann's column is well written, easy to understand. Comments on current news events were valid and of interest and value to the readers. Reader was informed as well as entertained by the column."

OPA Judge's comment: "Lehmann's Guthrie Daily Leader *is a three-time winner of the Oklahoma Press Association State Fair Better Newspaper Contest. (1968, 1972 and 1973). His regular column, 'By The Way,' earned him a monthly award as well as the Sweepstakes Award."*

Even a blind hog finds an acorn every once in a while!

RAYMOND FIELDS, PUBLISHER AND PATRIOT

With the April 22, 1889 Land Run, Guthrie became home for many distinguished publishers, reporters and correspondents. Frank Greer, Leslie Niblack, Marion Tuttle Rock, Fred W. Wenner and John Golobie were legendary and influential figures in journalism in Guthrie's early years.

Fields

The name of Raymond H. Fields should be added to this list. Fields was a community builder as publisher of the *Guthrie Daily Leader*, and a patriot for his service in WWI and WWII, and his long tenure of leadership in the national, state and local American Legion, and as a champion for veteran's affairs.

Fields served in France in WWI as a member of the famed 36th division. In the battle of Marne, Fields and another soldier buried the body of famed poet Joyce Kilmer (I think I shall never see a poem as lovely as a tree), who was killed July 30, 1918 by a sniper's bullet. Kilmer was later buried in the American Memorial Cemetery in Aisne, Picardy, France.

Fields was born near Center in Indian Territory July 5, 1897. His newspaper career began with the *Oklahoma News* in Oklahoma City as a reporter. He soon rose to the title of managing editor of the Scripps-Howard newspaper and was in fierce competition with the *Oklahoma City Times*, the evening edition of the *Daily Oklahoman*.

Yearning to own his own newspaper, Fields in 1925 had borrowed and saved $5,000 and set out to pursue a daily paper that might be for sale. He learned the *Guthrie Daily Leader* might be a candidate as publisher Leslie Niblack was anxious to move to Florida.

Niblack had come to Guthrie in 1892 from Indiana to head the *Daily Leader* that had been started by Col. Roy Hoffman. The paper was to be a Democratic voice in opposition to the *Oklahoma Daily State Capital* headed by Frank Greer, a staunch Republican.

Niblack soon became strong in Democratic circles after the Democrats had elected Charles Haskell the first governor of the state. Niblack was made a notary public and administered the oath of office to Haskell in Statehood Day ceremonies Nov. 16, 1907, in Guthrie. Niblack became Haskell's son-in-law after marrying Haskell's daughter, Frances, in 1909. The turn of events had the Democrats riding high and prompted the demise of the opposition Republican newspaper in 1910.

Leslie Niblack

Fields contacted Niblack and began negotiations with the publisher to purchase the newspaper. Niblack's asking price was $100,000, excluding the two buildings the paper occupied.

Believing the price too high, Fields and Niblack went by car on a high hill west of Guthrie to discuss the price. After "plying" Niblack with corn whiskey, Niblack refused to budge on the asking price.

One week later, the two made a second trip with a bottle to the hill west of town. After the bottle was drained, Niblack's price was $100,000 including the two buildings.

Believing the price still too high, Fields made arrangements to lease the basement of the Ione Hotel, telling the owner he intended to start a competing newspaper with the *Leader*. Fields knew the word would spread rapidly to Niblack. A call by Niblack was soon made to Fields suggesting they continue negotiations.

A third trip with a bottle was made to the West Guthrie hill. With the bottle exhausted, Fields had the price he felt was reasonable: $50,000 cash, no checks, for the newspaper including

Guthrie Leader, ca. 1900

the two buildings. $5,000 was to be placed in escrow with The First State Bank. A week was given to close the deal or Fields would forfeit the escrow money.

Fields immediately contacted a Tulsa oilman friend who had promised to loan Fields the money when a paper was found, only to learn the friend was building a downtown Tulsa office building and the promised loan was no longer available.

A distraught Fields returned to Oklahoma City, where he confided in a friend that the deal would fall through in a few days if he weren't able to find financing. The friend suggested he contact Lew Wentz, a very successful oilman in Ponca City that had found new riches in the Three Sands Field west of Ponca City. Wentz, Fields was told, had an interest in acquiring some newspapers to advance his Republican political philosophy.

Fields went to Ponca City unannounced and immediately gained an audience with Wentz, a bachelor who had quarters in the Arcade Hotel. Wentz lent an attentive ear to Fields and called Clyde Muchmore, publisher of the *Ponca City News* for his views as to the worth of the *Guthrie Daily Leader*. Assured by Muchmore the paper was well worth the price, Wentz handed Fields a letter addressed to Oklahoma City banker John Fields (no relation) to seek his advice.

Reading the letter from Wentz, the banker personally typed a reply, sealed it, and told Fields to deliver it to Wentz. Fields was on the next train to Ponca City where he delivered the letter to Wentz. Reading the reply, Wentz picked up the telephone, contacted J.W. Meek at the Security Bank in Ponca City and ordered $55,000 in cash be delivered to his office immediately.

Wentz

The letter from the Oklahoma City banker told Wentz that he had no interest in acquiring a newspaper property but if he did would be his first choice as a business partner.

A joyous Raymond Fields boarded the train at Ponca City for the two-hour ride to Guthrie, the $55,000 cash packed in a shoebox, tucked firmly under the arm of Fields. Arriving in Guthrie, Fields walked the three blocks to the bank where he told banker Beyer to summon Niblack to consummate the transaction.

Niblack left the *Leader* office hatless and walked a half-block to the bank where the ownership of the newspaper was transferred to Fields. $50,000 cash was deposited to the account of Niblack and $5,000 operating capital deposited to the account of Fields and the *Leader*.

Without comment, Niblack walked back to the *Leader* office, donned his hat and walked out the door, never saying a word to anyone of the *Leader* staff as he left about the change of ownership. Thus, Raymond Fields became owner of his own newspaper with financing made possible by oilman Lew Wentz.

With the relocation of the state capital from Guthrie to Oklahoma City in 1910, the town had suffered a tremendous financial loss. Business activity of all kinds had shifted to the new state capital city to the south. Lucrative state legal notices that formerly were published by the *Leader* had all gone south with the capital placing the *Leader* in financial straits.

Claimed paid subscriptions in the thousands by Niblack numbered only in the hundreds when an audit was conducted by Fields, with most of that going to political hacks and friends. Niblack's editor, Henry Derwin, had allowed the news coverage to contain mostly stories sent by the wire service with scant attention to local events.

Fields, his operating partner E.M. McIntyre as business manager, and Fields' wife, Mildred, faced a daunting task of turning things around. Fields began a column titled "The Referee," published daily on the front page. The column was devoted to local issues and events along with some editorial comment. An upturn in the credibility of the *Leader* was beginning to show improvement when The Great Depression hit the country in 1929.

The *Leader* struggled financially, with Fields telling the staff they were worth more than he could pay, but they could leave with his blessing if better opportunities came their way. Some bachelor staff members lived in upstairs efficiency apartments in the buildings rent free to relieve some personal expense. The bachelor quarters became known as "The Boar's Nest."

With the collapse of the Stock Market and the economic collapse of the country, Fields opened a soup kitchen in the newsprint storage area of the *Leader* where many were fed. Local grocers assisted the program by donating food.

In 1929, Fields and several other civic leaders who were members of the LeBron Post of the American Legion decided to stage an '89er Celebration event in honor of those making the April 22, 1889 Run to stake their claim to land opened for settlement. Original members included Fields as chairman, Merle Smith, Bert McKean, Bert Kemmerer, Gordon A.C. Bierer, Glen Farquharson, Ed McIntyre and Ralph Deming.

The '89er Celebration has continued as an annual event in Guthrie since that time.

A limited number of events were scheduled for the first Legion-sponsored celebration, but a parade with horses, buggies and bands was the central attraction. Pioneers who made the Run were registered and rode in the parade.

Attorney Merle Smith was distinguished events chairman that featured the national commander of the American Legion who attended. The group marched from the American Legion building, then on Oklahoma Street, to Highland Hall where a stage was set up. Smith called on Judge Freeman Miller to make a few remarks and Miller spoke for over an hour. Fields finally suggested that they "yank him down!"

Listening to the tales of the pioneer settlers inspired Fields to begin recording their voices and experiences on a tape recorder. Some of the stories made their way into the pages of the *Leader* at '89er Celebration time. Fields later presented his collection of recordings to Oklahoma Christian College in Edmond. The collection was added to other recordings in their Living Legends Library. It is now housed in the Oklahoma Historical Society audio collection in Oklahoma City, and is available for research.

Special guests for Guthrie's '89er Celebration since 1929 have been personalities of national renown as well as U.S. Senators, state governors, political officials, Hollywood stars, and Miss Americas. The early '30s brought presidential candidates to Guthrie: Alf Landon, Paul McNutt, governor of Indiana, and Bernar McFadden, publisher of health magazines and physical fitness advocate who ran for president of the U.S. twice.

Several Hollywood movie stars appeared in the celebration parade as distinguished guests, including Humphrey Bogart, Gene Autry, Leslie Nielsen, and many others.

One of the most popular distinguished guests to appear in Guthrie was Mayor Fiorello LaGuardia of New York City, who was the distinguished guest for the 1938 celebration. Fields gained an audience with LaGuardia on one of his trips to New York while on business for the American Legion. Fields invited the mayor to attend the celebration and LaGuardia accepted, much to the surprise of Fields. The mayor told Fields it would be good to get away, because "all I do is chase fire trucks and ambulances."

LaGuardia and his wife arrived in Guthrie, and the mayor was shown the car he was to ride in the parade.

LaGuardia

"Car, hell!" he replied, "I didn't come here to ride in a car! I want to ride a horse!" A horse was selected for him to ride. The mayor's wife rode in the car. LaGuardia, being short in stature, had to wait while the stirrups were adjusted on the saddle to accommodate his physical size. Spectators were amused to see his legs stand almost straight out in the saddle as he bounced along the downtown parade route, but ride a horse he did. Officials estimated the crowd at 100,000 spectators, one of the most ever.

The 1938 celebration in April must have difficult for Fields and his wife, Mildred. They lost their only child in a tragic accident February 18, 1938.

Patricia Fields, 13, died as a result of fire at a Washington's Birthday observance at the old Logan County High School. Patricia, dressed in a period costume made of crepe paper, was serving refreshments to the attendees, when she took a break and went to another room. Being warm, she and a companion raised a window to get some fresh air. A natural gas flame from a heating radiator was blown by the breeze from the opened window and ignited the dress Patricia was wearing. She fell to the floor and began rolling trying to extinguish the flames. Her classmates then heaped coats on her body to smother the fire, but too much damage had been done. She died at the Guthrie hospital a few hours later despite heroic efforts by physicians to save her life.

Patricia Fields

Patricia Fields was buried in Guthrie's Summit View Cemetery, which resulted in a permanent connection of the Fields' to Guthrie.

Wentz was adding more newspapers to his growing holdings during the 1930s and had appointed Raymond Fields to oversee their operation. Wentz's papers now included Blackwell, Ponca City, Guthrie, Holdenville, Wewoka and Okemah.

Fields was also busy with American Legion affairs on a state and national level. He served terms as the local commander and had been elected as Oklahoma State Commander for the American Legion. He was also serving as chairman of publications for the National American Legion.

With the Japanese attack on Pearl Harbor, December 7, 1941, America entered World War II. Fields entered service in the armed forces again. He had served in the famed 36th "Rainbow" Division ambulance units in World War I, but dutifully entered the service again, leaving the operation of the *Leader* to McIntyre and Mildred Fields. There was a period during WWII when the *Leader* had an all female newsroom staff.

Following the War, Fields returned to Guthrie resuming his duties as publisher of the *Leader* and supervising the other papers in the Wentz group. He remained active with veteran's affairs and served as chairman of the national publications committee for more than 40 years.

The death of Lew Wentz in 1949 meant changes for the newspapers and publishers in his group. Fields and McIntyre sold their interest in the *Daily Leader* in 1955 to Phil McMullen. Fields then bought the

The all-female newsroom staff: Marion Ewing, editor; Berniece Bond, proofreader; Myrtle Braun, society; and Ruth Moon, news and feature writer.

Guymon Daily Herald in the Oklahoma Panhandle. The Fields' managed the *Herald* until 1966 when they sold the Guymon property to Donald W. Reynolds, who built the Donrey Media Group into a giant media conglomerate including newspapers, television, radio stations, and advertising billboard outlets in the Western United States and the Hawaiian Islands.

After selling to Reynolds, the Fields retired and removed to Oklahoma City. Fields remained active with his American Legion duties.

Fields

Ironically, when Fields was editor of the *Oklahoma News,* he sometimes deliberated on which news story to feature on page one of the paper. Competition was fierce among the newspapers, long before the arrival of radio and television, and each vied for top street sales from newsboys hawking paper sales on the streets.

One particular street salesman, 14-year-old Donald Reynolds, was the star salesman for the *News*. Fields would seek out young Reynolds for his opinion on which story the youth would find the best for street sales appeal. Now Fields had just sold his newspaper to his star salesman who had risen to great heights as a media giant.

During Fields career, he guided many *Daily Leader* staff members to become leaders in journalism. Among those was Paul Miller, a recent graduate of Oklahoma A&M College who came to Guthrie as news reporter. Fields immediately recognized that Miller had the capability and desire to reach higher goals.

After a few months, Fields sent the young Miller to the *Okemah Daily Leader* newspaper as managing editor. From there, Miller's career blossomed and he became president of the Gannett Corporation, a world media leader.

In later years, Miller commented, tongue-in-cheek, that Fields had only promoted him at his young age to the position of news editor at the *Okemah Daily Leader* because "I was the only one qualified that could be hired for twenty dollars a week." Other members of the "Boar's Nest" that advanced to important journalism careers were Gerald "Cowboy" Curtin, a star football athlete at Oklahoma A&M who became publisher of the *Watonga Republican*; James Craddock, publisher of the *Weatherford Daily News* and "Bo" Belcher, a star baseball player for Oklahoma A&M College.

OSU President Kamm

Belcher was sports reporter for the *Leader* and later established the Chandler Baseball Camp at Chandler, Oklahoma, where young players honed their skills, many becoming stars in college and in the professional ranks. Raymond H. Fields had an illustrious career as newspaper publisher, civic leader and champion for veteran's affairs. His guiding hand was felt in the development of many others in shaping their achievements. He was an Oklahoma Publisher for more than 50 years, and is a member of the Oklahoma Journalism Hall of Fame. He served in offices of the Oklahoma Press Association; Commander of Guthrie and Oklahoma American Legion offices and served for 40 years as chairman of the national *American Legion Magazine* and publications.

Mildred Fields died in 1973 and was buried in Summit View Cemetery beside their daughter, Patricia. Raymond became a frequent visitor to Guthrie visiting their graves with his three poodles.

I was always delighted to see Raymond and his poodles as they visited me in my office at the *Daily Leader* after I became publisher of the *Leader* for the Donrey Media Group, who purchased the newspaper from Phil McMullen in 1959. Much of this article of remembrance is based on stories he related during those visits.

Raymond Fields with Bill Lehmann, 1976

Raymond always remained proud of Guthrie and his association with the community. He was very excited when we did a renovation of the *Leader* in 1976, converting the façade of the *Leader* into a Territorial era appearance.

He was particularly pleased when we decorated the wall in the foyer and business office using actual front pages of the *Guthrie Daily Leader* with the headlines of major events from Oklahoma Statehood to World War II.

Many of the pages were created during Raymond's tenure at the *Leader*. He gazed fondly at the pages, saying, "I remember that!"

Raymond Fields died in February 1979. I was honored to be one of his pallbearers as he was laid to rest with Mildred and Patricia in Summit View Cemetery. His estate was left to the Oklahoma Press Association.

Montage of front pages

THE GREAT ESCAPE

Guthrie has always been a very good news town. Seems like something is going on all the time that makes a good story. But one cold March day in 1970 Guthrie made the national network news.

A bus carrying some 50 soldiers convicted of crimes at Ft. Sill, Oklahoma, was transporting the men to federal prison at Leavenworth, Kansas, to begin serving their sentences. None were convicted of major crimes and were being transported on I-35 just east of Guthrie without restraints of any kind. A prisoner, for some reason, overpowered the only guard, took his pistol and ordered the driver to stop the bus. The men left the bus and scattered like a covey of quail. Some rejected the foolish idea and remained on the bus, but some took off on foot still in uniform.

Military escapes taken back into custody

Some of the prisoners were spotted near the Cimarron River, north of Guthrie. Logan County Sheriff's deputies, the Oklahoma Highway Patrol Troopers, and city police were first on the scene after the alert was sounded. They had captured a few and then the military arrived in force. The scene on the Cimarron River looked like something in a movie production. Two military helicopters, a small military airplane circled the river where the prisoner could be seen in the distance. Some were wading across the shallow river to get to the west side. An Oklahoma Highway Patrol sharpshooter fired shots at them but more of a warning to give up the effort. Bullets could be seen striking the water near the men and they gave up, hands in the air.

A dozen or so prisoners remained on the loose and still were in hiding at nightfall. The countryside was bleak in early March with no tall grasses or weeds to conceal the men. But the evergreen cedar trees in abundance in the countryside offered shelter, particularly from spotters in the air. The escapees could go inside the branches of the cedar trees, remain still and blend in with the tree in their green uniforms. The air search was called off for the night but resumed at daybreak the following day.

A sheriff's deputy and Sheriff Nolan Welch put cuffs on an escapee.

Most of the escapees were captured by day three. They were hungry and tired. Some were spotted still in their uniforms and gave up easily when authorities arrived. Three were still in hiding with reports coming in from eastern Logan County indicated the prisoners were active near Meridian, east of Guthrie. A farm home had been broken into and some civilian clothing taken that allowed the men to change from their military uniforms. Two more days passed and the two were nabbed when they tried to break into another farm home to steal some food. That left one more prisoner still on the loose and in hiding. The military, now knowing the identity of the last prisoner, told authorities he had been through survival training and could possibly live off the land and be difficult to apprehend.

Three more weeks had gone by and the last prisoner was still in hiding. Reports near Meridian told of rural home break-ins, missing food and clothing. Believing they had him cornered and capture was imminent, Logan County Sheriff Nolan Welch called and asked me to accompany him in the manhunt for the last prisoner. We spent the biggest part of the morning chasing leads that proved fruitless. At lunchtime we went to the little town of Meridian to Minor Bradbury's grocery store. We bought a loaf of bread, a couple of pounds of bologna, a jar of mustard, and some rat cheese to make some sandwiches.

Bradbury was retiring and wanted to sell the grocery store. Not having any buyers, he was preparing to have an auction to sell the property that remained. As I was paying for some food, I spotted a small printing press sitting on the counter. I asked about the press and Bradbury told me he used it to print weekend specials on a post card to send to his customers in the area. I asked if the press was for sale and he said it was and that he wanted twenty dollars for the item. I laid down a twenty dollar bill  and took possession of the tiny printing press along with a shirttail of type. The manhunt was soon called off because the missing prisoner was still in hiding somewhere out there in the wilderness.

Finally the last escapee was nabbed as he was spotted trying to break into a farm home. He was shirtless and barefoot. His body was covered with scratches, insect bites, and dirt from living in the wild. His survival training had paid off, but at an uncomfortable price. He survived by capturing frogs along the farm ponds and eating them raw. Sometimes he was successful in finding food at some the farm homes he had broken into, but it did not last long. He admitted he was relieved when finally captured because it meant hot food and a warm bed, even if it was in a prison. I still have the little printing press that came from Bradbury's grocery store. I am happy to have it among my treasured possessions along with the memories it brings about the manhunt and the great escape.

RESPONSIBILITY

"Jimmy," I said to the *Guthrie Daily Leader* carrier boy, "Mr. Jessup on your route complained that he has not been getting his paper on the porch. He says it's always in the bushes. Mr. Jessup is getting a little old, and it is is inconvenient for him to have to fish the paper out of the bushes. Do you think you might be able to get it on the porch for him from now on?"

"Well, I'll try," Jimmy said, "but it really isn't my responsibility."

I was completely caught off guard and astonished by his reply and said, "Not your responsibility? Just what do you consider your responsibility?"

"Well," Jimmy replied, "my responsibility is to come to the paper office after school, pick up the papers for my route, fold them and throw them to the customers. But once that paper leaves my hand it leaves my responsibility!"

Jimmy is now in charge of customer service at Cox Cable.

ASTRONAUT BALLS

"ASTRONAUT BALLS, ha-ha-ha!" the voice on the other end of the telephone line said to me, and then hung up. I had no earthly idea as to what the caller was talking about!

I looked at the headlines of *Pawhuska Daily Journal-Capital* of that day and didn't see anything wrong. Still baffled, I asked some of the employees if they knew what the call was about. The phone rang again and this time the news editor took the call, and the caller told him to look at a story on the society page.

There it was: A line in the story said, *"The room was decorated with astronaut balls hanging from the ceiling."*

I had to laugh myself!

"Maida," I said to Maida Williams, the society editor, "is this the wording you used in the story or is it a typo?"

"It's exactly as I wrote the story," she said. "I took the call on the telephone and the lady said they were having an outer space program at the church fellowship hall, and the room would be decorated with 'those little Sputnik things hanging from the ceiling—'You know, those little astronaut balls,' the caller said. I never thought another thing about it," Maida said. "I just put it in there the way she told me."

Pawhuska readers had a good time with the story for a few days. Chalk one up for newspaper bloopers. It made the bloopers in *Editor and Publisher Magazine* with worldwide circulation.

THE SECRET STASH OF CASH

Speeding down I-35 at 100 miles per hour is a scary experience. It is even more frightening when the driver has a coffee can between his legs into which he is spitting tobacco juice every few seconds. To complicate matters he has to hit the siren every once in awhile to get slower traffic in the left lane to let him pass.

This was the scenario as I was riding with Logan County Sheriff Nolan Welch as we sped to the south county line to investigate a home invasion and robbery. He was trying to quit smoking and had started chewing tobacco to satisfy the nicotine urge. This caused him to have to spit frequently. Plus withdrawal from nicotine made Welch as nervous as a whore in church. It was a scary ride to say the least. I was very relieved when we reached our destination.

The sheriff and I had a good relationship. Whenever something big happened he would want me to go with him instead of the news editor or reporter. He would call and say, "get you camera, Bill, I'll pick you up in a few minutes." I was glad we had such a relationship because it resulted in some good stories that would be features and headlines that might otherwise be just a few lines in the police notes.

"Somebody roughed up old Louis Martin and molested his wife," the sheriff said as we sped down the highway. Louis Martin was a known bootlegger, among other things. He was a gruff individual with an unkempt appearance, cussed like a sailor and always needed a shave. He wore a pair of overalls that always appeared to be searching for a washing machine. Martin had an 80-acre farm in south Logan County where he cooked and sold moonshine whiskey. The sheriff knew it as did everybody else, but if it is not harming anyone, let it be. Rumors were rife that Martin had cash buried in fruit jars in secret spots on his farm. Lots of cash!

Entering the Martin home it appeared a tornado had struck. Furniture was topsy-turvy and turned upside down. Drawers in chests were pulled out with contents dumped all over the floor and loose papers everywhere. Martin was sitting in a chair and had blood all over his face. His wife was nearby shaking and sobbing. A neighbor lady who had been visiting at the time said to the sheriff, "that nigger sonofabitch needs to be killed!"

Louis Martin and Sheriff Welch with electric cord used to torture Martin.

A pair of black men had come to the house in pretext of buying some eggs after seeing the sign posted in the screen door of the Martin home, Martin said. While his wife went to fetch some eggs, the pair overpowered Martin, tied him up, and demanded to know where his secret stash of cash was located. They grabbed the wife and neighbor and made them both lie down on the living room floor. Martin, using cuss words that would singe your hair, described what he told the men and denied having any secret stash of cash anywhere.

Repeated attempts to have Martin reveal the hidden places of his cash brought more cussing and threats of what he would do to the men if he got loose! The men then raised the dress of Martin wife, took down her panties and began to fondle her hoping this outrageous act would loosen Martin's tongue. It only resulted in more cuss words and threats by Martin.

One of the men then took a table lamp from the table and pulled out the electric cord from the lamp. Using a pocketknife he trimmed the insulation from the ends exposing the copper wire. He then separated the wire and plugged the cord back into the wall. He then touched Marin's ear lobes with the exposed wire causing the skin to fry and blood to ooze out. Martin was still defiant in the face of the torture and the humiliation of his wife.

The men finally realized they were getting nowhere with Martin. They took what loose cash they found in the house, but found a big wad of cash in the bib pocket of Martin's overalls. Taking this money the pair left. The neighbor loosened the bonds of Martin, went to her home next door and called the sheriff's office reporting the incident. Martin told the sheriff there was more than a thousand dollars in the pocket of his overalls.

The case was never solved. A good description of the men was not given other than they were black. Perhaps they were men from Oklahoma County, just across the line. Perhaps Martin knew them and didn't want to pursue the matter since his activities were illegal. Martin and his wife both died some years later. There is still talk that a secret burial place of cash is still to be discovered on the old Louis Martin farm.

The scary ride paid off in a good story for the *Guthrie Daily Leader*! Sheriff Welch went back to smoking cigarettes and gave up chewing tobacco, much to the relief of everybody around him.

History

*A few Old West tales
involving friends and ancestors.
Photo by Gene Lehmann*

THE STRANGE CASE OF ELMER MCCURDY

My office at the *Guthrie Daily Leader* was an occasional gathering place for some friends who shared an interest in history, particularly Oklahoma history. There was Fred Olds, western painter and director of the Guthrie's Oklahoma Territorial Museum, Glenn Shirley, author of 14 books on Oklahoma lawmen and outlaws, and Ralph McCalmont, a Texan-turned-Okie when he bought the First National Bank in Guthrie.

While we were visiting over coffee and rolls, I asked if they had seen the article about the body found at the wax museum in California. None had, so I told them they were filming a scene in the *Six Million Dollar Man* television episode when someone knocked over one of the figures during a chase. The impact knocked off one of his arms, and they discovered it was human when a bone became visible.

Elmer In His Coffin

"They called in the medical examiner and he determined the body was human and very old and probably been preserved by arsenic. The wax museum had bought the figure from a side show exhibit several years ago and they are trying to determine who it is and where it might have come from," I concluded. "The owner of one of the sideshows suggested to authorities the body might be connected to an Oklahoma outlaw killed in a robbery back in the teens," I said.

"Well, that might have been a train robber killed in Okesa about 1911," Glenn Shirley suggested.

"What do you think they will do with the body?" Olds asked.

"Aw, they'll probably incinerate him and scatter the ashes in the Pacific Ocean," I said. "If that is the Oklahoma outlaw, we need to get him back and give him a decent burial," Olds said.

Olds then went to the telephone, called the Los Angles medical examiner's office and got Robert Naguchi on the line. Naguchi told Fred the investigation was ongoing and they did not know the identity of the body. Fred then told Naguchi we wanted to do some research here and if the body was truly the train robber, we wanted him returned for burial. Naguchi told Fred he would be notified before any decision was made concerning disposition of the body.

The train robbery happened in Okesa, Oklahoma, in 1911 according to Glenn Shirley, the leading authority on lawmen and outlaws in Oklahoma. Okesa was in Osage County near Bartlesville. My son, Gene Lehmann, was a photographer and reporter for the *Bartlesville Examiner-Enterprise* at the time. I got on the phone and told him to look in the newspaper archives and see if he could find a story on the robbery. He soon called back telling us he had found the story of the event and gave us the name of the outlaw who was slain shortly after the robbery by Osage County deputies. His name was Elmer McCurdy.

McCurdy and a couple of others had robbed the train at Okesa, believing a bounty of $400,000 in Osage Indian oil royalty payments was aboard. The train they were seeking had already passed a couple of hours before. They robbed the wrong train. All the bandits received were $46 in cash, a gold watch and two gallons of whiskey. Deputies traced McCurdy to a barn on a ranch near Pawhuska. A shootout occurred according to the story and McCurdy, being drunk on the whiskey by then, was slain in the shootout.

McCurdy's body was taken to Johnson Funeral Home in Pawhuska. I had moved from Pawhuska to Guthrie and called my friend, Dorsey McCartney, who was manager of the Johnson Funeral Home. I asked him to check his records to see if he could find anything on the slain outlaw. Mc Cartney soon called back and said he had found the record. Charles Johnson probably thought it would be a long time before anyone claimed the body for burial, so he embalmed Elmer's body with arsenic, legal until 1922. Arsenic would preserve a body in a mummified condition, McCartney said.

McCartney then said Mr. Johnson had stood the preserved body of McCurdy in a standing position in the corner of on the rooms in the funeral home. Elmer stood there five years. Many people knew of the preserved body and curiosity seekers came by the view the remains from time to time. Finally some men came in claiming the body was of the missing brother and claimed it for burial. Paying the funeral home bill, they left with the remains, according to records. Mr. Johnson had taken a photo of the body and it was available for viewing, McCartney told me.

Armed with this information to tie the robbery to the body in Los Angeles, we ran a series of stories in the *Guthrie Daily Leader* on the events and called for McCurdy's body to be returned to Oklahoma where he would receive a decent burial next to Bill Doolin, Little Dick West, and Charlie Pierce, slain Oklahoma outlaws that rested in the boot hill section of Guthrie's cemetery. United Press International and Associated Press news wire services picked up the story and circulated it to news media outlets worldwide.

Fred then got on the phone and called Naguchi and said we thought we had the body identified and wanted to know how we could claim it and bring it back to Oklahoma. "Not so fast," Naguchi said to Fred, "this is the body of a human being and there are many procedures we need to have to positively identify the body." Naguchi told Fred. An anthropologist would probably be needed as well. Fred picked up the telephone and called his good friend, Dr. Clyde Snow at Oklahoma University seeking his assistance. Snow was a world authority on identifying ancient remains of bodies uncovered around the world. Snow said he would be glad to help.

Dr. Snow, Olds, and McCalmont boarded a plane to Los Angeles to meet with the medical examiner and present some scientific information available to identify the body. Olds, dressed in his cowboy attire of a big ten-gallon cowboy hat, Levi's, and nearly knee-high cowboy boots, attracted much attention on the plane and in Los Angeles. Snow presented a graph made of the photo of McCurdy. This matched perfectly with the scan of McCurdy's head. It was McCurdy! Naguchi said they would release the body to the men but did not want the funeral to be a "Roman Holiday" of publicity. Agreeing to the conditions, the three left with McCurdy returning in a cardboard box in the freight section of the airplane. The fare was paid by McCalmont.

Back in Guthrie, a pine box was built for a coffin for McCurdy with a simple cross on the top about 12 inches long made of half-inch material. McCurdy's body that looked like leather had been painted and waxed from so many years as a sideshow attraction. It brought a few tears among those of us who believed that a dignified, decent burial was long overdue to the disfigured body after being bandied about for 66 years, gawked at, jerked on, painted, and waxed.

Glenn Shirley, Fred, and I were members of the Indian Territory Posse of Oklahoma Westerners, an international group active in preserving history of the Old West. Shirley appealed for their help, and they agreed to be the sponsor. Max and Leland Warren of Warren Monument Company donated the large granite marker to go on the grave. We needed a minister to conduct the funeral. No Guthrie minister would agree to speak over the body of that sinful outlaw. Fortunately, Dr. Glenn Jordan of the Oklahoma Historical Society, being an ordained minister, agreed to conduct last rites.

I told Fred I remembered an old motorized hearse from my days in Ponca City that dated back to 1920 era. I called Trout

Funeral Home in Ponca City and told him we would like to use the old hearse if it was still available. "I have something better than that," he said, "I have an old horsedrawn hearse that hasn't been used since 1929. The hearse was last used at the request of an old cavalryman

and performer with the 101 Ranch Wild West Show," Troth told me. "It is sitting in a barn at Stillwater, and if you will send a trailer, I will let you use that."

The old horsedrawn hearse really excited Fred, and he immediately called Truman Moody, a rodeo and parade stock producer in Wynnewood, Oklahoma. Moody agreed to pick up the old hearse and drive it with a team of his horses in the procession from the museum to Summit View Cemetery, some four miles. The event was carried on all the major television networks with Walter Cronkite, Peter Jennings and Dan Rather delivering the news to every household in America.

Everything was lined out for the funeral of the old outlaw. Guthrie's mayor, Dr. Robert Ringrose, and several others were to lead the procession on horseback. The sheriff of Osage County, George Wayman, and Osage County Senator John Dahl agreed to take the casket from the hearse and hand it to the pallbearers to be laid on wooden planks and lowered into the grave. I was to ride shotgun on the hearse with Moody. Olds and Don Odom, Guthrie historian, would follow in a wagon and team of horses driven by Olds.

The procession started from the museum in downtown Guthrie to the cemetery. Several hundred spectators lined the route along the way. By the time we reached the cemetery, there was a crowd of some 250 people awaiting the ceremony. A large group of television cameramen gathered discussing the event. It was obvious the news media were more interested in McCurdy's burial than the general public. Cameramen from Germany and Norway were present to record the event for viewers in their countries, where interest in the American Old West is surprisingly very high.

The single rose placed on the casket by a young lady.

Taking the casket off the old hearse were pallbearers Osage County Sheriff George Wayman; Senator John Dahl; Historian Don Odom; Museum Director Fred Olds; Banker Ralph McCalmont, and I, publisher of the *Guthrie Daily Leader.* We placed the casket on planks across the open hole in the ground where it would be lowered by ropes in traditional fashion of an Old West burial. The crowd gathered around the casket. A slender girl, perhaps 16, in a long cotton print dress, long blond hair and large eyeglasses, dropped a single rose on the casket as it sat on the boards. She wiped away a tear.

"Ashes to ashes and dust to dust," began the remarks of Dr. Glenn Jordan. "We come not to judge the deeds of the deceased but to grant him a respectful burial due any man on his journey to where final judgment will be rendered by higher authority."

Jordan continued with his eloquent comments for the somber occasion and called for the wooden casket to be lowered by the ropes to its resting place at the bottom of the hole. The casket and the single rose were lowered, the ropes retrieved, and Elmer McCurdy was finally at rest after 66 years. Olds placed cardboard over the casket and had two yards of concrete poured on top to discourage any future disturbance of Elmer.

Fred Olds, Don Odom, Ralph McCalmont, Bill Lehmann hear eulogy by Dr. Glenn Jordan.

Interest in the Elmer McCurdy story has drawn the attention of two authors that have written books on McCurdy, tracing his roots back to the state of Maine. The McCurdy events have been written about in many magazines. McCurdy has been the subject of several television features and documentaries. Elmer McCurdy has gained far more fame in death than he ever received in life.

Oklahoma has produced many exciting outlaws and lawmen during the course of its early history. Elmer McCurdy pales in comparison to any of them. He was a born loser, really a creature to be pitied rather than celebrated. Born in Maine to an unknown father, he drifted west as a soldier in the U.S. Army where he had a lackluster service record. After the service, he was arrested as a petty thief and associated with other losers. Even the train robbery was botched when they robbed the wrong train. The autopsy by the Los Angeles medical examiner suggests he may have been shot while drunk rather than in a shootout as deputies described. But if anyone needed to be put away with at least a little dignity, it was Elmer McCurdy. We provided that for him.

In 1990, a producer of documentaries from the British Broadcasting Company (BBC) was at a cocktail party in Paris, France, when he heard of the strange events surrounding the life and death of McCurdy. Fascinated, he began researching the events and brought a team to America to produce a documentary. He traced the life of McCurdy in Osage County to California, interviewing people connected with the sideshows and burial. Titled *Timeline—the Oklahoma Outlaw*, the film has been shown worldwide with decidedly British accent in the commentary.

Fred Olds and I were a part of the BBC documentary when they came to Guthrie to record events of the burial. No actual television film footage from the networks or metropolitan TV stations survives that were filmed during the funeral and burial. Many still photos taken by Gene Lehmann have been used extensively by BBC and national magazines among others.

The Burial Committee of the Indian Territory Posse of Oklahoma Westerners: Mounted on horses, left: State Rep. John Dahl, Osage Country Sheriff George Wayman and Jim Cummings. Foreground: Ralph McCalmont, unidentified, Fred Olds, Max Warren, Leland Warren, Bill Lehmann, Glenn Shirley, Don Odom and Dr. Glenn Jordan. (Gene Lehmann photo.)

Of the original members of the meeting in my office that day in January, 1977, only McCalmont and I remain. Fred Olds and Glenn Shirley have gone to their just rewards. McCalmont said after our lives are over and done, whatever good deeds we have done will be forgotten, but our exploits in the strange case of Elmer McCurdy will be remembered above all else. Perhaps so. There will be plenty of books and film left behind to be a reminder and perhaps spark the interest of another generation.

But I hope ol' Elmer finally is at peace and has a smile on his face while he enjoys a drink of whiskey and gets dealt a poker hand by his outlaw buddies in Boot Hill.

RIP Elmer McCurdy.

McCurdy burial photos by Gene Lehmann

WILD BILL POSEY: CREEK OUTLAW

One of the most brazen outlaws in Texas and Indian Territory history was one "Wild Bill" Posey. Posey and his gang of henchmen rode roughshod over a wide swath of Texas and Indian Territory in the 1870s. The mere mention of the Posey name provoked fear and panic among the people when the gang was present in their area.

While not one of the Wild West's most famous outlaws, Posey's antics caused destruction to all he came in contact with. Even his own family was destroyed when he lynched his brother-in-law, Matt Wallace, in the middle of the night before the terrified eyes of Wallace's pregnant wife and their two-year-old daughter.

Wallace's wife, Sarah Ann (Miller) Wallace was the grandmother of this writer.

Posey's reign of terror began in 1872 on Tehuacana Creek, six miles east of Waco, Texas. It ended when he was killed in a bloody shoot-out with the Creek Lighthorse in Indian Territory in 1877.

William Andrew Jackson Posey was born June 16, 1846 in Talapoosa, Alabama, the fourteenth of fifteen children and youngest son of Benjamin Franklin Posey and Eliza Berryhill. His parents were first cousins, each was one-half Creek Indian, making each of their children one-half Creek. There were seven girls and eight boys. [1]

The Benajamiń Posey family migrated to Texas in 1847, first to Nacogdoches, then to Horn Hill, northwest of Groesbeck, in

Limestone County. Many of the Alabama Posey-Berryhill families migrated to Indian Territory just prior to the 1830 forced Indian removal. They settled along the Arkansas River from present Wagoner to present Tulsa. For reasons unknown, Benjamin Posey relocated his family to Texas. Bill Posey grew up a cowboy and was an excellent horseman, as were all the Posey men.

Elizabeth Posey

Bill Posey married Elizabeth Wallace July 18, 1865, in Limestone County. [2] They settled on Tehuacana Creek in McLennan County, east of Waco. Elizabeth's brother, Matthew Alexander Wallace, had married Sarah Ann Miller and the couples lived near one another on the land inherited by Sarah following the death of her father, Robert T. Miller, in 1853. [3]

Waco was a town of only three thousand residents by 1870. [4] But the city had furnished six generals and a host of colonels to the Confederate States Army (CSA) in the Civil War. All the Posey and Wallace men served in the Civil War. [5]

There was plenty of land in Texas, and the wide-open spaces seemed to have a Longhorn beef behind every mesquite bush. Cattle were worth $3 per head in Texas, but worth $15 at Kansas railheads. [6] Thus came the birth of the Chisholm Trail and the movement of cattle to the eastern marketplace. The Poseys and Wallaces began gathering cattle and trailing them to Kansas. The Kansas cattle market brought newfound wealth to the families following the war.

Bill Posey began purchasing land around Waco.[7] He bought some 500 acres on the Brazos River east of Waco. Then bought 666 acres of land inherited by Sarah Miller Wallace. The deed called for a purchase price of $5,000 payable at $1,000 per year for five years. [8]

Cattle and horses with brands of others began showing up in Posey herds. He and the Wallaces were charged with theft in McLennan County. The Wallaces began distancing themselves from Posey's operation and unsavory characters began associating with Posey. Newspaper accounts tell of Posey's gang brazenly driving off livestock of all descriptions from nearby ranches.

Posey was charged with the theft of six horses in McLennan County but was acquitted. [9] His defense attorney was Waco attorney Richard Coke, who would be a future Texas governor. Posey was soon charged with the theft of two mules.[10] Coke could not get him off this charge and he was convicted and sentenced to a five-year term in state prison.[11]

Financial troubles then hit Posey in lawsuits brought by Coke for unpaid legal fees, and by Dr. S.A. Owens for unpaid medical services. [12] The litigants won the lawsuit and Posey was unable to pay. The court took Posey's land and several hundred head of livestock to satisfy the ruling of the court.[13]

Posey attempted to deed back the property he had purchased from Matt and Sarah Wallace, but it was too late. The land had been lost and the deed was filed too late to avoid the loss.[14] The land was divided into 40-acre parcels and sold to settle the debt. The court also took much of Posey's herd of horses and cattle. [15]

Posey was lodged in the McLennan County jail May 30, 1873, to await transport to state prison.[16] The Posey gang staged a jailbreak, freeing Posey and four other prisoners. The gang went on a rampage throwing terror into nearly every citizen around Waco. They killed a deputy sheriff named Blankenship in a fierce gunfight near the Posey home [17] before escaping to the "Posey Thicket," near his father's home at Horn Hill. No lawman was brave enough to enter the Posey Thicket.

Outlawry Runs Rampant in Texas

The outlawry running rampant in Texas during Reconstruction had the citizenry outraged. The killings in and around Waco, coupled with the theft activities, drew much criticism about the inept state police and the court system.

In 1873, attorney Coke announced his candidacy for the office of governor of the state of Texas opposing the unpopular Reconstruction governor E.J. Davis. This was the same lawyer who successfully defended Bill Posey in the early theft charges. Coke had gained five acquittals for Posey before losing on the two counts of mule theft resulting in Posey's conviction and prison term sentence.

Richard Coke
1874-1876

Coke was a man of large stature, with a massive bald head, a heavy growth of beard, and a voice that "roared like a bull when angry." He was said never to be without the Bible he carried in his pocket.[18]

Coke defeated Davis in the fall election by a huge majority. One of the campaign planks was to eliminate Davis' state police force, which most considered ineffective and oppressive. Coke was inaugurated in January 1874, but Davis refused to give up office. He fortified himself with his Negro state police guards on the first floor of the capitol and wired President U.S. Grant to send reinforcements to back him. Grant refused and Coke was ushered into office.[19]

The election of Coke was like the dawning of a new light following the dark days of Reconstruction that shrouded Texas. Coke and the new legislature quickly abolished the state police and ushered in the strengthened Texas Rangers. Texas citizens cheered the election. The new administration ended radical rule and restored Texas government to the people.

Bill Posey was still on the loose and reportedly causing havoc among the farmers and ranchers over a wide area of central

Texas. The Texas press reported Posey's gang was stealing horses, mules and cattle in broad daylight. It was said the gang would ride up to a ranch, round up a herd, and drive it off, the owners powerless to stop the brazen thieves.

Posey next surfaced in McLennan County, it was reported, driving a herd of stolen horses ahead of him. He had taken the horses in broad daylight from the ranch of a German in Hill County. He was quickly recognized and word got to the sheriff that Posey was again in the area. The sheriff dispatched a posse and started after him. He was cornered in the Brazos River bottom just a few miles from his home and Waco. A spirited gun battle ensued, but Posey was able to slip by the posse. This time he headed for the Indian Territory and sanctuary among friends and family.[20]

The tragedies on the Tehuacana had caused great sadness. A grieving Elizabeth Posey waited with her three sons at the Posey home, distraught and heart-broken at the events that had shattered their lives.

The Hanging

In the dark of night on June 30, 1873, the Posey gang appeared at the home of Matt and Sarah Wallace. They entered the house and forced Wallace outside.

Sarah Ann Wallace

They tied his hands behind him, placed a noose around his neck and over a limb of a live oak tree. The tree proved not to be tall enough, so they placed another rope around his feet and secured it to another tree. The writhing body of Matt Wallace soon was silenced by death. A grieving Sarah Ann Wallace and bewildered two-year-old-daughter, Sarah Emmaline, were left behind with the lifeless body as the horses thundered off, carrying the shouting mob.[21] Sarah was also six months pregnant with Matthew Wallace II, their second child.

Posey and some of the gang members then headed for Indian Territory, where he had kin and was well known. Indian Territory was a haven for outlaws, but Posey was Creek Indian and allowed to choose land at will. Posey may have been forgotten in Texas had he stayed out of the state, but the gang kept making forays into Texas stealing cattle and horses and driving them north to the Kansas markets. This caused the Texas governor to place a $500 reward on Posey for his return to Texas to serve the prison sentence.[22]

Before their departure to Indian Territory, Posey and the gang paid late-night visits to Dr. Owens, the attorneys, and the prosecutors who were responsible for his convictions and ruining his life. They threatened the lives of all. Posey's former attorney, Richard Coke, was governor. Waco citizens petitioned him to boost the reward on Posey's head to $1,000, which he did.

In a letter to Gov. Coke, district attorney Pearson pleaded with Coke to take speedy action to capture Posey. The letter concluded with the observation that "Posey is a perfect terror to this community. It is supposed that he hung M.A. Wallace in Waco a short time ago. A few nights ago, he was at M.D. Herring's house at night with his party with a view to kill him, whose life he has threatened. He has also threatened to kill Dr. S.A. Owens of Waco."[23]

Posey and some of the men then headed back to Indian Territory and his sanctuary on Cane Creek, a few miles west of Muskogee.

Posey Sends for Sons

The death of her brother, Matt Wallace, the loss of land and the estrangement of the families Posey had caused, was too much for Elizabeth to bear. She died in 1876 of a broken heart, family members said.[24]

Posey and Elizabeth had three sons, Matthew, 10, Albert Washington, 7, and Robert, 5. Following the death of Elizabeth, the boys were living with Elizabeth's father, Washington S. Wallace.

Learning of the death of Elizabeth, Posey sent an emissary to Waco to retrieve his sons with the threat he would return and kill the rest of the Wallace family if his demand was not met. The boys were sent and joined their father for a new life in Indian Territory. (25)

Posey had two homes in the Creek Nation. The main home was a blockhouse on Cane Creek between Okmulgee and Muskogee. The other was near Concharty Town and Red Fork on the Arkansas River in the northern reaches of the Creek Nation. Posey had taken a new wife, a woman named Susan. The family was known to attend church and buy supplies in Muskogee and Okmulgee, but Posey was never challenged—his ever-present guns and reputation a deterrent.(26) Muskogee had only recently been settled. It was formerly a water and fuel stop for the MK&T Railroad as it was constructed through the area 1873-74.

Posey Captured in I.T.

Texas authorities had been alerted Posey was living on Cane Creek. On June 29, 1874, Texas officers from Sherman, consisting of J.L. Hall, Bill Everheart, S.D. Ball and Burt Douglass arrested Posey. On the Sunday before the arrest, the party arrived within five miles of the ranch of Posey, and halted for the night due to a severe storm. Just at daybreak on Monday, they started and, in a short time, came in sight of the ranch.

J. L. Hall

They discovered Posey starting out on the prairie in search of his horses. The officers divided, and a part secured position in the stables or lots. Two of the men started out to watch his movements. He shortly returned to the house, when his son, Matthew, saw the two men, attempted to warn his father. Ignoring the warning of the youngster, Posey proceeded to the stable, and the officers stepped out with guns drawn and ordered him to surrender, which he did, though reluctantly. The lawmen left at once with the prisoner for Muskogee.

There they boarded a train, transporting the prisoner back to Texas. Posey's three sons were left with relatives. [27]

An article in the *Denison Herald* of July 14, 1874, reported that deputy sheriff Hall "had returned from Muskogee, in the Nation, where he had put the cuffs on W.A.J. Posey, mule thief and fratricide."

Jesse Leigh Hall would later become a fabled Texas Ranger.

Posey Escapes Prison

Posey arrived in Huntsville July 19, 1874, [28] to begin serving his five-year sentence. The Texas prisoners were leased to corporations at the time and they were forced to work on road gangs and other projects of hard labor. Posey was an incorrigible prisoner. He was constantly subdued by the guards by water baths, clubs and often was in solitary confinement.

Another punishment was to be placed atop "The Horse," a wooden platform that was sharp at the top where the prisoner was forced to sit. His feet were not allowed to touch the ground and many times weights were added to the feet of the prisoner to further subject him to grueling pain. Posey was subjected to this punishment many times. The "horse" was placed in a position so all prisoners could view the agony.

Posey had served 20 months of his sentence. He was working on a road gang March 4, 1876, when he spotted his opportunity for freedom. Texas newspapers reported he had a 12-pound ball attached to his ankle as he worked. Posey managed to get behind a guard whom he felled with a rock to the head. Taking the guard's rifle, he shouted a challenge to the other guards to come and get him and he would kill them all. He mounted a horse, placed the ball between his legs and rode away to sanctuary to his father's home at Horn Hill. There, his shackles were removed and he gathered guns and ammunition and headed again for Indian

Territory. [29] The officers tracked him to the Posey Thicket, but, again, none would enter the thicket.

Posey Spotted In Indian Territory

Soon after Posey's escape, The *Eufaula Indian Journal* reported Daniel Childers, with two assistants, found the trail of many cattle that were headed for the north but were stopped by the high water stage in the Arkansas River. They separated while searching, and Childers unexpectedly came upon a cave in the hills about 30 miles north of Childers Ferry. Childers' attention was attracted to smoke coming from the cave, and he decided to check it out. It was just breaking daylight, and Childers concealed himself to observe the events. Soon after, Bill Posey, who had just escaped from the Texas penitentiary, and a woman came out of the brush with a pail of milk, and entered the cave. They passed so near Childers' hiding place he could have easily dispatched them. But now, being alone, he let them pass. Soonafter, two men came out of the cave whom he recognized as white men by the name of Withers. Leaving the cave, Childers followed the trail of Posey and the woman and was rewarded by finding a corral hidden in a ravine in the woods containing nearly 400 head of cattle stolen in Indian Territory. Childers took command of the cattle and headed them toward Childers Ferry and turned them over to his ranchmen. Childers was again joined by his assistants, and they started on the trail of a large herd of cattle that had been crossing the ford. Following the trail, they overtook two men with 40 head of steers. The men put spurs to their horses and escaped, but the cattle were taken and driven back to the ferry and safety. [30]

The Beginning of the End

Posey might have remained safe in the Territory had he stayed out of Texas. But he kept making forays back across the Red River stealing horses and cattle, bringing the herds back to the Territory and to the subsequent Kansas markets. His notoriety in Texas was wide spread now, but he remained one step ahead of the law.

The Chicago Sun-Times reported Posey enlarged his home on Cane Creek, where he and his three boys, and the new wife enjoyed family life. They planted beans, corn, squash and the other crops commonly raised. He kept hogs and chickens, and supplemented the family meat supply with the abundant wild game. Always mindful of his wanted status in Texas, he added a second story to their home, which permitted a wide view of the countryside, and observation of approaching visitors. In the winter of 1877, Susan presented the family with another son, Henry.[31]

Meanwhile, back in Texas, Coke had served a two-year term as governor and was up for re-election in 1876. He won a second term handily but resigned shortly thereafter to take a vacant seat in the United States Senate. Coke's successor to the governor's mansion was Lieutenant Governor Richard B. Hubbard. [32]

Richard B. Hubbard
1876-1879

Hubbard was no ordinary man, and his administration was far from ordinary. He was the biggest and loudest governor Texas ever had. He weighed over 400 pounds, and it was said his voice could be heard for miles. He carried his bulk well. He was an extremely impressive man, commanding respect from all with whom he came in contact. He had served as a Confederate colonel in the Civil War, and a term in the Texas Legislature.[33]

Posey's continued antics in Texas were apparently troublesome to an extent Hubbard wanted an end to it. At the urging of Waco citizens, Hubbard finally decided to place a new reward on the head of Posey — dead or alive.

Gov. Hubbard petitioned Principal Chief Ward Coachman of the Creek Nation to apprehend Posey and return him to Texas authorities. The petition from Hubbard, dated March 27, 1877, read:

"To the Superintendent or Chief Executive Officer of the Indian Territory: Whereas, it appears by the annexed documents, which are hereby certified to be authentic, that W.A. Posey stands charged with the crime of 'Theft' committed in the State of Texas, and information having been received that the said W.A. Posey has fled from justice and has taken refuge in the Indian Territory.

"Now, therefore, I, R.B. Hubbard, Governor of the State of Texas, have thought proper, in pursuance of the provisions of the Constitution and laws of the United States, to demand the surrender of W.A. Posey, as a fugitive from justice, and that he be delivered to Daniel Childers, who is hereby appointed the Agent on the part of the State of Texas to receive him.

"Given under my hand, and the Great Seal of the State affixed, at the city of Austin, this 27th day of March, A.D. One Thousand Eight Hundred and Seventy Seven, and of the Independence of the United States One Hundred First and of Texas the Forty Second year. R.B. Hubbard, Governor."

Included in the petition to Chief Coachman were certified copies of the McLennan County court documents showing the conviction of Posey on the charge of theft of two mules, Cause No. 1436.[34]

Chief Coachman received the requisition from Gov. Hubbard and issued the following dispatch to the Creek Lighthorse:

Whereas it appears from documents placed in my hand as to the crimes committed by W.A. Posey now in the jurisdiction of the Creek Nation and a demand having been made in accordance with the law and truly by R.B. Hubbard, Governor of the State of Texas to receive him. Now therefore, I, Ward Coachman, Principal Chief of the Creek Nation do issue to any lawful officer, Greeting: You are hereby commanded in the name of the Creek Nation to arrest said W.A. Posey and deliver him safely to said Daniel Childers—herein fail not as the law directs, Given under my hand and seal of the office the day and year above written, Ward Coachman, Principal Chief."[35]

Coachman summoned Suntharlpee, a Lighthorse captain of the Uchee Town district to effect the arrest of Posey, who was known to be a resident of the district. Coachman instructed the captain to select two of his best men to assist in the arrest. They knew Posey and understood his arrest was going to be a difficult task.

Chief Ward Coachman was a pleasant and popular leader of the Creeks. He was born in Wetumka, Alabama, in 1827, and went to neighboring schools in Macon County. He was the youngest son of

Chief Ward Coachman

Mushlushobie (who adopted the Christianized name of Coachman), a full-blood Creek. His mother was Pollie Durant, who was a one-half Creek. Coachman lived with his uncle, Loughlin Durant, until he was 22 years old, when he went to the Indian Territory on a scouting mission. Finding the new country favorable, he returned to Alabama and began making preparations to move some remaining Creeks to the new country. A party of 65 Creeks arrived in the new country six weeks later, guided by Coachman.

Coachman became a trader among the so-called "wild tribes" to the west, but a band of Caddos returning from a hunt carried off his stock. He was nearly killed but managed to make it back home. He then entered retail business near his home in Wetumka, I.T., and was involved in agriculture until the Civil War broke out. He served in the Confederate army under Col. Chilly McIntosh as a lieutenant. At the close of the war, he became a leader among the Creeks and was elected Chief in 1875. (36)

The Creek Lighthorse

Duties of the Creek Lighthorse as defined by the Creek General Council in the Uniform Code adopted for the Nation in 1840, were to "destroy all spiritous liquors brought into the Nation, and inflict penalty and levy a fine upon all persons found guilty of introducing it, or commission of other offenses." The code also mentioned the Lighthorse should monitor the "ever-present cattle herders passing through the Nation on their way to the northern markets, and to watch for lawless bands roaming the Territory."

A Lighthorse company consisted of a captain and three or four privates. Their compensation was $400 dollars per year for the captain, and half that for the privates. The Lighthorse members were elected by a vote of the people in their respective districts for a term of two years. The Lighthorse were furnished guns and ammunition in order to carry out their duties. There was no official uniform, but they were supplied with a badge for identification purposes. The Daniel Childers named in the documents by Gov. Hubbard as being authorized to receive Posey for the State of Texas, was a captain of the Creek Lighthorse.

Following the removal of the soldiers at Fort Gibson after the Civil War, the Lighthorse became the only law enforcement in the Territory. They were poorly equipped and not enough in number to adequately provide protection. Murder was commonplace and the number of unsavory characters traveling through the Territory was growing because of inadequate law enforcement. Life was cheap in the 1870s in Indian Territory. Some said there was no Sunday (a day of rest) west of St. Louis, and no God west of Fort Smith.[37]

Federal Law in Indian Territory

Judge Isaac Parker

The government had seated Judge Isaac Parker on the bench of the federal court at Fort Smith in 1875. His jurisdiction was to include the Indian Territory in an effort to stem the lawless tide. In his first court term Parker sentenced eight men to be hanged. This was carried out with great public ceremony on gallows erected next to the federal courthouse in Fort Smith. He quickly gained the title of "Hanging

Judge Parker," and his system of justice was carried out eighty-eight times in the twenty years he presided over the court.

Those two decades also saw 65 of his deputies killed in the line of duty in attempting arrests of the lawless breed that inhabited Western Arkansas and Indian Territory. Some said the record showed both a persistence of his efforts in effecting a death penalty for major crimes, but the lack of success in bringing law and order to the region.

The government, the courts or local authorities were never able to contain a population that included renegade white and black outlaws and Indians of every conceivable blood mix that preyed on the Territory. The same record could be applied as well to the state of Texas during this period.

The Chicago Sun-Times, who kept a correspondent at Fort Smith and regularly reported news of the Territory, (mostly the bad news), reported Judge Parker had dispatched two deputy U.S. Marshals to the Territory in an effort to take Posey into custody. The paper reported deputies approached Posey's home on Cane Creek, and attempted his arrest. Posey, the article said, agreed to accompany them to Fort Smith, but invited the deputies into the house for dinner before they left on the 75-mile trip. He placed chairs at the table and was making preparations to leave, "but he suddenly reached in under his couch, brought out his six-shooter and sent one ball through the thigh of one deputy and another through the eye of the other, and drove them from the house.

"He ordered them to throw up their hands, and then cooly asked for the writ (arrest order). This he destroyed and compelled the outwitted and conquered officers to go in and partake of the meal prepared for them, and let them go back to report their failure."[38]

Posey continued his operations out of the Territory for some 15 months after his escape from the Texas penitentiary. He and his family moved openly in the Territory, where they were well received. He participated in the fall and spring roundups with other stockmen in the area, never seeking to throw a "sticky loop" over any of his neighbors' livestock. Cattle ran the open range and the estray law prevailed during this period before the invention and use of barbed wire, which fenced off the owners' property. Life and activity of the times regarding the estray law was found in the pages of the *Indian Journal*, published at Eufaula, I.T.:

"Rounding Up Estrays"

With each recurring spring comes the gathering of horsemen and rounding up, or surrounding a large tract of country, and all approaching a common center, driving before them with a merry shout and loud halloos, the cracking of whips and hard riding, all the unbranded and estray cattle within the circle. They often come from many miles to seek their own. This year they all met at the rock quarry, where a field enclosed with a stone fence will hold the wildest steer. Nearly one hundred men had gathered nearly fifty head. The owners selected all that could be identified, branded them and drove them back to their range. "The estrays will be advertised for six months and sold if unclaimed. Many of the cattle roaming on the broad prairie will wander twenty miles or more from home. After they get wonted to a range they seldom leave, and, as with ponies, if driven off, will return from long distances at certain seasons."

In the same issue, it was reported a local rancher, Montford Johnson, had lost a number of cattle recently—"stolen and driven north." He learned they had been driven towards Childers Ferry and crossed at Red Oak Ford, on the Arkansas.

The open ranges provided easy accumulation of livestock. The Territory was sparsely populated, and one could move around undetected for days without seeing another human. It was said the range was full of unbranded horses and cattle, easy pickings by Posey and his men, who made regular forays into Texas and Southern Indian Territory gathering herds that were taken to Coffeyville and sold.

For some unknown reason, Posey broke his rule of not bothering local livestock. He had been accused of cattle theft in the pages of the *Indian Journal*, but denied the charge, even sending in a compatriot to lodge complaint with the editor.[39] But now the U.S. Marshal at Fort Smith had received a formal complaint by Charles Clinton, that Posey and a man named Charles Cain had stolen 40 head of his cattle, valued at $400.[40]

Clinton, a white resident of the Indian country, Western District of Arkansas, signed the complaint. Witnesses were listed as Clinton; Dan Childers, and Fred Severs, a highly respected Creek citizen living on the Arkansas River in the northern Creek country. Severs would later become secretary for the popular Creek Chief, Pleasant Porter, and would build the Severs Hotel in Muskogee, the largest hotel in the area at the time. Though the alleged cattle theft was committed on the first of June 1876 the arrest order for Posey and Cain was not issued until April 5, 1877.[41]

Texas authorities appeared to be under pressure to bring Posey to justice in Texas. The executive order from Gov. Hubbard to Chief Coachman for Posey's arrest could not be ignored. Now came troubles with Judge Parker's court and with citizens in the Territory in which he lived. The cattle stealing complaint lodged in Fort Smith was a federal law violation, even more serious than state laws. With these new developments, the outlaw career of Bill Posey appeared to be nearing an end.

Posey's Bloody End

Susan was now with a Posey child and they spent the winter near Red Fork where she could be near her family at the time of delivery. Another son, Henry, was born in the spring of 1877. Posey was readying the wagon to move the family back to their home on Cane Creek. He had placed the wagon on jacks and was making repairs. The wagon slipped from a jack and landed on Posey's right index finger, nearly severing it at the second joint.

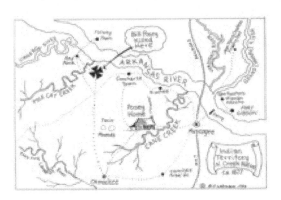

He left for Okmulgee the next morning to buy supplies and have the finger treated by a doctor. The finger could not be saved and it was amputated at the second joint. Posey left the doctor's office with a heavily bandaged hand.[42]

Learning Posey was in town, Chief Coachman dispatched Creek Lighthorse Captain Suntharlpee and two picked assistants to apprehend Posey for the Texas authorities. They tracked him to the northern reaches of the Creek Nation at a point where Polecat Creek enters the Arkansas River, near present Jenks, Oklahoma. Posey was driving six head of stolen horses ahead of him. They ordered him to surrender, but Posey refused, determined not to be taken back to Texas and prison.

Posey reached for his 16-shot Henry repeating rifle, but his heavily bandaged hand prevented him from getting off a shot. A blast from a shotgun of one of the deputies tore into Posey's right shoulder, rendering it useless. He was reaching for a revolver with his left hand when another charge from the shotgun blasted his left shoulder. With both arms dangling helplessly by his side, Posey dug his spurs into the flanks of his animal, sending it charging into

Suntharlpee's mount, knocking them into a tributary to the creek. He was charging his horse into the deputies, and they were firing at him with revolvers, one striking him in the nose and blowing it away. Suntharlpee regained his footing and charged up the ravine in time to catch Posey with a pistol shot to the jaw, sending the bullet crashing into his brain, killing him. Posey was only 31 years of age.

Newspaper accounts of Posey's killing were telegraphed worldwide. *The Chicago Sun-Times* said, "Too much praise cannot be awarded the Creek authorities. Chief Ward Coachman and Suntharlpee with his brave posse, for ridding the world of one whose crimes are seldom equaled, and whose daring bravery, if directed in another cause, would have been worthy of admiration."

A white man named Henry Riggs, claiming he was Posey's brother-in-law, charged Suntharlpee and his men had kept Posey's weapons, and he wanted them turned over to him. This claim caught the attention of Jacob Barnett, a Judge of the Deep Fork District of the Creek Nation, who wrote a letter to Chief Coachman, dated June 22, 1877:

"Dear Sir: This man Riggs, a white man living near Col. Robinson's in the Deep Fork District, and a brother-in-law to Bill Posey is meddling himself I think too much for a man in his position and status in this country. I have learned that he has written a letter to some of the U.S. Marshals concerning the killing of Posey and also about Captain Suntharlpee taking Posey's arms. I have no idea that he can do anything but it goes to show that he wants to meddle where he has no business—and cause trouble so I must advise you to revoke his permit immediately and report him as an intruder and let the Nation get rid of him for I think he is a bad man."

It is believed Riggs was a brother of Posey's second wife, Susan. His name was Henry Riggs, and the new Posey son had been named Henry. All Posey's sisters had married except one, who still resided with her parents in Limestone County. None of Posey's sisters were married to a man by the name of Riggs.

A letter signed by Judge Micco of the Deep Fork District, dated September 25, 1877, told Chief Coachman that the prosecuting attorney for the district had informed him that Henry Riggs was, indeed, "an intruder in the Muskokee (sic) Nation" and his permit to reside in the Territory had expired some time before.

Relatives buried Posey where he was killed, near a large boulder. His mangled body was wrapped in a blanket sent by his mother when the Posey sons were sent to be with him in the Creek Nation.[44]

Thus ended the life of William Andrew Jackson Posey, in a violent and bloody shoot-out in the wilderness of Indian Territory. He had spent the last five of his 31 years as a fugitive from the law. He had lost his land, his wife, his herds of livestock, and his dreams with them. At the end he did have his sons, perhaps his most prized possession.

And he kept his vow not to be taken alive and sent back to prison in Texas.

The Aftermath

Following the death of Bill Posey, Susan and the infant Henry Posey went to live with her family near Concharty and Red Fork. The three other Posey sons were taken in by their Berryhill-Hopwood kin but were soon kicked out because of Matthew. Matthew was troublesome and difficult to control. They drifted to Utah and Idaho, where they worked as cowboys. They returned to Indian Territory periodically to visit family. Matthew lost an arm at the shoulder in a bank robbery shootout, reportedly as a member of the Dalton gang. Matthew's daughter said he never talked about his past or the loss of the arm. He could roll a Bull Durham cigarette with one hand, she said.[45]

Bill Posey's sons were each one-quarter Creek. Each was awarded a 160-acre allotment of land by the Dawes Commission. The land was soon sold, however, and they continued to live in Indian Territory and Utah.[46]

Dan Childers

The former Creek Lighthorseman went berserk in the summer of 1885. He first went down to Muskogee, where he had a tombstone made for himself with only the date blank. He then drove his light wagon up the trail to Tulsa, lashing his team and raving incoherently. He then stopped at a store and bought three coffins, drove out to Red Fork, and killed his sister-in-law. He loaded the body into the wagon and returned to Tulsa, raging and terrorizing the town. Childers headed out to the ranch of George Perryman, bent on more murder. He was shot dead as he approached the house. Perryman, a kindly Creek Indian, took the dead man's children into his family and reared and educated them as his own.[47]

Captain Suntharlpee

Suntharlpee, the Creek Lighthorse Captain who delivered the fatal shot to Bill Posey, became prominent in Creek politics. He built a house and a blacksmith shop near Euchee Town and served as a member of the U.S. Indian police in the Tulsa area. He also served as a cattle inspector at Red Fork, I.T.[48]

Charles Clinton

Clinton was the white rancher who claimed Bill Posey and Charles Cain had stolen 40 head of cattle from his range. He was intermarried with a Creek woman and formerly lived in Okmulgee. He built a 10-room home on a hilltop outside of Tulsa and moved his family there. His wife was a former student at the Tullahasse Indian School. She was a teacher in the neighboring schools. Clinton built a ferry across the Arkansas River near Red Fork, which was a big shipping center for cattle in later years. [49]

William Crabtree

William Crabtree was a Limestone County punk who had come to Texas from Arkansas in the late 1860s. He was in and out of jail accused of many crimes and was a known member of the Posey gang. He was implicated in the lynching of Matt Wallace and jailed at Waco, but the charges were dismissed for lack of evidence. The 1878 murder of J.T. Vaughn, a citizen of Bosque County, Texas implicated Crabtree. The Horrell brothers out of Lampasas had been charged with the murder with the trial being held in Meridian, county seat of Bosque County. Crabtree had turned state's evidence during that trial in testimony about the brutal robbery and murder of Vaughn resulting in the conviction of the Horrell brothers. Crabtree was shot to death on November 28. His body, bearing six bullet holes to the chest, was found in a ravine near the Meridian courthouse. Lawmen attributed the killing of Crabtree to friends of the Horrell brothers, revenge for his testimony against the men. (50)

Last Posey Member Caught

A Waco, Texas dispatch October 21, 1887 said: "Twelve or fifteen years since there was a desperate gang of horse and cattle thieves located in the jungles of Tehuacana, about ten miles from Waco, under the lead of the celebrated desperado Bill Posey. The band had consisted of Posey, Bud and Ben Fuller, William Crabtree, the Sweats and others. Posey was since killed. Crabtree was killed. Sweat served a five years sentence, and yesterday morning Deputy Marshal Waller arrested Ben Fuller near Caddo, in the Indian Territory, and landed him in the Waco jail.

Fuller had been a fugitive from justice for seven years and only lived with his Winchester constantly in his hand. Waller only succeeded in arresting him by some neat strategy for which he is noted. Fuller has been indicted for horse and cattle thefts in many cases." Thus fell the last member of one of the most desperate bands of lawless outlaws and ruffians with which the frontiers of Texas and Indian Territory had been infested.

End Notes:

Bill Lehmann is a retired former publisher of the Guthrie Daily Leader, *Guthrie, Oklahoma.*

1. Eliza Berryhill Posey family Bible records, original held by Louise McIntire, Gladewater, Texas.

2. Ibid

3. Ibid

4. Federal 1870 census records for McLennan County, Texas.

5. The Waco Medical Association, History of Waco, by Dr. W.O. Wilkes, (1942) held by the McLennan County Library, Waco, Texas.

6. Ibid.

7. Warranty deed record, Book O at Page 35, February 27, 1871, office of the McLennan County Clerk, Courthouse, Waco, Texas.

8. Warranty deed record, book O at page 29, February 24, 1871, office of the McLennan County Clerk, Courthouse, Waco, Texas.

9. State of Texas, County of McLennan, Cause No. 1381, September 4, 1871.

10. State of Texas, County of McLennan, Cause No. 1436, December Term, 1871.

11. State of Texas, County of McLennan, Cause No. 1436, conviction December 15, 1871.

12. State of Texas, County of McLennan, Coke, Henning and Anderson, Cause No. 2103, April 18, 1873; Dr. S.A. Owens, Cause No. 2081, May 2, 1873

13. Sheriff Deed, McLennan County, Texas, filed July 3, 1871.

14. William A. Posey to S.A. Wallace and Matthew Wallace, Warranty Deed Q at Page 48, filed with the McLennan County Texas Clerk, June 1, 1872.

15. Sheriff Deed, McLennan County, Texas, filed October 6, 1872.

16. Compiled from newspaper accounts of the lynching, including The Waco Examiner, Waco Advance and Dallas Herald, July 25, 1873.

17. Ibid.

18. Texas Governor biographies, McLennan County Library, Waco, Texas.

19. Ibid.

20. A compilation of newspaper articles from the Waco Examiner, Waco Advance, Galveston News *and* Dallas Herald.

21. *Family legend and* Dallas Herald, *July 12, 1873, Page one column three.*

22. *Official collection papers of Governors E.J. Davis, Richard Coke and Richard B. Hubbard, Texas State Library, Austin, Texas.*

23. *Ibid.*

24. *Family legend interview with Ora Posey Nielsen, American Fork, Utah, granddaughter of Bill Posey and Elizabeth Wallace Posey, September 6, 1992.*

25. *Ibid.*

26. *A compilation of newspaper articles including the* Chicago Sun-Times, *who kept a correspondant in Fort Smith, Arkansas to report area news including Indian Territory.*

27. Eufaula Journal *and* Waco Examiner *June 29, 1874.*

28. *Texas State penitentiary records.*

29. *From stories published in the* Waco Examiner *and* Galveston News.

30. Eufaula Indian Journal, *June 16, 1876.*

31. *Family Bible records.*

32. *Texas Governor Archives, Texas State Library, Austin, Texas.*

33. *Ibid.*

34. *Creek Indian Archives collection, Oklahoma Historical Society, Oklahoma City, Oklahoma.*

35. *Ibid.*

36. *Ibid.*

37. *Excerpts from* West of Hell's Fringe *by Glenn Shirley, Oklahoma University Press, 1978.*

38. *Compilation of reports by Fort Smith, Arkansas Corresponent for* Chicago Sun-Times.

39. *Compilation of news articles published in the* Eufaula Indian Journal, *Eufaula, Indian Territory.*

40. *Federal Arrest Warrant, Western Didtrict of Arkansas. Federal Records Center collection, Ft. Worth, Texas.*

41. *Ibid.*

42. *Interview with Ora Posey Nielsen, American Fork, Utah, September 6, 1992., granddaughter of Bill Posey.*

43. *Compilation of newspaper articles regarding the death of Bill Posey, including the* Eufaula Indian Journal *and the* Chicago Sun Times.

44. *Interview with Ora Posey Nielsen, American Fork, Utah, September 6, 1992, granddaughter of Bill Posey.*

45. *Interview with Ora Posey Nielsen, American Fork, Utahm, September 6, 1992, granddaughter of Bill Posey. Interview with Inez Posey Colson, October 17,1992, daughter of Matthew A. Posey.*

46. *Dawes Commission Rolls for Creek Nation, 1899. Indian Archives Collection, Oklahoma Historical Society, Oklahoma City, Oklahoma.*

47. *Excerpts from the book "TULSA, from Creek Nation to Oil Capital," by Dr. Angie Debo, Oklahoma University Press, 1943.*

48. *Ibid.*

49. *Ibid.*

50. Bosque County Herald, *Meridian, Texas, November 26, 1878.*

WHERE IN THE WORLD ARE YOU, MAX LEHMANN?

By Lynda Lehmann French and Bill Lehmann

A nine-line story appearing on page one July 14, 1904 in the *Galveston Daily News* was a discovery we had been seeking since 1986. Thank God for the Internet!

Finally a lead was found in the search for the circumstances surrounding the mysterious disappearance of our grandfather, Max Lehmann.

> **KILLING NEAR CARRIZO.**
>
> **M. M. Lehman Was the Victim—Particulars Are Lacking.**
>
> SPECIAL TO THE NEWS.
>
> Carrizo Springs, Tex., July 13.—M. M. Lehman was shot and killed at an early hour this morning about three miles east of town on the McCaleb farm. No particulars of killing have been learned.

Many stories among family members were mere speculation. No one knew exactly what happened to Lehmann. He had just up and disappeared. Some thought he went to Mexico. Some said he was killed over a soured racehorse deal. Others said he was done in by a jealous husband who discovered he was delivering something other than the mail to his residence.

The newspaper story now revealed his fate. Now we knew what happened to him, and where. But it opened up a whole new set of questions that are still unresolved: Where are you, Max? Where are you buried? We would like to place a marker on your gravesite.

Max Lehmann, 1954-1904

Max Lehmann was murdered July 13, 1904. He was shot to death in the early morning hours on the McCaleb farm just outside the tiny town of Carrizo Springs, Texas.

The killing was under mysterious circumstances. And today, 110 years later, the event remains shrouded in mystery and the burial place of Max Lehmann's body is yet to be discovered.

Max Lehmann was a victim of a murderous crime, and also a victim of a flawed judicial system. Perhaps it was even a cover up to protect the respected (or feared) family name of the murderer.

The failures of the system to Lehmann were many. There were 14 recorded deaths for Dimmit County in 1904. Max Lehmann was not among them. There are no recorded cemetery records of his burial in Dimmit County. No coroner's report can be found. There is no record that can be found of the disposal of his personal property. Lehmann was owner of a horse and buggy among other personal effects, and they were never returned to the surviving family members.

Another large roadblock is the victim is never identified in criminal charges, only the person charged in the crime. No cross-references; no nothing. The victim is a forgotten individual in criminal cases involving murder.

In 1904, communication and travel were primitive. The basic means of communication was by mail and telegraph. Lehmann was killed a hard two-day ride from his normal home in Wilson County. Family legend says when the family learned of Lehmann's death, authorities said the body would be sent by train to Wilson County to be claimed by the family. The body never arrived.

Dimmit County Sheriff records for 1904 are reportedly lost in the jungles of storage areas in the courthouse labyrinths. Likewise, 1904 newspaper copies of the *Carrizo Springs Javelin* that might contain stories of the event have mysteriously disappeared between the *Javelin* and the microfilm producer.

Lehmann was killed by John A. Tumlinson, the son of legendary LaSalle County Sheriff Joe Tumlinson, a popular and powerful individual. The Tumlinsons were descendents of Capt.

Peter Frank Tumlinson, a member of Stephen F. Austin's "Old 300," the original group that established Austin's Colony in early years before Texas' independence from Mexico. The "Old 300" are regarded as Texas "Royalty." Tumlinson was appointed one of 25 "Rangers" that kept law and order in the colony and engaged in forays against marauding Indian bands that raided the colonists.

The descending ranks of the family were prominent in Texas law enforcement, with several serving as Texas Rangers. The family name was either revered or feared, depending on which side of the law you were on.

Following the killing of Lehmann, Tumlinson headed for sanctuary in Mexico, crossing the Rio Grande River near Eagle Pass, Texas. He soon decided to return to Texas, but was apprehended by Texas officials in Mexico and returned to Texas where he was lodged in the Dimmit County jail at Carrizo Springs, where he faced murder charges.

Tumlinson was the only witness to the killing, but his daughter, Dora Hyden, was a key player in the slaying. A sheriff's deputy interrogated Dora soon after the killing. In a deposition to the deputy, Dora testified she and Lehmann were to be married. Upon hearing this news, Tumlinson grabbed his gun, saddled his horse and raced to the McCaleb farm where he confronted Lehmann, shooting the unarmed victim to death. She testified Tumlinson then retuned and told her he was headed to Mexico and he would send for her.

Dora had recently given birth to a baby boy, but was estranged from her husband, Alfred A. Hyden. She and the son were apparently living with her father, a widower since 1897. Dora named the infant John Tumlinson Hyden, using her father's name.

Why Lehmann was in Dimmit County is a mystery. Had he known Dora in Wilson County before coming to Dimmit County? He was a relative stranger there. Had he taken a new mail route in Dimmit County? Did he work on the McCaleb farm where he was killed? All are unanswered questions. It is believed he followed

Dora there and she formerly lived in Wilson County and was a resident on his mail delivery route.

Max Lehmann was a hard 50 and had lived a hard life. He emigrated from Germany in 1854 as an infant, with his father and brother. He had learned the butcher trade while growing up in the German community of Indianola, a seaport on the Gulf of Mexico.

A rolling stone, Lehmann had been a drover on the Chisholm Trail with the Halliburton Ranch out of Gonzales, gathering cattle from the mesquite thickets around Cuero and Gonzales. He met and married Sarah Ann Miller-Wallace, a widow with two children. They had six children of their own. Lehmann had lost two farms to the mesquite-laden lands near Cuero and Gonzales. He took a job as a rural mail carrier to make ends meet, and even that was not enough to ward off the bankers and hard economic times. Sarah died in 1900 leaving him with four children still at home.

Dora was a young 18 years old. Perhaps this is the reason Dora's father took umbrage to the thought of her marriage to Lehmann. Dora and her husband were estranged and in the process of divorcing. It is possible the baby she was carrying might have even been a result of the relationship with Lehmann.

While Tumlinson was being held in the Dimmit County jail awaiting trial, the state of Texas was preparing the case against him. There were no eyewitnesses to the crime, but Dora was apparently the only person with direct knowledge of events. A subpoena was issued for her to appear in court as a witness. The subpoena couldn't be served because the deputy could not find her whereabouts.

Authorities heard she was in LaSalle County and traced her to a residence, but she had relocated to Webb County. From Webb County she had scooted off to El Paso, staying a hop, skip, and a jump ahead of the process servers.

1904 turned into 1905 and the court was still preparing documents laden with legalese, wherefores and whereases that lawyers like to waste pen and paper on. By final account, it amounted to one continuance to another because they couldn't locate Dora for her testimony.

Growing tired of confinement, John Tumlinson busted out of the Carrizo Springs jail in July 1905, and headed again for Mexico. Sheriff Buck struck out after Tumlinson and arrested him again in C.F. Diaz, Mexico. He was brought back to Texas, but this time lodged in the Laredo jail, a more secure facility.

In 1906, Dora fled Texas and was living in San Diego, California. She had changed the name of the son from John Tumlinson Hyden to Joseph Delbert Hyden, possibly not knowing the true identity of the father. She married Isaac Brock Thayer, a longshoreman and deep sea diver, in San Diego on April 28, 1906.

Feeble attempts by the Texas court to bring Dora back to Texas for testimony were a complete failure. The court could have placed her under oath in a deposition and forced her to answer questions, but they didn't; one more failure to deny justice to Max Lehmann.

Documents obtained at the Texas Ranger Museum in Laredo reveal the court finally decided without an eye witness and no testimony from Dora. There wasn't much chance for conviction. The case was dismissed December 12, 1906, and the charges against Tumlinson dropped.

Tumlinson was freed and immediately scurried to California with his son, Joe Tumlinson, to join Dora in San Diego.

Out of 96 pages of legal-size hand-written documents in the case against Tumlinson, only one reference carried the name of the victim, Max Lehmann. That reference was in the deposition taken by a sheriff's deputy in interrogating Dora following the murder of Lehmann where she stated her father had done the killing in a fit of rage over the possibility of the marriage between Dora and Lehmann.

Dora must have had a charm that attracted men. She married five more times, bearing children by each, before her death in 1947 in San Diego. She and her father were regular visitors back in Texas to see relatives.

Ironically, John A. Tumlinson disappeared in 1938 without a trace. In a letter to the editor of the Yuma, Arizona, newspaper, Dora appealed for the public's help in locating Tumlinson who had been missing for a year.

In the letter dated July 30, 1939, Dora stated Tumlinson was en route to Texas from San Diego and had sent a postcard from Yuma to the family. A year had passed and they had not heard from him again. Dora described Tumlinson as being slight of build and weighing about 111 pounds. He had blue eyes and gray hair with a gray mustache, the letter said. Like Max Lehmann, Tumlinson had just up and disappeared.

Fast forward to 2014:

Dink Frazier, of California, a former resident of Carrizo Springs, heard a story about the unearthing of a body on the former McCaleb farm in the 1940s. A crew was digging a water tank on the farm when they uncovered a body that had been buried on the site. Without notifying authorities, the crew just covered up the body again and erected a wooden cross to mark the spot, then moved the water tank to a new location a few yards away.

On a recent visit to the area, a descendant of the former owner of the McCaleb farm went to the location, drew a map and marked the spot of the unearthed body with an "X."

Could this be the final resting place of Max Lehmann? Could friends or relatives of Tumlinson gone to the scene after the killing and buried Lehmann? No body — no evidence.

Frazier and Dimmit County historian Bert Bell have been helpful in finding documents and information concerning the case. The Internet and Ancestry.com have also been very helpful in finding information not known previously.

Dora's testimony was vital in revealing reasons Max Lehmann was in Dimmit County, her relationship with Lehmann and what happened to his body following the killing. She and Tumlinson died with lips sealed.

Frazier says a descendant of the Tumlinson family remembers the "old men" talking about the event, but they simply passed it off with the comment that Lehmann "needed killing." Maybe that is reason enough to kill somebody when the eyes of Texas (and the law) are upon you, stranger!

Perhaps some equipment exists today that can locate a possible burial gravesite. Should remains be discovered on the old McCaleb farm location, two grandsons of Max Lehmann stand ready to provide DNA samples that might confirm the identity and reveal the final resting place of Max Lehmann.

A granite marker will be provided instead of an "X" to mark his final resting place.

Being killed over the love of a young, pretty woman may not be a preferred way to die, but it surely is way up there on the list. At least it beats getting killed over a horse!

MAX LEHMANN'S LAMENT

He came down from Wilson County
To fetch his future bride,
A two-day trip to Carrizo Springs
It was his last and fatal ride.

Dora was a rounder
Married to another at the time,
The child she carried belonged to Max,
You can bet your bottom dime.

Dora was unfaithful
To the man she didn't love,
Max had taken up his place
And was to wed the soiled dove.

Max Lehmann was a widowed man
50 winters old,
Dora had only 18 years
But lived life fast and bold.

Dora's beauty attracted many men
The reason you might guess,
The thing that all men covet
Lay beneath young Dora's Dress.

She had gone to see her father
In Carizzo at the time,
When told she planned to marry Max
The father lost his mind.

John Tumlinson loaded up his gun,
Spurred his horse into a lather,
Went off to confront old Max
And settle up the matter.

He arrived where Max was staying
Before the sun was up,
Called him out and shot him dead
And left him lying in the dust.

He went back to tell young Dora
He killed Max and had to go,
So he crossed the Rio Grande
And was swallowed up in Mexico.

Friends went to find the body
And buried Max into the ground,
No murder has been committed
If a body can't be found.

A posse rounded up 'ol John
In a sleepy border town
Lodged him a Laredo jail
To await justice to come down.

Only two men could tell the story
Only one was left to say,
What happened on that fatal morn
Or where Max's body lay.

They tried to find young Dora
To tell the court of what she knew,
But she had fled to California,
To start her life anew.

John spent a year in Laredo's jail
But freed without a trial,
Texas needed Dora's tale
And Max's body that was vital.

John went west to join Dora
Where she was living very nice,
She had married two more times
Leaving Max to pay the price.

John went back and forth to Texas
But in Arizona dropped from sight,
Perhaps it was in the cards of fate
When he murdered Max that night.

No tombstones can be planted
On their places in the ground,
Both men lie in unmarked graves
Only God knows where they're found.

The voice of old Max Lehmann
Cries out in Texas wind,
Find my body; dig me up
And bury me with my kin.

Place me next to Sarah
And take away our gloom,
Cover our grave with Live oak shade
And Bluebonnets in full bloom.

By Bill Lehmann, grandson 2/3/15

Guthrie History

INAUGURATION OF GOVERNOR FRANTZ—JAN. 15TH, 1906.

BILL LEHMANN

BICENTENNIAL OUTLOOK: GUTHRIE AWAKES

(This article appeared in the October-December 1975 edition of *Historic Preservation Magazine* published by the National Trust for Historic Preservation. Author was Bill Lehmann, publisher of the *Guthrie Daily Leader*.)

An unusual American city has announced a preservation plan equally unusual as the nation enters its Bicentennial year.

Guthrie, Oklahoma will celebrate its 87th birthday April 22, 1976. There's nothing particularly startling about that. Many American cities are much older than Guthrie, but most cities have changed over the years. Guthrie hasn't.

Guthrie is virtually the same as it was when it was the center of attention during the most colorful and turbulent period of Oklahoma history. Guthrie was the territorial capital of Oklahoma and was the state capital after Oklahoma became a state in 1907. But in the dark of night on June 10, 1910, the governor of Oklahoma had the state capital changed from Guthrie to Oklahoma City. With the state capital designation went Guthrie's future importance in political and economic affairs.

Guthrie street scene, 1910

Guthrie entered a period of stagnation. There was no development, but neither did the city decline. It just lay there, much like a modern Rip Van Winkle and slept while the rest of the world progressed.

Today Guthrie looks much the same as it did in 1910. The brick streets have been covered with blacktop, and neon signs and bright streetlights have been installed. But they light the same buildings that were seen and used by territorial and state political leaders and townspeople who built the city on a raw prairie as "America's last Frontier."

Guthrie's birth as a town came April 22, 1889, in the first of four land runs used by the United States as a method of distributing land to settlers anxious to find their own piece of America. The Oklahoma bill authorized the opening of an area in the center of Indian Territory for settlement April 22, 1889. The method for claim and settlement was unique. Those desiring land were to line up at a given point bordering the land to be settled and, at a signal, run to the land they desired to settle, drive in a stake to their claim and register with the Federal Land Office. Thus was established the Land Run.

Guthrie street scene, 1889

Although Oklahoma was comparatively unknown, people began gathering by the thousands along the southern border of Kansas, particularly at Arkansas City where trains would embark for the Oklahoma Territory line. Those making the Run from the north came principally from the northern states. Those lining up along the southern boundary of the Territory came from the southern states.

The rich, the poor, the refined, the ignorant, the white, the black, the men, the women, the northerners and the southerners all joined in the onward rush for land ownership in the new Oklahoma Territory.

Fully 10,000 people clamored to be aboard the first train leaving Arkansas City at dawn on April 22 for the Oklahoma

Territory boundary near present Orlando. One by one the trains left the Kansas depot loaded with would-be settlers.

The 15th and last train left at 11 a.m. to line up behind the others on the Santa Fe tracks for the rush southward. At the territorial line were other settlers who had gathered in wagons, on horseback, in carriages, on bicycles and on foot to await the signal to enter the new land and stake their claims.

The cavalry officer took his signal position at the line with a flag in one hand and a bugle in the other. Precisely at noon, he raised the bugle to his lips and gave the signal blast while dropping the upraised flag. Then began the race for homesteads—a race beyond the power of the pen to describe. Cheers and shouts from 100,000 souls were joined by the shrill whistles from the trains as they embarked on the southward journey into the virgin territory in the mad dash for land.

From the southern border the scene was much the same. Trains entering from the south carried passengers that would settle Norman, Oklahoma City and Edmond. Settlers from the north stopped at what would become Orlando, Mulhall and Guthrie.

Guthrie had the advantage over all the other towns from the start. It had been designated as the capital of Oklahoma Territory and was the site of the Land Office that was still under construction at the time of the Run. With Guthrie's advantage it had naturally received more publicity and was the focal point of most settlers entering the new lands.

At noon on opening day, Guthrie was but a watering stop on the Santa Fe railroad line that had been built through the Indian Territory two years before to connect the Texas cattle country with the eastern markets. A few government and railroad workers and a contingent of cavalry troops assigned to the Territory to preserve peace and keep out "sooners" were all that greeted the first settlers as they arrived.

In two hours the beautiful green of the new country was so completely covered by settlers' tents that the scene the appearance of a vast army bivouac. By nightfall 15,000 people had settled

Guthrie, seeking a new life and prosperity. Though the settlers were from all walks of life, there was never a more resourceful group of people that made so much of so little. *Rome may not have been built in a day, but Guthrie was!*

Trains carrying needed lumber and building supplies followed the settlers into the territory. Frame buildings began rising on the virgin Oklahoma soil the afternoon of the run. The dust had not settled from the rush of settlers when newsboys were barking the headlines of the first daily newspaper published in the territory, *The Oklahoma Daily State Capital*, issued from a tent on the afternoon of the run. In a month the first brick building had been built for the Guthrie National Bank, and was occupied. By July a full city directory had been printed and circulated. The Guthrie Chamber of Commerce had also been organized and was functioning by July.

Guthrie National Bank, 1890

Election of city officers was held the day following the run. Though city government prevailed in Guthrie, no other law prevailed. Oklahoma, as a territory, did not come under the jurisdiction of state or federal law. Congress approved Territorial Laws in May 1890, a full 13 months after the opening, yet the settlers got along without laws better than the people in the more "civilized" states. In the year without laws, Guthrie recorded no murders and order generally prevailed.

With the grant of territorial government in 1890, President Benjamin Harrison appointed George Steele of Indiana as first governor of Oklahoma Territory. Following the election of representatives, the first territorial legislature convened in Guthrie on August 27, 1890. The legislative assembly heard routine business. Then a blockbuster bill was introduced by members of the southern delegation. The legislature speedily approved Council Bill No. 7 which called for the permanent designation of Oklahoma City as the territorial capital.

Governor Steele quickly vetoed the bill, much to the chagrin of the Oklahoma City forces. Steele later resigned and returned to Indiana because of the bitterness caused by his veto.

The battle line was drawn, nevertheless, and though Guthrie would remain the capital for another 20 years, the move to make Oklahoma City the permanent capital would continue.

Foucart's office building, where he designed his unique buildings

As the territorial capital, Guthrie continued to be an important city. It was the hub of business and commerce in the territory. The city boasted six railroads, six banks and five daily newspapers during its territorial heyday. The first architect in the territory, Joseph Foucart, designed and constructed many distinctive buildings that remain in Guthrie today, including the Gray Brothers Building (1889) that was used by the Bank of Indian Territory, the Bonfils Building (1890) and the *Oklahoma Daily State Capital* Building (1902).

Foucart was educated in Belguim. His architecture reflects the influence of European and Russian design, with turrets, cupolas, bay windows and ornamental tinwork galore. Most of his buildings were constructed in Guthrie, but he also designed the first territorial college buildings and public buildings in other areas.

When the bid for statehood came in 1906, Guthrie was designated the site for the Constitutional Convention. Delegates were elected from the Oklahoma and Indian Territories and they convened in Foucart's Guthrie City Hall building to draft the nation's most lengthy constitution. The constitution was approved by vote of the people of the two territories resulting in the granting of statehood to Oklahoma November 16, 1907. Guthrie was to be the state capital until 1913, at which time the people would select a permanent capital by popular vote.

Greer's *Daily State Capital* Newspaper

Frank Greer, editor of the Republican *Oklahoma Daily State Capital,* was an arch rival of Oklahoma's first elected governor, Charles N. Haskell, a Democrat. The newspaper conducted a venomous attack on Haskell and his administration. As the attacks continued, Haskell became more attentive to the talk of those who wished to make Oklahoma City the state capital. In 1910, Haskell pushed through a bill calling for an early election to choose a permanent location for the seat of state government.

Greer's **Daily State Capital** *Newspaper*

On the ballot as choices were Guthrie, Shawnee and Oklahoma City. One June 10 the election was held. Haskell was in Tulsa that evening. The polls had barely closed when Haskell declared Oklahoma City the winner. Although Guthrie had been designated the state capital until 1913, Haskell wired his secretary, W.B. Anthony to go to Guthrie and remove the state seal and bring it to Oklahoma City. Anthony went to Guthrie in an automobile furnished by the Oklahoma City Chamber of Commerce and removed the state seal to Oklahoma City, thus establishing a new capital.

State seal removed from this building to Oklahoma City creating new State Capital

Guthrie later lost heated court battles in which both the State Supreme Court and the United States Supreme Court upheld the action of Haskell. The relocation of the state capital spelled economic doom for Guthrie. The city fell asleep.

As America approaches its Bicentennial year, a new Guthrie appears to be rising from slumber. Much like the legendary Phoenix, Guthrie is experiencing renewed life. Nearly 80 percent of the houses and commercial structures in Guthrie are the same as they were in the 1889-1910 period.

The entire city within its 1907 limits (7 blocks) has been placed in the National Register of Historic Places as the only totally intact territorial capital and state capital remaining in America.

The historic Carnegie Library, built in 1901, has become an Oklahoma history museum and is now being developed with an adjacent new building as the Oklahoma Territorial Museum by the

Carnagie Library

Oklahoma Historical Society. The library was the scene of the inauguration of Oklahoma Territory's last governor, Frank W. Frantz. It was also the place where Oklahoma's first elected state governor, Charles N. Haskell, took his oath of office. Statehood Day ceremonies here November 16, 1907, saw the symbolic wedding of Mr. Oklahoma Territory and Miss Indian Territory when the two territories became one state—Oklahoma.

Guthrie donated the building to the Oklahoma Historical Society by an overwhelming vote after the city built a new municipal library.

Other museum plans call for the establishment of the *Oklahoma Daily State Capital* Newspaper and Printing Museum in the building that housed Oklahoma's first daily newspaper. The building was designed by Joseph Foucart to replace the original structure which was destroyed by fire on Easter Sunday 1902.

The *Oklahoma Daily State Capital* was the leading newspaper in Oklahoma during territorial and early statehood days. Its fiery editor, Frank Greer, left Guthrie shortly after the state capital was relocated. The newspaper advertising and subscription lists were absorbed by the *Guthrie Daily Leader*, but the *Daily State Capital* printing and bookbinding business continued to operate in the building as the Cooperative Publishing Company until 1974. The 1902 furnishings and printing equipment are unchanged.

Through public subscriptions of $25,000, matched by the Oklahoma Bicentennial Commission, the building will be developed by the Oklahoma Historical Society, with help from the Oklahoma Press Association as a museum of newspaper publishing.

The Carnegie Library and *Oklahoma Daily State Capital* building are both listed on the National Register of Historic Places individually as well as within the Guthrie Historic District.

A Guthrie Preservation Trust has been proposed to establish the means of revitalizing Guthrie's downtown historic district while maintaining its historic streetscape. Application has been made to the U.S. Department of Housing and Urban Development for financial assistance to accomplish this bicentennial goal.

Administered by the Guthrie City Council, the trust would acquire a facade easement for each building in the historic district through donation by each building owner. In return for granting control of the building facade to the trust, each owner would be assured that the facade would be restored or preserved by the trust to its original appearance. The trust would also be charged with the responsibility of perpetual maintenance of the facade. The building owner would retain control of the ownership and business rights behind the facade.

Guthrie National Bank, 1890

Foucart's Gray Bros. Building, 1889

In addition to preservation and maintenance of the building facades in the district, the trust would be responsible for maintaining street scenes typical of the territorial period.

All parking meters in the district would be removed, portions of the original brick streets in the historic district would be exposed and maintained, and historically related businesses would be encouraged to occupy historic structures. Suggested businesses are a livery stable with horse-drawn tour vehicles, and restaurants in buildings that housed such early-day establishments as the Reaves Brothers Casino, Blue Bell Saloon, Yeller Dorg Saloon and Same Old Moses Saloon.

In January 1975, the first expansion of the Guthrie business community came in the form of a shopping center located on the outskirts of town. With a new highway bypass and another shopping center in the offing, the downtown historic district may be in economic danger unless the preservation project can be proven profitable and can make the historic district more desirable to merchants than a shopping center location.

The citizens of Guthrie, Oklahoma would like to prove that a plan melding history with present community life and future growth in a compatible, mutually profitable force can succeed.

We think we can do it.

JOSEPH FOUCART, FATHER OF GUTHRIE'S SKYLINE

Those visiting Guthrie for the first time are amazed at the different world they are plunged into after leaving the straight and boring stretches of I-35.

There before their very eyes are buildings that look as if they belong in a Russian nightmare and certainly, at first glance, do not appear to belong on the flat Oklahoma landscape. But there they are. They do not disappear in a wisp as if the beholder were caught in a dream world. They are permanent. After the initial shock wears away, the more the designs are examined, the more beautiful they become and finally, they belong.

Joseph Foucart

The buildings are as unusual as the history of Guthrie itself. Mysterious yes. They were the product of Jos. Foucart, a Frenchman who was educated in Belgium. A man of mystery himself, that adds even more excitement to the beauty and romance of the buildings that bear his trademark. Foucart was the first of his profession to locate in Oklahoma Territory having come to Guthrie, the territorial capital, in June 1889.

Foucart was born in Arlon, Belgium in 1848, the son of John Pierre and Katherine (Mater) Foucart. His lineage was from a prominent French family with ancestry traceable by records back to the year 1560. His grandfather, Domnick Foucart, was born in France and was an agriculturist. He served under Napoleon in the French army. Foucart's father was French as was his mother. His father removed to Belgium where Jos. was born. He was one of five children and the only one of the family to immigrate.

Foucart completed classical studies in the Royal Atheneum at Arlon before studying civil engineering and architecture at the school of Ghent from which he graduated in 1865. The next four years found Foucart as an assistant engineer for a Belgium railroad. From there he went to Longwy, France as a mining and civil engineer.

With the beginning of the Franco-Prussian war he entered the Tenth Regiment of Artillery, Fifth Battery of the French Army. He was taken prisoner at the Battle of Sedan but made good the escape from his captors after only five days and returned to Longwy. Foucart served as a non-commissioned officer until the surrender of that fortress in 1871. After the peace treaty was signed, he was granted an honorable discharge.

In 1872 Foucart became associated again with his profession and superintended the construction of the castle of Roussle of Viere, Belgium. The venture took a full two years to complete and cost a whopping $400,000 – a fortune in its day. In 1875, Foucart entered the service of M. Govaerts, private architect to the King of Belgium. Foucart superintended the erection of the King of Lacken's Winter Garden. After that project was finished, he superintended the construction of Brussell's Grand Central Hotel. Next came the Courthouse of Charteroi, Belgium at a cost of $328,000. The next year, 1879, he saw to the erection of the Pouhon at Apa. 1880 saw Foucart in Paris as chief draftsman for drawing, detailing and finishing of the new Paris City Hall, which cost $16,000,000. The remainder of his time in Europe saw Foucart in practice for himself as architect and supervisor of building. He immigrated to America in 1888.

Landing in the U.S., Foucart spent three months in Texas before opportunity beckoned in Kansas City. He remained in Kansas City until the opening of Oklahoma Territory. Seeing an opportunity in the new land, Foucart came to Guthrie, the territorial capital, where he established his business and immediately set out designing and superintending buildings in the newly opened frontier town. It was to be the most productive period of his life with the majority of this works still standing.

Foucart's unusually designed buildings still dominate the Guthrie skyline. In addition to the remarkable design was the manner in which they were constructed. Being an engineer as well as an architect, Foucart put together buildings that were practically indestructible. Some of Foucart's creations that have been demolished in later years were most difficult to bring down.

While Foucart's creations still prevail and are admired by thousands of people today, the man himself was clothed in mystery. His name rarely appears in any of the early day books and periodicals whose biographical sketches included superlatives on all the pillars of the community and territory. Perhaps it was because he was too frugal to purchase space in the early publications, save a small advertisement. Even so, Foucart's architectural drawings were the most sought-after in the territory. But none of these stories ever featured a story or photo of Jos. Foucart. A small advertisement appeared occasionally with a mere listing of "Jos. Foucart, Architect and Building Superintendent."

Just who was Joseph Foucart?

Little is known about Joseph Foucart's personal life. Some who knew him described the architect as having a heavy European accent in his speech. Others described him as very aloof and secretive, with a desire to work alone.

Mrs. James D. Burke, leader of the choir and pianist for Guthrie's St. Mary's Catholic Church for 15 years, described Foucart as having an excellent and "delightful" baritone voice as a choir member.

Foucart may have been aloof to some, but he was a member of several fraternal organizations in Guthrie and held office in many. He was a member of the International Order of Odd Fellows (IOOF), Knights of Pythias, Elks Lodge, where he served as Exalted Ruler and was elected a Life Member. Also Sons of Herman, the Guthrie Commercial Club, Guthrie Gun Club, where he was described as being an excellent marksman. He was said to be a staunch Republican politically. Records of purchases at Lillie's Drug Store show a penchant for fine cigars.

Foucart was married in France to Henriette Jacques who was born and died there. They had two children, Pierre Julian Foucart who was a pharmacist in Paris. Also a daughter, Marie Julia Foucart who was born in France, married Theodore Toye and immigrated to the United States. Foucart married again in France to Mary Jacquard and had no children.

Architects describe Foucart's style from Old World European and Russian influence with the use of cupolas, bay windows and turrets. His style is also said to include many Victorian Gothic and German Renaissance features.

Foucart later teamed up with another French architect by the name of Villeroy. The names of the pair of architects appeared on many of the drawings of buildings between the 1890-1895 period. Villeroy's name soon disappeared from the drawings and advertisements just as quickly as it had appeared in the first place. Villeroy vanished as mysteriously as he appeared.

Guthrie became a tent city overnight when the settlers first came to the new land. In only hours, frame buildings began to rise from the prairie. Many were replaced as quickly by permanent brick and frame structures. Foucart appeared on the scene two months after the Run. He had time to design and build about six native sandstone and brick buildings before the calendar turned to 1890.

His 1889 creations included the Gray Brothers Building that was the Bank of Indian Territory. The building at the corner of Division and Oklahoma still stands. It remains as one of Foucart's most unusual and beautiful buildings. Among other 1889 creations was the McKennon Opera Building that would be the site for the first territorial house and senate meetings and the home of Oklahoma's First daily newspaper, the *Oklahoma Daily State Capital.*

The E.T. Patton building at Division and Harrison was also an important early building designed by Foucart. This building housed retail businesses on the ground floor. On the second floor were offices for the territorial governor, territorial marshal and other territorial officials. The building has since been razed. The site is now a used car lot.

Other buildings coming from Foucart's pen were the International Building on the southeast corner of Second and Harrison. This building contained Foress B. Lillie's drug store, the territory's first licensed druggist. Upstairs was the apartment of the first Territorial Governor, George W. Steele. The building has since been razed and a vacant lot remains where the important building once stood.

International Building

Capitol National Bank

Foucart is also credited with the DeStegieur Building that housed the Guthrie National Bank that was built by German immigrant brothers. The building still stands in the 100 Block on East Oklahoma Avenue. Another important Foucart creation in 1889 was on Guthrie's most important corner during the first years. Foucart designed the Capitol National Bank, or Commercial Bank in 1889. The building was directly across the street from the Land Office, becoming one of the busiest corners in the territory in the early years.

Many sources credit the Commercial Bank as being the first brick building in the territory, but it wasn't. The First National Bank on the corner of First Street and Oklahoma was the first brick building having been started in May 1889. This building was not a Foucart design.

1890 saw many Foucart creations arise, many of which still stand in Guthrie. The Bonfils Building in the 100 Block of South Second Street is a Foucart creation. The building was built by Fred Bonfils, a Kansas City confidence man who came to Guthrie on the first train with a bag full of confidence schemes. His deceptive antics were soon discovered by the pioneers he had bilked, and he left town just ahead of the committee in charge of tar and feathers. But Bonfils did leave a reminder of his presence in the building that bears his name. "Bonfils" is etched in native sandstone atop the building. Bonfils later teamed with a man named Tammens and the pair established the *Denver Post* newspaper and became millionaires.

Foucart's Bonfils Building, 1889

Another 1890 creation of Foucart was the castle-like structure in the 100 Block West Harrison. The building was built by the E. T. Patton Company, according to an 1891 drawing. Foucart himself had an office in this building on the second floor. The "castle" on the third floor was reached by a steep flight of stairs where a small room contained the drawing table and instruments used by Foucart in designing the

Foucart Building

unusual buildings that would be built so extensively in Guthrie and Oklahoma Territory.

The DeFord Building in the 100 block South Second is another beautiful creation from the pen of Jos. Foucart. The 1890 structure is relatively unchanged from its original construction.

The year 1891 was an important year for Foucart when he designed and built three brick buildings next to his offices on Harrison. The buildings were built by Tontz and Hirshi and A. H. Waite. Tontz and Hirshi buildings housed hardware, implements, and a harness shop. The A. H. Waite building, later became the west building occupied by the *Guthrie Daily Leader* when the *Leader* was begun in 1892.

DeSteigier Block

The period from 1890 to 1902 saw some of Foucart's most beautiful and unusual, creations in both Guthrie and in the territory.

St. Joseph Academy

Foucart was in great demand during these years and many of his buildings still stand while others have been razed. Buildings constructed during this period included the huge St. Joseph's Catholic School for girls that sat atop the high hill in West Guthrie. The St. Joseph's Academy operated for many years, later adding a nursing school until the Benedictine Sisters moved their Order to Tulsa. The school building, affectionately known as "Big Red," sat vacant for many years. It became a part of the Guthrie Job Corps system, but was razed in the 1970's.

The Victor Block

The huge four-story Victor Block came in 1893 and is considered a Foucart classic today. Built by W. S. Smith, who was beset by ownership legal challenges for several years before winning his case, he named the building the "Victor" Block in celebration. The structure was full of horse-shoe-shaped windows and sculpted tin gingerbread across the building top, a Foucart trademark. Foucart moved his offices to this building where they remained until he left Guthrie.

Two known residential homes designed by Foucart during this period include the F. J. Heilman home at Cleveland and Ash Streets. Heilman was a harness maker with a shop on South Second Street in downtown Guthrie. This home is claimed to be the first brick home in Oklahoma Territory having been built in 1892. It has the classic Foucart trademarks of a turret, bay windows and horseshoe-shaped window on front.

Heilman House, first brick home built in Oklahoma, 1990

Miller Home   *2002 West Noble*

Another residential home designed by Foucart is the Miller home at 700 East Warner Street built in 1893. Both homes are still occupied today and are in magnificent upkeep condition. The brick residence at 2002 West Noble Street is believed to have been designed by Foucart, but cannot be documented as such. The house has all the trademarks and design of a Foucart building, with the typical Foucart archway and large circular window.

Other buildings during this period were the Royal Hotel and Brooks Opera House; several school buildings in Guthrie; Williams Hall Library building at Oklahoma A&M College, Stillwater; Northwestern Normal School at Alva, known as the "Castle on the Plains," and a host of smaller business buildings and homes in Guthrie and throughout the new country. Most of Foucart's work shows a striking resemblance to the fortress-like structures of his early life in Normandy and Brittany.

None resembled a fortress more than Oklahoma A&M College's (now Oklahoma State University) Williams Hall, which fell victim to the headache ball in June 1969. A new building for performing arts has since replaced the old structure.

While Williams Hall was under construction, Stillwater had little to offer in the way of rentable rooms, so Foucart pitched a tent to be near his work. From there he could supervise all construction. The closest railhead was at Orlando, 18 miles away. Brick and other materials not available locally were hauled from Orlando by wagon and mule teams. Stone for the window arches and the coping and belt courses were quarried east of Stillwater. Foucart is remembered as a very particular taskmaster with every stone being completely matched in color and size, otherwise it was culled and sent back.

By late 1899 the building's east portion was complete but the west portion and a lean-to on the north side remained. The lean-to was an afterthought of college president Angelo C. Scott, which offended the sensitivities of the architect, Foucart. To add insult to injury students now and then would lend unsolicited assistance to the project, much to the distress of president Scott and Foucart.

Those attending class in the completed portion of the building found the stored materials being used on the uncompleted west wing most inviting. The stacked brick was particularly appealing. One dark night a half-dozen students found their studies a little dull and decided to break the monotony by bricking up the main entrance to Williams Hall. The job was almost complete when a stern voice from the darkness demanded a cessation of activities. All promptly ran to escape the vengeance of Foucart, but much to their surprise, they were called into President Scott's office one by one the next day and told that their after class hours would be spent in tearing down the bricks they had so carefully placed in the doorway. The chore was one for the students to be remembered. Another challenge to the minds of the students was the thirteen peaked turrets of the building. More than one morning workmen arrived to find barrels fitted over the peaks of the turrets that added to the decoration of the unusual building.

Williams Hall

Two of Foucart's most famous and classic building designs came in 1902 when he designed and built the *Oklahoma Daily State Capital* newspaper building and Guthrie City Hall. The structures were classic in design with the turrets and towers so prevalent in Foucart's work.

Old Convention Hall And City Hall Bldg.

The City Hall building was important historically because it was the meeting place for the Constitutional Convention in 1906 when delegates from Oklahoma Territory and Indian Territory convened to draft Oklahoma's Constitution that was necessary before the state could be admitted to the Union. The building saw the most influential and important men of Oklahoma pass through the doors and draft the bill that would be the most important document in the formation of the new state. Many future governors were in attendance at the Convention—Charles Haskell, Lee Cruce, Alfalfa Bill Murray and a host of other leaders in early Oklahoma Territory and later the state.

In 1956 the Guthrie City Council bowed to the demands of the time and voted to raze the Foucart creation in the name of "progress," and construct a not-so-beautiful modernistic city hall to replace what some called the Foucart "monstrosity" and nothing more than a pigeon roost. The "headache ball" pounded away at the 1902 creation that was only being held together with powdery lime mortar and pioneer spit. The building was so

Razing "the Monstrosity"

strong that many times when the headache ball struck the building's old sandstone brick nothing happened. Bystanders cheered at the stamina and determination of the building with too many guts to go down without a fight.

Daily State Capital Building

Another Foucart classic that still stands today is now one of the most unique museums in America, the *Oklahoma Daily State Capital* newspaper museum building at the corner of Second and Harrison. The imposing 4-story, 50,000 square foot structure was designed and built in 1902 by Foucart especially for Frank Greer's newspaper and printing business. Greer's *Daily State Capital* had been destroyed by fire on Easter Sunday, 1902. The building was in the old McKennon Opera House. Greer constructed the new Foucart-designed building and the newspaper and printing plant was again operating by early fall, 1902.

Foucart's classic design fitted Greer's plans to a "T". Beautifully matched oak business cages were especially designed for the newspaper as well as the matched oak filing shelves for legal documents which Greer printed and sold all over the southwest. In addition, Greer produced an influential morning newspaper that was the leading newspaper of its day.

The building is still the same today as when it was built in 1902. The steam boiler room which furnished power to the equipment and heat to the building is still intact with its 1902 date cast into the massive cast iron furnace frame. The equipment is still the same as well as the type, type cases, printing presses, and other equipment relating to the operation as a newspaper. It is as if the printers and pressmen left their aprons and makeup rules on the printing stones and left for the night, but never returning.

Greer was so conscious of fire following the destruction of the paper in 1902 that Foucart designed fireproof vaults on each floor of the structure that still exist today. The building also features a huge six-inch water main on each floor with a fire hose that will reach any point of the building in case a fire should break out.

Foucart's activity after 1902 is obscure. It is not known whether Guthrie's building activity slowed to the extent to cause him to look for greener pastures elsewhere, or whether he just felt it was time to move on. It is not really known when he decided to move from Guthrie, but records indicate his presence in the oil boomtown of Sapulpa, Oklahoma in 1910 where he built a building identical to the Guthrie Victor building. He can later be traced to St. Louis, Missouri where he lived with a daughter, Marie Julie Foucart Toye and her family for a short period to time.

Some known Foucart ties with St. Joseph and Springfield, Missouri also exist. Family records also indicate Foucart had patents on a gasoline engine which the Wright Brothers of airplane fame either used or were interested in. He also was said to have an invention to convert used motor oil into gasoline.

Then he vanished.

Trying To Find Joseph Foucart

Don Odom, Guthrie historian and retired history teacher, had spent two decades attempting to trace Foucart's whereabouts after leaving Guthrie in 1909. All leads proved fruitless until Odom was contacted by Foucart's great granddaughter living in Texas. Among some papers was a note that Foucart had died in 1917.

Odom began searching archive files of the *Guthrie Daily Leader* and finally found a small item dated April 11, 1917, saying the former Guthrie architect had died in Muskogee. Finally a solid lead! "Joe Foucart, well-known architect, dead at Muskogee," the article read. "The local Lodge of BPOE Elks was notified of his death. His wife died some time ago. Foucart was past Exalted Ruler of the local lodge and was voted a life membership. He will be buried by the Muskogee lodge." Odom found Foucart's death certificate citing the cause of death as carcinoma of the liver and spleen.

Checking burial records at Muskogee's Green Hill Cemetery officials found Foucart was buried in the BPOE section in the cemetery. It was an unmarked grave. The Guthrie Elks Lodge had paid for the burial through Foucart's life membership in the Guthrie lodge.

Only one known building in the Muskogee area can be traced to Foucart's design. The Odd Fellows (IOOF) Lodge home for aged in Checotah is a Foucart creation and still exists on the old highway 69 Highway north of the city.

The search for the mysterious and elusive Joseph Foucart finally came to an end in 1999 with Odom's discovery. Joseph Foucart seemed to have disappeared from the face of the earth. It had been a 90-year search by family members and historians, but the elusive Foucart had finally been found. The family had a tombstone placed on his grave in the Green Hill cemetery in Muskogee.

Odd Fellows Lodge

Plans for a memorial to Foucart's presence and influence in Guthrie's architectural treasures are to be announced in the future. He leaves a grandson, Alex Toye, an architect in Kansas City, Mo. to follow in his footsteps.

GUTHRIE RESTORATION LEADERS

Representative/Restauranteur Donald W. Coffin; **Guthrie Daily Leader Publisher Bill Lehmann; First National Bank President Ralph McCalmont and bank vice-president Jay Hannah on November 6, 2014, Guthrie City Council meeting citing Lehmann for his service to the projects.**

Fred Olds

One of the most colorful figures during Guthrie's restoration period was Fred Olds, artist, sculptor, writer, poet, lecturer and teacher. As Artist in Residence for the Oklahoma Historical Society, Fred Olds' paintings and sculptures at Oklahoma's museums will be a lasting legacy with the giant cowboy boot footprint he left behind. Fred and his wife, Flo, developed the Oklahoma Territorial Museum from the architectural design to the finish. He also he created the heroic size sculpture of the symbolic wedding of Oklahoma Territory and Indian Territory at the entrance. His sculptures and paintings are on display at other state museums. Olds delighted in presenting to public school students the history of Oklahoma and the West. He taught painting and sculpting classes, teaching a blind student how to sculpt by feel.

RALPH MCCALMONT: PREACHER, BANKER, PRESERVATIONIST

Architect Joseph Foucart created Guthrie's picturesque Victorian skyline. Ralph McCalmont saved it for future generations to enjoy.

Ralph McCalmont

Before arriving in Guthrie in 1974, Ralph McCalmont found himself in an extremely difficult wrestling match. His opponent was himself—Ralph McCalmont. The winner would affect the rest of his life: Should he enter the ministry for which he had studied for four years, or should he enter the banking business that he had been a part of during his collegiate years? He decided to pursue the banking career but he never forgot his faith. It was a good choice for him and the community of Guthrie after he left Ft. Worth, Texas, to purchase the First National Bank there. Guthrie would not be the same as he found it.

McCalmont was born and raised in Texas but became interested in the preservation movement that had ignited a new interest in the historic city that had fallen asleep after losing the Oklahoma state capital to Oklahoma City in a 1911. Guthrie had been a long slumber, but there was an awakening. Many of the historic buildings of the former territorial and state capital period had been razed but many remained. The historic Carnegie Library was to be replaced with a modern new library, but the city had designated saving the old library as a museum, a giant step forward in changing the mindset of Guthrie's future potential as a tourist Mecca.

Preservationists on a national scale had become aware of Guthrie's historic importance and had placed the entire Guthrie city limits of 1911 on the National Register of Historic Places, the crown jewel of recognition. The Oklahoma Territorial Museum construction was underway under the guidance of the Oklahoma Historical Society and there was new excitement in the air.

As McCalmont toured Guthrie's historic sites with local historians and learned their history, the more he became interested in the movement and decided more could be done. He initiated the Logan County Historical Society, made acquaintance with state preservation leaders. He flew his own airplane to Washington D.C. touring national historic sites, became acquainted with the movers and shakers gaining their favor an interest in Guthrie's movement. He succeeded in getting the feature story in National Preservation magazine with many photos of Guthrie's important historic structures, most still standing. He even met and married the director of the Historic Houses of America near Williamsburg, Va. museum complex bringing her to Oklahoma.

Guthrie had many of its downtown historic structures covered with a false aluminum fronting that hid the Victorian era architecture. This was done in the 1950s in an effort to "modernize" the appearance of the city. To restore the appearance of the early days era the false fronting would need to come off the buildings. This was not an easy sell because of costs. McCalmont brought in Donald Coffin, a former state legislator, to spearhead securing federal grants to assist the building owners in joining the effort. Jay Hannah, a vice-president at the bank, also assisted in meeting with the business owners.

Overall plans included a federal pact with the city to replace all downtown concrete sidewalks with new bricks and to install Victorian era street lighting. The efforts of the three men were successful in coordinating the plans with the city of Guthrie, the federal government and the business owners. It was not easy and many obstacles were overcome to achieve the success of the project. Work was begun in 1978 and finished by 1980. The appearance of Guthrie's downtown had been restored to its original appearance of early statehood where very little had changed since 1911.

With McCalmont's leadership Guthrie was a busy place. Hannah spearheaded the restoration movement to restore business fronts to their original appearance; Coffin was active in the Guthrie Arts and Humanities Council in bringing world-class performers such as Itzack Parlman, Victor Borge and Isaac Stern to Guthrie's Scottish Rite Temple auditorium. Coffin also helped establish a permanent theatre base of actors to present stage plays at the restored Pollard Theater.

1970s facade

The *Guthrie Daily Leader* took down the old false building front and erected a new Victorian design front while completely remodeling the interior to Victorian period; the historic *Daily State Capital* newspaper was acquired and being developed as a printing and publishing museum by the Oklahoma Historical Society. With McCalmont's assistance, a Guthrie couple, Pete and Donna Cole, bought the five-story Victor Block building, creating a Victorian style shopping

1980 Restoration

mall on the interior and building the upscale Sand Plum restaurant on the top floor. Artist Fred Olds painted a giant 40x40 foot mural on the wall, depicting Guthrie at Statehood in 1907. Guthrie was receiving much attention both nationally and statewide.

As a result of its restoration program, the National Historic Preservation Trust honored Guthrie as the "Small City of America." The nationwide "Main Street America" program initiated by the Trust used Guthrie as a model for its program.

In 1977, McCalmont helped coordinate and bankroll the return of an Oklahoma outlaw, Elmer McCurdy, killed in 1911, for a proper burial in Guthrie's Boot Hill cemetery section. The event received worldwide publicity. Other celebrations and events now make Guthrie a destination. Guthrie resident Byron Berline, national champion fiddle player, established an annual International Bluegrass music festival where bluegrass music enthusiasts gather, camp, play and watch national and international professional performances.

Despite all this activity in Guthrie, McCalmont was becoming involved with state activities. He was elected to the Board of Directors for the Oklahoma Historical Society. He made his airplane available to the director of the Oklahoma Bicentennial Commission personally flying the director to events and speeches in Oklahoma during the 1976 bicentennial year. In Texas, he rescued and restored a cemetery located near Nacdoeges, Texas, where his ancestors were buried and published a two-volume set of genealogy family history books of ancestors dating back to the 15th century. Governor Brad Henry named McCalmont the interim director of Oklahoma Parks and Recreation where he served one year.

McCalmont sold his Guthrie banking interests to BankFirst in Oklahoma City where he serves as a member of the board of directors. McCalmont's wife, Susan, is director of Creative Oklahoma, a program devoted to education and creativity. He is a frequent visitor to Guthrie. The historic Victorian city will feel his presence for generations to come.

THE GUTHRIE RESTORATION PROGRAM

When I first came to Guthrie in 1966 as publisher of the *Guthrie Daily Leader*, I thought I had entered another world. I couldn't believe the architectural wonders that made Guthrie a jewel on the plains. It was unlike anything I had seen in any other Oklahoma town.

Guthrie in 1910 and today

Many of the downtown buildings were built between 1890 and 1900. They resembled old European fortresses and castles with onion domes, cupolas and sculpted tin works. Beautiful Victorian homes dominated the residential area of the city. I would learn later they were mostly designed by French architect, and Belgium-educated, **Joseph Foucart**, who came to Guthrie at the opening of Oklahoma Territory to settlement on April 22, 1889.

Guthrie was designated the capital of Oklahoma Territory following the great Land Run of 1889. Guthrie was also the capital of the state of Oklahoma following statehood in 1907. But the capital was moved from Guthrie to Oklahoma City in 1910. The removal of the state capital was devastating to Guthrie economically.

Also suffering was the town spirit. Like Rip Van Winkle, the city fell asleep and the slumber lasted for more than fifty years. Nothing much happened during this interval, which was perhaps a godsend for its future. Thanks to a preservation movement begun in the 1970s, Guthrie has awakened and is now thriving.

The 1950s saw an effort to modernize the business district. The 100 Block on West Oklahoma Street had many of the original buildings covered with aluminum false fronts manufactured in various colors and designs. The 1950s and 60s also saw many of the old historic structures meet the wrecking ball. Among these victims was Guthrie City Hall, where the Constitution for the State of Oklahoma was framed in 1906.

Others were the Brooks Hotel and Opera House where the leaders of the territory and state were housed. Other victims included the Mineral Wells Bath House and Ione Hotel.

With the importance of Guthrie in the early history of Oklahoma, I was astounded that nothing was in place to recognize this history. If ever a community needed and deserved a museum to commemorate its importance in state history, it was Guthrie.

The opportunity presented itself in 1968 when the Guthrie City Council placed the need for a new municipal library among bond issues to be presented to voters.

The existing library at that time was the Carnegie Library, built in 1901 after a donation of $25,000 by steel magnate Andrew Carnegie. Nothing had changed since. The furnishings were the same. It was like walking back to 1901. Some new books had been added over the years, but the old ones were still on the shelves as well.

A new library was needed, but the old library did not deserve the wrecking ball as many of the other buildings had experienced. The Carnegie Library was historically significant. It was the scene of the symbolic marriage between Indian Territory and Oklahoma Territory at statehood day ceremonies, November 16, 1907.

Statehood Days Ceremonies at Carnegie Library, Nov. 16, 1907.

Thousands had gathered to witness the ceremony and the inauguration of Charles N. Haskell, Oklahoma's first state governor. The Carnegie Library would make an ideal museum for Guthrie.

The Guthrie Daily Leader petitioned the city council editorially to preserve the old library as a museum, which it unofficially agreed to do upon approval of bonds to build a new facility.

Don Odom had long sought a place in which to showcase the history of Guthrie and Oklahoma Territory. He was instrumental in developing my interest in Guthrie history. He took me to the historic buildings explaining their history and importance.

The popular history teacher had an enthusiastic audience over the years, but I had a barrel of ink and a printing press to reach a wider audience than his classroom, so we began an editorial campaign to preserve the Carnegie as a museum.

A bond issue was introduced to provide funding for a new library. Also on the ballot were improvements to the fire station, paving the sod runway at the municipal airport and three other issues. Bonds were approved for the new library and fire equipment. Approval of the others would take renewed attempts later. But the new library bonds were approved overwhelmingly.

The city council then appointed a museum study committee to make recommendations to convert the Carnegie Library into a museum facility. Committee appointees were Bill Lehmann, chairman; Don Odom, Guthrie High School history teacher and Charles Gerlach, president of the Guthrie Chamber of Commerce.

Odom had a deep interest in Guthrie and Oklahoma history. Odom and his history students had been responsible for the placement of granite markers at historical points of interest in Guthrie. Gerlach was descended from early day Guthrie citizens and business owners. As a native Guthrian, he also had an interest in, and supported the need for, a museum.

Now what? Our plea for a museum had been supported overwhelmingly by the council and by the vote of Guthrie citizens to provide bonds to build a new, sorely needed, library.

Now the council had handed the ball back to us to determine the course of action to make the proposal a reality. It was time to put up or shut up!

The study committee looked at the premier museums in Oklahoma that consisted of Woolaroc, Philbrook, Gilcrease and The Cowboy Hall of Fame. All had been funded by trusts and collections of oil millionaires. The Cowboy Hall of Fame was established by funds provided by prominent businessmen and ranchers from all over the western United States. Guthrie had no one who could match that wealth. It was a very real dilemma.

I attended an Oklahoma Press Association meeting in the old Biltmore Hotel in Oklahoma City and had a lengthy conversation with George Shirk, mayor of Oklahoma City, about the Guthrie museum possibilities.

Shirk was one of the most respected historians in the state and had tried in vain to preserve some of the Oklahoma City landmarks from being destroyed during the 1960s Urban Renewal of Oklahoma City that resulted in the destruction of many Oklahoma City historic treasures. Guthrie still had most of its treasures intact.

Shirk suggested we get in contact with Elmer Fraker, executive director of the Oklahoma Historical Society, for his professional advice. Returning to Guthrie, I told committee members about

Shirk's suggestion and a meeting was scheduled with Fraker to come to Guthrie and tour the Carnegie library.

As a historian, Fraker was very familiar with Guthrie and its importance as the early capital of the territory and state. He loved Guthrie so much he had even brought his bride to Guthrie to take their wedding vows many years before.

After a tour of the historic library, Fraker immediately told the committee the Oklahoma Historical Society would love to have the facility as a part of its operation. The museum would offer the professional staff of the historical society to house, maintain and develop the Carnegie Library as the Oklahoma Territorial Museum.

One problem solved, but our work was only beginning! We needed approval of the city council and the historical society needed to obtain funds for operation from the Oklahoma Legislature.

Logan County had recently elected Donald Coffin as state Representative. Fraker and Coffin petitioned legislators to support the addition of the Carnegie Library to the OHS museum operations, which they voted to do.

As chairman of the Museum Study Committee, I presented the OHS proposal to the city council and the council accepted the proposal unanimously.

The Guthrie City Charter did not allow the city to dispose of any city property with a value of over $5,000 without a vote of the people. Not wanting more election expenses at the time, the city attorney, Merle Smith, drew up a 50-year lease that was accepted by Guthrie and the society and work was begun.

George Shirk was also state preservation officer. He put his staff to work on criteria to make Guthrie eligible for federal funding and recognition in certain areas of national historic preservation. Historian Kent Ruth, of Geary, Oklahoma, headed this department.

Ruth immediately began work to promote Guthrie and was successful in having the federal agency declare the entire city limits of Guthrie recognized on the National Register of Historic Places, the only city in America with such recognition.

Ruth was paraplegic and confined to a wheel chair from an early age. A sister cared for Kent, and gave up a personal life to do so. Ruth was author of "Window On The Past," a weekly column in the *Daily Oklahoman* newspaper. He devoted many articles to our museum efforts that added greatly to our overall publicity campaign.

Even before construction began on the new library building, my office at the newspaper began to look like a mini-museum. Folks started bringing in items they wanted to donate to the museum. I accepted the item and gave them a copy of the donor form provided by the historical society. I even traveled to Stillwater to bring in a plow used to cut sod for the early sod houses of the initial settlers. I went to Perry to receive a chair made from buffalo and steer horns that had been part of an early day saloon.

Brooks Opera House and Hotel Royal.

Don Odom paid me a visit when it was announced the city was going to demolish the Brooks Opera House and Royal Hotel.

"Let's go see what we can find in room 17," Don said. "That was Governor Haskell's office, and we might find something of interest even after all these years." The rooms were entirely vacant and we found little there, but Odom suggested we take off the door to Room 17. I acquired a screwdriver, and we took off the entire door that had received multiple coats of paint since 1907. Don took the door to his home and applied several coats of paint remover until he found

The Museum Study Committee: Front row: Bill Lehmann, chairman, with OHS officials Elmer Fraker and Martha Royse Blaine. Back row Charles Gerlach, Attorney Carl Morgan, Guthrie City Manager Ronald Anderson, and Don Odom.

the solid brass doorknob to the room still had the state seal of Oklahoma on it. Another treasure for the museum!

Interest in the museum continued to mount as the Carnegie was being prepared for a different function and the new library was under construction. A regular visitor to Kenneth Mitchell's Jelmsa Abstract Company was Orlando farmer and rancher Fred Pfieffer. Pfieffer had watched development of the museum and suggested to Mitchell he would like to help in the effort. Mitchell contacted me and I put Pfieffer in contact with Fraker. Fraker told Pfeiffer an immediate need was visitor parking and suggested buying two homes directly across the street that had no historical significance for parking.

A large two-story frame home on the east side of the library would also be ideal for expansion if it could be acquired. Pfeiffer's first contribution was $30,000 to purchase the homes. Pfeiffer later told me he would like to do more and suggested he would like to build an addition to the Carnegie in memory of his wife and brother, Ruth and Otto Pfeiffer. A meeting was set up with Fraker and city officials. The John Turnbull architectural firm of Oklahoma City drew up plans for the Pfeiffer Memorial Annex and were accepted. Pfeiffer then contributed an additional $350,000 to build the annex to the museum. This allowed needed expansion for displays as well as an elevator to connect the two buildings for convenient visitor and handicapped access.

Fred Pfeiffer

In 1975, I had a call from Myrtle Jackson, owner of the Cooperative Publishing Company, which had been the home of Oklahoma's first daily newspaper, *The Oklahoma Daily State Capital*. She suggested the *Guthrie Daily Leader* might entertain thoughts of buying the building and relocating its newspaper there. A tour of the 50,000 sq. ft. building with Mrs. Jackson left me with only one impression: What a mess! There's no way it would serve as a functional modern newspaper plant.

The Oklahoma State Capital newspaper had one of the most colorful histories in the state. Begun by Frank Greer, the newspaper issued its first edition from a tent on the very first day of the April 22, 1889 land run. By the time of statehood, it had become the largest printing and bookbinding operation west of the Mississippi River.

The *Daily State Capital* newspaper was the voice of the Republican Party and boasted the largest circulation in the state. Its chief rival was the *Guthrie Daily Leader*, the Democratic voice, led by Leslie Niblack, begun in 1892.

The election of Charles N. Haskell, a Democrat, as the state's first governor was devastating to Frank Greer. Greer's paper began a ceaseless tirade against Haskell, and the Democrats, from the time Haskell took office. And it didn't help Niblack had become Haskell's son-in-law and was a notary public in administering the oath of office to Haskell during inauguration statehood ceremonies. Many believed Greer's editorials were a major factor in causing Haskell to prematurely move the state capital from Guthrie to Oklahoma City in 1910. *The Daily State Capital* ceased publication in 1911. Greer moved to Tulsa, where he became engaged in the oil business. The business then became the Cooperative Publishing Company with a new owner, Ted Harmon.

Charles N. Haskell

Greer

Harmon continued the printing business and was the leading publisher of legal forms, official courthouse ledgers and bookbinding. The company also continued as publisher of the official textbooks for the Oklahoma state school system. It was also the location for regular Saturday night poker sessions among the town's business leaders until Harmon's death.

Myrtle Jackson had acquired the company, but the business had faltered by competition of more modern printing methods that went to other plants. The printing plant was much the same as it was when built in 1902.

The original State Capital building had been destroyed in an Easter morning fire in 1902. The new State Capital building was designed by Joseph Foucart, the architect who designed so many of Guthrie's now historic buildings.

To walk into the building was to walk into 1902. It was as if the printers had placed their aprons and makeup rules on the stones and gone home for the night. The plant contained four floors of ancient printing and book binding equipment. Its future could only be one thing—a museum. The asking price was $50,000—one dollar per square foot with all the equipment intact.

The new State Capitol Building

The Oklahoma Historical Society said they would accept the facility as a museum if it could be purchased. The Oklahoma Press Association also agreed to lend support. Contact was made with many interested parties and many tours were conducted.

Gladys Warren had been named to head Oklahoma's Bicentennial Commission to commemorate the 200th year of national independence. She agreed to provide $25,000 in matching funds to purchase the publishing plant as a bicentennial project if the community would raise the remainder.

The Donald W. Reynolds Foundation, owner of the *Guthrie Daily Leader,* immediately pledged $10,000 for the purchase of the plant. In short order the remaining $15,000 was raised from 143 donors that included Oklahoma newspaper publishers, Guthrie business leaders and individuals.

A major problem developed when Guthrie raised its portion before federal bicentennial funds became available. A solution was reached through the Guthrie Chamber of Commerce. With a $25,000 loan and the funds raised, the chamber become owner until the federal funds were secured. After receiving the funds, the facility was then turned to the Oklahoma Historical Society for operation as the largest museum in the country devoted to printing and publishing.

In the early 1970s, the Logan County Historical Society was formed and a preservation plan for Guthrie began in earnest. Spearheaded by the leadership of First National Bank President Ralph McCalmont, the plan was initiated. Assisted by Jay Hannah and Donald Coffin, the team was successful in garnering support from local businessmen and obtaining available federal grants to completely restore Guthrie's downtown to its original territorial appearance. The false facades on the buildings were removed and the building fronts restored to their original appearance. The early day appearance was accented by installation of period streetlights and brick sidewalks throughout the downtown area.

In 1975, *The Guthrie Daily Leader* began a remodeling project to coincide with the Guthrie preservation effort and the bicentennial observance. Since 1892, the newspaper offices were located in two buildings that adjoined but had entirely different architectural designs. A false façade had been placed on the front of these two buildings in the 1950s. A new design was created that would be architecturally representative of Guthrie history circa 1900.

The 1950s facade of **The Leader**   **The Leader's new "old" look, 1996**

Photos of early Guthrie were enlarged and placed throughout the building. Wainscoting, tin ceiling panels and stained glass from the old *Leader* building were incorporated in the design. The south wall of the business office featured actual front pages of the *Daily Leader* and the *Oklahoma State Capital* newspapers denoting the major historical news events that had transpired from statehood to the world wars. An open house was staged in July 1976.

Viewing the new facilities were officials from Guthrie, the Oklahoma Press Association, The Oklahoma Historical Society and citizens of Guthrie. A special guest, Frances Haskell, daughter of Oklahoma's first governor Charles N. Haskell, and former wife of Leslie Niblack, delighted the crowd.

Guthrie's preservation efforts have been realized by dedication of many local citizens combined with the assistance of historians and preservationists on a state and national level. The city now boasts five museums and is a mecca of tourism, which has given the city new life. With its many attractions and festivals,

Frances Haskell

Guthrie is now a destination. Guthrie's past *has* become its future.

"Holes of vice and dens of iniquity"

GUTHRIE SALOONS RAN WILD IN TERRITORY

The saloons and gambling halls of early Guthrie pale in comparison to the glitz, glamour and bright neon lights of today's casinos run by Oklahoma's Indian tribes. But the pioneers had their days at the saloon rails and gaming tables.

Dust had barely settled from the rush of settlers until saloons and games of chance were in full operation in tents hastily erected on Guthrie town lots claimed in the new Oklahoma Territory's Land Run April 22, 1889. One of the most popular was the Reaves Brothers Casino tent located on the northwest corner of Second and Harrison Streets.

Dick Reaves was a "Sooner," having hid in the sand plum thickets on the Cimarron River north of Guthrie. Waiting the opportunity to come from hiding, he quickly rushed a mile south and staked his first claim on a 160-acre quarter section of land on the northwest edge of Guthrie. Leaving his brother, John, to hold the claim, he rushed to the area marked for Guthrie town lots, staked a claim, pitched a tent and opened his casino on April 23.

The Reaves were among the first to open a saloon, but other saloon operators were equally as quick in setting up shop. Making the Run from Dodge City. Kansas was Bat Masterson and brothers Bill and Frank Tilghman, who also staked claims to town lots and had saloons in operation in short order. Masterson and Bill Tilghman were famed lawmen in Dodge City. Masterson soon sold his claim and returned to Dodge City. The Tilghman's operated their saloon until Bill was appointed a U.S. Marshal, leaving the operation to brother Frank.

Other saloons making their debut in Guthrie was the Same Old Moses Saloon, run by Moses Weinberger and the Blue Bell Saloon-brothel across the street from the Reaves Brothers where

Tom Mix was a bartender before leaving for Hollywood and starring in silent and later talkie Western movies. The Red Dog Saloon was another big attraction vying for the settler's money.

The Guthrie News was one of five daily newspapers to operate in Guthrie shortly after the Run, and the race was on to see which one could outnumber the other, a daily newspaper or a saloon. The editor of the   called the saloons "Holes of vice and dens of iniquity" and called for regulation, but there was no law before the territorial legislature met the following year to establish territorial law. So the saloons ran rampant.

By June 1889 the Reaves brothers had erected a two-story frame building with the saloon and gaming operation below and a hotel-brothel filling rooms in the upper portion. The saloon was painted a gleaming white, which was a beacon among the drab tents and colorless frame buildings that dotted the Guthrie landscape at that time. The saloon was a busy place operating 24 hours a day to satisfy the desire of settlers to wet their whistle and plunk down a few coins for possible riches.

A gleaming new white Reeves' Brothers Casino opened in June following the Land Run April 22, 1889.

The early saloons were notorious for trouble and the Reeves Brothers Casino was no exception. A sign was posted in the saloon warning that if trouble came it would be dealt with quickly.

The sign read: *"We the citizens of Guthrie are law-abiding people. But to any one coming here looking for trouble, we always keep it in stock with a written guarantee that we will give you a decent burial. We will wash your face, comb your hair, and polish your boots. Place your sombrero on your grave, and erect a momento as a warning to others saying.... 'He tried and failed.'"*

As business prospered, plans for expansion began to take place. Reaves had territorial architect Joseph Foucart draw up a proposal in 1891 for a three-story Reaves Brothers Business Block to replace the frame building. The building was never built, perhaps because the looming possibility of statehood would bring prohibition. Sure enough, when statehood came to Oklahoma on November 16, 1907, national prohibition came with it, closing all the saloons and casinos operating in the new state. When the Reaves Brothers closed the saloon at inauguration of the governor no one could find a key to lock the doors. The casino had operated for 18 years never having closed.

Always a crowd at the saloon

The Reaves sold their farm claim to J.E. Oliver, bought another farm east of Guthrie and retired to obscurity. Mamie Oliver, daughter of J.E. Oliver continued to live in the farmhouse built by Reaves until her death in the 1970s. She recalled the orchard started by Reaves was productive for many years and the Reaves family retuned often to gather fruit during the seasons.

Of all the early Guthrie bars the Blue Bell Saloon was the only survivor. They ceased selling whiskey after prohibition in 1907, but operated as a beer hall until prohibition was repealed in Oklahoma in the 1960s. Today it operates as a restaurant-bar, and alcoholic drinks are still available. The original Blue Bell Saloon building and furnishings, along with the original back bar, are still in place.

The old Reaves Brothers casino building was later demolished and never replaced. It is now a memorial park honoring veterans. The Reaves farm on the northeast corner of 12th and College Streets in north Guthrie is now used for a wheat and cattle operation.

The early saloons and casinos are but a memory, replaced by the glamorous casinos operated by the Oklahoma Indian Tribes that feature top Hollywood and Nashville entertainment, hotels and restaurants that would rival Las Vegas, and, of course, gambling.

BILL LEHMANN

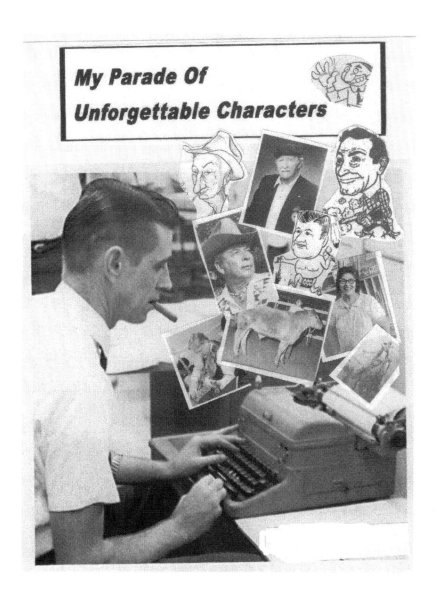

HILDA WALKED THE MILE IN DIFFERENT SHOES

I loved Hilda Harris. She was one of the most unique women I have ever known. She walked down the path of life with a beaded moccasin on one foot and a high heel slipper on the other. It was not an easy path but she maneuvered the difficult journey with dignity and grace, never tripping.

Hilda Harris was full-blood Otoe-Missouria Indian, with a touch of Sioux mixed in. She married a full-blood Irishman, Walter (Bud) Harris, which made her journey down that path of life much different than the ordinary American couple. The Irishman was very outgoing, with an infectious, hearty laugh and was always talking and smiling. This personality my have affected Hilda because she adopted some of the same characteristics which were different than your average Indian personality.

Hilda Harris

Many whites believe Indians to be reclusive and withdrawn. Indians, in their own culture, are outgoing and communicative. They tend to be highly competitive and challenging. In mixed cultures they may not say much, but it is not reclusiveness—just caution. Indians hear everything and give it careful analysis. When they get to know you, be prepared for a soft, subtle humor that will be far over your head if you haven't paid attention. If you are engaged in sports with an Indian, expect fierce competition. They do not like to lose! Hilda had all these traits, but was effervescent and communicative in both cultures.

But Hilda was Indian and proud of it. She would not say she was Native American, she would say I'm Otoe NDN-the "ia" in Indian not being pronounced. She would not be offended by the Washington Redskins mascot. I can see her taking a young Indian lad by the ear, privately (who might believe the term to be offensive), and telling him or her to worry about something more important. Hilda was a leader in the Indian community working to promote education. She also worked in the white culture as well in education and other community projects. She fitted in beautifully with both cultures.

Hilda, in front of her mother, Laura Moore; Madge Dent, Rhoda Dent Compron, and daughter Ca.

Hildegard Moore was born in 1904 on the Otoe-Missouria Indian Reservation at Red Rock, Oklahoma Territory. She was only one generation removed from life on the tribal homelands of southern Nebraska. There the tribe lived in tepees, feasted on buffalo, venison, small game and the pantry of nuts, fruits, and herbs provided by nature on the Plains. The tribe was removed to Oklahoma Territory by the U.S. government in 1870.

Hilda's father, Charles Moore, was an Otoe tribal official and was called to Washington D.C. periodically to confer with the Bureau of Indian Affairs regarding tribal affairs in education, housing, and land management. Moore's wife, Laura, would never accompany her husband on the trips to the nation's capital because she "did not trust the white man." She had good reason because the government broke every treaty ever negotiated with the American Indian.

Hilda was the last hereditary Princess of the tribe through ancestry of her mother, Laura Jones Moore. Laura's grandfather was Missouri Chief, who was chief of the tribe in their homeland. Hilda was inducted into the tribe as princess in special ceremonies on her 13th birthday. The ceremony was held in a teepee on the old Otoe camp rounds and conducted by her uncle, Henry Jones, a tribal leader. She received her early education in the Otoe School, Chilocco Indian School, and Red Rock High School.

Hilda got her first car, a Model T Ford Roadster, in her early teens and could be seen speeding around Red Rock, kicking up clouds of red dust. She was the envy of most girls (and boys) who could only dream of having their own automobile. She used the car to attend Chilocco Indian School in northern Kay County, returning home on weekends. Hilda caught the eye of an oilfield roughneck, Walter Harris, who was working on a rig in the area for Marland Oil Company. Her free spirit captivated him, and after a short courtship, they were married in 1923 when Hilda was 19.

Hilda's Roadster

The marriage of the fullblood Indian girl to the fullblood Irishman troubled Hilda's father. He cautioned that the difference in cultures might be difficult. "You will be living among the white people and will have to adapt to their ways. But never forget your Indian heritage, and be proud," he told her.

The couple lived in Ponca City where Hilda became the typical American housewife. They had two children, Walter, Jr. and

Virginia. Hilda became involved in raising the children, both outstanding athletes, attending their school activities and participating in the PTA. Ponca City was near Red Rock, and Hilda was able to visit family and allow the children to learn about their Indian heritage from family elders and tribal friends.

World War II changed the life of the Harris family, as it did most families in the country. Walter, Jr. had attended Oklahoma University on a football scholarship but had left to become a part of the New York Yankees. His professional career was interrupted by service in the 101st Airborne Division, where he was a paratrooper and engaged in combat in Europe. Virginia was attending Oklahoma State University. Walter, Sr. (Bud) was now working for Cities Service Oil Company and was assigned to duties in Louisiana. Hilda was away from her tribal family for an extended period this time but never forgot her roots.

Following the war, Bud retired, and the couple moved to Guthrie, where Bud assumed the position of regional director of the American Red Cross. Hilda began to make up for lost time among her tribal family and friends. She began service in many areas of tribal affairs, particularly in education. But she found time for play as well. Virginia was home during the summer and teaching golf at the Guthrie Country Club. Hilda would take Virginia to her lessons and watch as the students went through the sessions. Hilda decided she wanted to learn to play golf, and Virginia taught her the fundamentals. Hilda became a championship golfer in women's circles, winning many tournaments in Guthrie and Oklahoma City.

Education was important to Hilda. She had worked in educational programs with the Otoe children to impress the importance of education in their lives. In addition to all her other activities, she enrolled at Oklahoma University in 1960-62, obtaining a degree in business administration. Hilda became dedicated to affairs of the Otoe-Missouria tribe. Her service included five years as secretary for five Indian tribes: Otoe-Missouria, Osage, Pawnee, Tonkawa and Kaw. She was also

Secretary to the Indian Health Service Advisory Board. She was secretary to the Oklahoma Environmental Health Board. In 1979, Hilda received a plaque for outstanding and dedicated service to the Oklahoma City area Indian Health Service. Twice she was a delegate to the National Congress of Indian Women and held chairmanships in the Oklahoma Federation of Indian Women.

If service to her people weren't enough, Hilda was highly active in affairs of the white community. She stood side by side with Bud Harris in helping distribute Red Cross supplies in times of regional disasters. She was active in the American Legion and Legion Auxiliary and Eastern Star of the Masonic Order. She was a regular speaker to Girl Scouts relating tribal customs and dress, even teaching them how to make "Indian fry bread."

Hilda at age 95

Active in politics, Hilda was a favorite among state political leaders including several governors, U.S. Senators, Congressmen and Speaker of the House of Representatives Carl Albert. Hilda was chosen as a representative from Oklahoma to march in the inaugural parade for President Bill Clinton. She marched alone in her tribal dress to the cheers of onlookers. Hilda served many years as a "Pink Lady" volunteer with the Logan County Hospital Auxiliary and was named Volunteer of the Year in 1972.

Hilda and Bud were frequent visitors in my office at the *Guthrie Daily Leader.* They were delightful as individuals and as a couple. Both were always happy, which tended to make others happy. Through them I could keep up with activities of their son, Walt, Jr., with whom I had worked at the *Ponca City News* in the 1950s. Walt, Jr. had become an acclaimed Indian artist, his works being displayed in museums and other venues and private collections in the Southwest.

I have no treasury of wealth, but I do have some personal treasures that are more valuable to me than dollars. Among them are some Indian artifacts Hilda gave me during the span of our friendship. One is a beaded ceremonial gourd rattle used in an untold number of Otoe stomp dances. The handle is covered in deerskin, and there is a place where the hide is worn, exposing the gourd handle from the thumbs of the dancer(s).  Another treasure is a beaded bolo tie and a beaded hatband, or necklace, with a feather. But the greatest gift Hilda gave me was the joy of knowing her. Hildegard Moore Harris died in 1999 and is buried beside her fullblood Irishman in Guthrie's Summit View Cemetery. She was buried in her tribal finery. Hilda was the oldest Otoe-Missouria Indian at the time of her death at age 95.

A truly unique individual, she was a treasure and one of a kind. She dedicated her life to and walked the path of two very different cultures. Walking with a moccasin on one foot and a high heel slipper on the other may sound ungainly, but Hilda made it appear as smooth as an Olympic skater gliding on ice. She was elegant and proud with a spirit and dedication to be envied and acclaimed.

Hilda was proud to be NDN. And she loved the Washington Redskins!

And everybody *loved* Hilda.

WALT HARRIS, INDIAN ARTIST

Known as the "Happy Indian Artist," Walt Harris came about the title from his warm, smiling and laughing demeanor. When a smile wasn't on his lips it was in his friendly eyes. He was happy and happy to be doing what he loved—painting Native American subjects. He had a knick name for you the minute you met, and it stuck!

Walt Harris, Indian Artist

The jovial attitude came from his father, Bud Harris, who was a fullblood Irishman. Facial features were identical; the eyes, the smile, the hearty laughter. The only difference was the skin color: Walt had the darker skin of the Indian ancestry of his mother, Hildegard Moore Harris, a fullblood Otoe-Missouria Indian of the Bear Clan.

As a child, Harris soaked up the tales of the ancestral tribe at the feet of his grandfather, Charles Moore. The tales of tribal history from their native homeland of southern Nebraska Harris would later put on canvas and paper. His paintings would be displayed in museums, public buildings and private collections cross the United States and in Europe.

Before his claim to fame as an artist, Harris had served in the famed 101st Airborne Paratroopers seeing combat in WWII. A very gifted athlete, he had attended Oklahoma University on a football scholarship, but gave it up to join the New York Yankees minor league baseball system. Then came service in the military. He went back to professional baseball for a time, but an arm injury forced him to give up the profession. He then became a printer in his hometown at the *Ponca City (OK) News* where he was a printer and was also a cartoonist.

All was not work at the newspaper. Harris kept his interest in sports alive by recruiting his fellow members of the newspaper staff to play basketball and baseball. I had only worked at the *News* a short time until Harris organized a basketball team. I was a tall, skinny six feet in height and had played basketball in high school, so I was one of Harris' recruits. He told me one day that we had a game that same night.

Ponca City News *Baseball team: Top, l to r: Tom Keith, Pat Sclessinger, Walt Harris, Joe Monday, Aaron Linebarger and C.W. Schwab. Front row, l to r: Bill Lehmann, Richard Oney, Bill Parsons and Kenneth Linebarger. Ca. 1955.*

"But I don't have any shoes," I told him.

"No excuse," he said, "I have shoes for you." My feet were as slender as the rest of me and the shoes he provided were far too large, but I went ahead and played. During the game I jumped up to get a rebound. I turned to pivot and head down court. My feet pivoted, but the shoes didn't. I felt a pain but went ahead and played, thinking I had sprained my foot. As I got out of bed the next morning and stood on my feet, a pain shot from my foot to the top of my head! After x-rays, the doctor said I had broken two bones in my foot. I wore a cast on my leg from the knee down for three or four weeks.

Then came baseball season. Harris got a team together to play baseball—not softball, but hard baseball. A superb athlete that had played professionally, Walt was the star, captain, and manager of the team, playing any position. He pitched, caught, but most times played shortstop. I played first base. Our opponents in baseball and basketball were usually Indian teams from White Eagle, Red Rock, and towns of the area with large Indian populations. We had some very spirited games, sometimes so spirited I became concerned for our safety when outside Ponca City, especially when our team was ahead. Indians are extremely competitive and dislike losing.

Harris and I had a good friendship that extended beyond the sports activities. We hunted and fished together. We both had an interest in art and attended a men's painting class taught by a tiny German-Frenchman, Jacques Hans Gallrein, who was always accompanied by his very large wife, who managed his affairs. Gallrein was the typical iconic figure of a Frenchman; short, very thin and weighing scantly more than 110 pounds. He had a thin pencil-line mustache and wore the traditional artist smock and French tam that covered his thinning hair. He walked around viewing the works of his students slightly hump shouldered with arms behind his back, smoking a cigarette placed in a cigarette holder. Gallrein was an excellent landscape painter.

"Tecumseh" by Walt Harris

Walt Harris attended Gallrein's classes to learn techniques, but his interests were not in the landscape teachings of Gallrein. He experimented with colors, oils, and watercolors. It was obvious his painting interests were in the Native American subjects and two-dimensional techniques. A talented sketcher with excellent anatomical skills, Harris viewed other works and actually developed his own signature style by sheer determination, focus, and discipline. And he remembered the tales of his tribal history related by his grandfather when he was a child.

Walt Harris became an acclaimed Indian artist with his works on display at the Kennedy Arts and Humanities Center in Washington, D.C. He also painted "And Suddenly There Were No More," for vice presidential candidate Walter Mondale. His paintings are also displayed at the Cowboy Hall of Fame, Gilcrease Museum, and the Marland Mansion in Oklahoma. Harris described his signature style as "a three dimensional effect to traditional Indian art with a touch of realism."

"We Were Many, Now There Are None"

Harris' work caught the eye of the leadership in Scioto Historical Society of Ohio. A group approached Harris to paint a picture of legendary Shawnee Indian Chief leader Tecumseh for the cover of their annual Tecumseh Pageant program brochure. They furnished an old tintype photo image of Tecumseh's grandson as a model. They observed Harris himself bore a strong resemblance of the tintype image and suggested he use some of his own features in the painting. Harris painted the picture in his Ponca City studio and flew to Chillicothe, Ohio, to meet with the group, where it was overwhelmingly accepted. Harris was flown to the annual pageant several times to participate in the convention honoring the Indian leader. His paintings were featured five consecutive years by the Scioto Society annual program cover.

Harris and his wife, Gloria, were preparing for a showing of the artist's works in Colorado Springs, Colorado. As they began the journey from Ponca City, Harris told Gloria he was not feeling well and needed to see a doctor. Leaving duties to an assistant who had already arrived in Colorado with paintings and prints, the Harrises sought their family physician. X-rays and diagnosis indicated lung cancer. Harris had been a heavy smoker. He was hospitalized in a Tulsa hospital, but the disease was too far advanced for treatment.

An old Indian tradition is to have a vision of a family elder who had passed to visit and guide you to the "Great Beyond" when it is your time to die. Harris' mother, Hilda, and sister, Virginia, were visiting with Harris in the hospital. He told them his time was near as he had a vision of his grandmother, Laura, at the foot of his bed motioning him to follow her. Walt Harris joined his ancestors the next day at age 70.

FRED OLDS, ARTIST AND SCULPTOR

Walking into Guthrie's Oklahoma Territorial Museum one morning I saw Fred Olds working on a mural painting that was to go to the Chisholm Trail Museum at Waurika, Oklahoma.

The 4 x 16 foot mural depicted a cattle drive as it meandered over the broad landscape of what would become the state of Oklahoma in later years. Clouds of dust and a seemingly endless string of Longhorn cattle originating in Texas and bound for the railheads in Kansas stretched across the vast panorama. The herd was being pushed over the rough terrain by ten or twelve drovers, who were guiding the cattle along the proven path.

As is the custom of many artists, Fred first roughly blocked in the faces of the cowboys, showing the desired lighting with finishing details to come later.

There was only one problem—all the cowboys looked like Fred Olds.

"Fred," I remarked, "Einstein says it is impossible for one man to be in ten places at the same time."

"Oh, dammit," he said, which was one of the worse words I ever heard Fred utter, "sit down here and I'll put you in there." So I sat for a few minutes while Fred painted my likeness on a horse, swinging a lariat to keep an errant steer in place. My likeness showed a few days' growth of beard along with a big cowboy hat and big bandana neckerchief to ward off the clouds of choking dust should it become necessary.

My grandfather, Max Lehmann, had been a Texas cowboy, raised in Cuero, where many of the herds were assembled to begin the long trek over the Chisholm Trail from South Texas to Kansas. Max was the son of a German immigrant, Carl Ludwig Gustav Lehmann, who had come to Texas in 1854. Max himself had been born in Germany but came to Texas as an infant with Gustav and an older brother Paul. Max served an apprenticeship as a butcher in his youth, and later became a ranch hand for the Halliburton Ranch out of Gonzales. Max had made the trip with the Halliburton crew before meeting my grandmother on a cattle drive through Waco, and deciding married life would be better than life on the trail. Fred said it was only fitting that the likeness of a descendant of a Chisholm Trail drover be included in the mural.

The mural was finished and shipped to Waurika in March, 1975. It was unveiled in ceremonies opening the Chisholm Trail Museum operated by the Oklahoma Historical Society. Several thousand visitors attended the event, which included a rattlesnake hunt.

Frederick Albert Olds was one of a kind. A prolific painter of the Old West and the characters associated with the era, Fred had an undying love for the cowboy, Indian, and the horse. He knew the anatomy of the horse and always had one or more horses in his stable. But he was also a sculptor, teacher, author, poet and, above all, just an all-around good man. He loved children and delighted in bringing stories of the Old West to schools, where he lectured with tales and sketches to his enthusiastic audiences.

Fred stood out in a crowd with his oversized cowboy hats with rattlesnake hatbands, Indian belt buckles, bolos, and Levi's tucked into his knee-high custom-made cowboy boots. His boot design included a rocking horse emblem embedded in the leather tops. The signature adorning his paintings and sketches included the rocking horse inside an Indian war shield, and Indian style horse tracks.

I first met Fred in the early 1970s when he was appointed director of the new Oklahoma Territorial Museum in Guthrie. Fred was also Artist In Residence for the Oklahoma Historical Society, doing paintings and exhibits for some of the other museums in the state. His wife, Flo, was director of exhibits at the museum and they worked together as a team to bring life and times in Territorial Oklahoma to the new facility. As a newspaperman, I had a keen interest in Oklahoma history and the developing museum. Fred and I hit on an immediate friendship.

Oklahoma Statehood came November 16, 1907. Guthrie had been territorial capital since the opening of Oklahoma Territory to settlement in 1889. It became the Oklahoma State Capital when Oklahoma Territory and Indian Territory were joined in ceremonies conducted on the steps of Guthrie's Carnegie Library. A symbolic wedding between Mr. Oklahoma Territory and Miss Indian Territory was solemnized and the two territories became one state.

A heroic-sized sculpture depicting this event was one of the first projects Fred began.

Fred first started the project with a 17-inch sculpture of modeling clay. The figures of a cowboy holding his hat behind his back while holding hands with his Indian maiden bride were depicted as they pronounced their wedding vows. The heroic-sized bronze now graces the entrance to the museum facility in Guthrie.

Fred Olds and "The Wedding"

As a fund raising project for museum needs, 50 of the smaller size wedding sculptures were to be cast and sold for $1,000 each. Fred had made arrangements with the Turkey Track Foundry at Nelagoney, Oklahoma to do the casting. I volunteered to drive Fred and the sculpture to the foundry located in the pristine, tall grass prairie of northern Oklahoma. I also wanted him to meet Jim Hamilton, another sculptor friend of mine whose ranch and studio were located at Foraker in the Osage Hill country.

We left the clay sculpture of the wedding in my pickup truck while we went inside to visit with Hamilton. Jim Hamilton had been a cowboy and rancher all his life. His wife, Dorothy, had a ladies' wear shop in Pawhuska and had an interest in the arts. When she took Jim to an art show once, he looked at some sculptures and decided, "Hell, I can do that."

Without any prior training, he accumulated the necessary tools and began to sculpt. He had looked at the backside of cows from a horse all his life, and in just a short time he became an acclaimed Western sculptor.

In Jim's corral were several Brahma cows. He also had a Brahma bull that was very gentle. Most people view Brahma bulls as the mean, angry variety associated with bull riding at rodeo events. But Jim's bull would sidle up to you and place his head on your stomach and want you to scratch his ears. Fred and I both had our pictures made on the back of Jim's bull. We were going to tell everybody that we "rode that bull to the ground."

After visiting with Jim we went back to the truck to continue on to the foundry. Forgetting to lower the windows while we were gone, we were greeted by a crumpled mass of clay lying in a molten heap. Fred took the piece back inside and placed it in the freezer, and in a few minutes the clay sprung back, stiff enough to reconstruct. We then hurried to the foundry with the truck's air conditioner going full blast.

Fred smoked "at" a pipe. He preferred the simple corncob variety but spent more time lighting and relighting than actually smoking it. He'd light the pipe, take a few draws or two, and lay it down to start painting again. In a minute or two it would be out, so he would relight the tobacco with a box of matches he kept at the ready. I gave him a nice lighter one time, but Fred gave it to a friend and went back to his box of matches.

Thinking Fred needed a little vacation with the boys, I took him with me on my annual Kansas pheasant hunt one year. The Brady Hood family of Kingsdown, Kansas, played host to some 30 or so friends who congregated at their ranch for the opening of the pheasant season in mid-November. I had been a grateful guest for many years and enjoyed the camaraderie of the participants who came in from several states to participate and renew acquaintances. Fred was a hit with them all.

We had hunted about a half-day on opening Saturday when it began to rain. The hunt suspended, we retired to the ranch house to escape a steady downpour. Fred began telling some of his stories to the Hood children, who were completely mesmerized with his personality and drawings. He spent the afternoon doing what he did best—relating to children. The adults were equally entertained, and the afternoon went very quickly.

That night the men struck up a friendly poker game to pass the time, and a few drinks were poured from a bottle of Brady's prime scotch whiskey. Fred and I participated, but we all went to bed early in hopes the rain would end overnight and we would be allowed a good hunting day for Sunday. The rain showed no signs of ending the next day, so Fred and I headed back to Guthrie, disappointed, but both deciding it was an enjoyable trip.

Upon our return, Fred resumed work on a drawing commemorating the centennial of the Chisholm Trail for the Oklahoma Historical Society. A hundred or so numbered prints were made available, and Fred gave me an autographed copy. Fred's dry sense of humor was evident by the inscription on the drawing: "To my old drinking buddy, Bill Lehmann," the inscription said. This was in obvious reference to the Kansas poker game. Fred had only one drink, and he didn't even finish that. Some "drinker," Fred!

Fred Olds' paintings and sculptures can be found in many galleries and museums in Oklahoma. His paintings also grace the walls in homes of many people who came in contact with Fred. Many were gifts. I watched many times when Fred presented one of his paintings to some of the dignitaries that visited the Guthrie museum. Flo would roll her eyes and say in a hushed tone, "Why sell them when you can give them away!"

That typifies Fred Olds, perhaps the kindest and most gentle man I ever knew.

PAUL PARKER'S MAVERICK CHAMPION STEER

Paul Parker yearned to be a farmer and stock raiser. But there was a problem. He was a city boy with no place to keep farm animals. Paul's father owned a hardware store in Guthrie but had been a victim of the Walmart expansion to Guthrie that had affected most small locally-owned businesses when the giant retailer moved into a community.

Laurence Parker had closed the store and was now circulation manager at the *Guthrie Daily Leader*. He was responsible for distribution of the newspaper to customers and directed about 25 schoolboy carriers including his two sons, Paul and Greg. Through good management the boys had saved profits from their paper routes and had built a sizable nest egg for future activities, as they grew older.

Paul was active in the Future Farmers of America (FFA) program at Guthrie High School. His savings from the newspaper helped fund his first livestock projects, but he had no place to keep them. Then two stalwart supporters of the FFA programs came forth with the opportunity Paul desired. Vance Kellogg, a farmer and stock raiser west of Guthrie would provide barn space for the animals.

Paul and Kellogg's son, Dennis, were friends and became close friends in FFA. Paul would go to the farm with Dennis and help with the feeding and care of the livestock. This friendship helped spark his interest in farm and ranching operations. Dennis was killed in a motorbike accident during wheat harvest. Paul volunteered to help with the farm duties during their period of grief. The Kelloggs (Vance and Carletta) took Paul under their wings, nurturing his passion in livestock even further.

Former Guthrie FFA agriculture teacher George Chiga offered to provide a steer for Paul to groom and show. There was only one obstacle: the steer was a maverick that neither George nor his ranch hands had been able to control! The animal was always busting out of his stall, turning over feed troughs, kicking other animals and just generally making a nuisance of himself.

Chiga was a successful cattle breeder specializing in the Red Angus breed. Always an innovator, he was experimenting by cross breeding the white-colored Charolaise breed with the Red Angus in his herd. The steer Chiga sold Paul was ¾ Charolaise and ¼ Angus. It had characteristics of both breeds; with the lighter color predominate with the Charolaise variety.

Originally bred to be a commercial herdsire, this magnificent bull prospect was so rank even experienced ranch hands were unable to handle it. Chiga agreed to sell this maverick to Paul at market price on the condition that he would be "steered." Rank dispositions like the one this bull had was not what George built his reputation on. Chiga would sell Paul the animal at market price, considerably less than the value of the blooded animal. This was a daunting task for a young schoolboy, but Paul's dream had come true and he quickly accepted the offer.

Paul bought the steer, and they delivered it to the Kellogg farm and its new stall. Paul had also added some sheep to show and started building a flock. The sheep were no problem, but as expected, the steer was a hell-raiser—into everything, overturning feed troughs and kicking and headbutting anyone or thing that came into range, including Kellogg's animals. Every time he broke out of his pen, it was all Paul, Kellogg, and others sharing the barn could do to round him up and get him back in and repair the damages. Paul was in a dilemma: his dream had been realized but he needed to find a solution to control that rank steer. Paul named him "Big Bad John" because of the steer's maverick ways.

Paul thought of the old adage "Music calms the savage beast." He decided to give it a try. Every day after school, Paul would play soft, classical music on a radio in the steer's stall. As he brushed and groomed the steer, he would talk to him. Paul selected classical music of Brahms and Beethoven. The soothing strains of piano and violins—no rock and roll or rowdy country barroom music, thank you—Paul was developing a steer with class in Big Bad John! He even read the poetry of Walt Whitman to Big John and left the radio on the classical music station at night to keep the steer company.

Showtime came at the spring show and sale of the livestock the students had spent the fall and winter grooming. First was the Guthrie Fair competition. Paul's stomach churned with butterflies and nervousness as the judges examined the many entries. They were meticulous in their assessment. Paul stood with Big John with crossed legs and fingers, hoping his steer would be on its best behavior. It won first place in the Guthrie show!

Paul and his maverick steer, Big Bad John

Next up was the Logan Country show, where the animals from all the FFA students in the county were entered for the eyes of the judges. Big Bad John decided all this "good boy stuff" was for the birds! He went on anther rampage, busting out of his stall and running amuck. When he was finally captured and under control, miles from the fairground he escaped from, Paul discovered several lacerations on the steer, probably from an encounter with barbed-wire fencing while he was on the loose. Big John lost over 80 pounds in that escape, but after some patching and grooming, Paul and Big John once again stood before the judges.

The judges carefully eyed the steers lined up for review. A grand champion would be named from this group. Paul sang quietly in the ear of the steer and talked to the animal while the judges poured over him from every angle. Paul's calming influence resulted in its best behavior. The steer won reserve grand champion honors. Paul's efforts had been richly rewarded. The judges told Paul his maverick steer would probably have won grand champion honors had it been a little "fatter" and if his hair color was darker. It was a lighter color of the hair from the cross breeding of the Charolaise and Angus breeds. The judges were *picky, picky, picky!*

The auction that followed the show brought a tidy sum for Paul's maverick steer. Paul used it for tuition at Oklahoma State University, where he pursued his degree in Agriculture Economics and Education. The experience he gained from raising Big John and from the Kelloggs helped prepare him for future leadership roles in agriculture—State FFA Vice President, Vice President of OSU Agriculture Student Body, and Oklahoma Senate Legislative Intern. Paul is now on the board of directors for the National Cattlemen's Beef Association and is senior marketing manager, Beef Cattle, for Zoetis, Inc. (formerly Pfizer, Inc.) and lives in Morristown, New Jersey. Zoetis Inc. is the world's largest Animal Health Pharmaceutical Company.

The Parker siblings chose different paths in life after graduating Guthrie High School. Paul's sister, Gloria, sought an opera and performing arts career and went to New York City, where she has been in numerous opera and musicals on and off-Broadway and around the world. She still performs in some productions but now is a successful talent and booking executive in NYC.

Paul's brother, Gregory, graduated from the United States Naval Academy in 1979. Working his way through the ranks, Gregory served aboard multiple attack and Trident class submarines before earning the rank of Captain of the *USS West Virginia* (a Trident Class nuclear submarine) patrolling the under seas of the world, protecting the interests of the United States. Greg also served as the Deputy Commandant of the Naval Academy for two years. He has recently retired and lives in Fernandina Beach, Florida. I love success stories, don't you?

DUFFY MARTIN'S FART BOX

Once you meet Duffy Martin you will never forget him.

A big man standing about six foot five inches tall, Duffy's big hand will swallow yours when he shakes hands with you. His smile and personality are as big as he is. Very friendly and outgoing, he will not be forgotten after the parting, and you will hope to meet him again real soon.

Another reason you won't forget Duffy is he farts a lot.

But Duffy's farts don't stink.

You see, Duffy many years ago invented an apparatus that fits in your hand and when squeezed sounds like you are emitting a fart. When standing with your hands together at about crotch level it is very realistic. Duffy can do this while talking to you and without cracking a smile. After many years of practice, Duffy is a master at using his gadget. He can squeeze off a tiny high-pitched fart or a big, fat bubbly one that sounds like he just messed his pants. He puts on a good hard-of-hearing act that gives the appearance he is completely unaware that he is breaking wind.

Duffy Martin

Oh, and has Duffy ever had fun with his toy. Getting on an elevator in Oklahoma City with an obvious farm couple, Duffy squeezed off a big fart when the door closed and the elevator began moving up. The wife of the couple slapped him on the shoulder and said, "Damn you, Lem, you're not on the farm now. Quit doing that in public!" The husband's protests went in vain.

In Amarillo, Texas, Duffy was in a big department store with his wife, Juanita. He wandered away while she shopped and began following a couple of lady shoppers. He squeezed off a few while acting as if he were shopping as well. One of the ladies went to a clerk and asked for store security, leaving Duffy with a lot of explaining to do. Fortunately Juanita got him out of that encounter. Some look down their noses in disgust, but most just laugh. Duffy says his favorite place to pull off a stunt is in a crowded elevator.

But Duffy is not all foolishness. He is a very serious businessman that came up the hard way and developed a golfing empire near Guthrie, Oklahoma. He has built four multi-million dollar championship golf courses that are very popular and challenging. People come from Oklahoma City to play his courses. He also built an RV Park between courses that draws mostly retired golfers from many states to come and park their rigs where they might stay several days and play golf.

Duffy Martin

Duffy Martin was a taxicab driver in Oklahoma City in his early years. He saved his money, did a little gambling and built a small 9-hole golf course in south Oklahoma City. He did most of the building himself using the construction equipment associated with the development. It was a popular course and became a very valuable piece of real estate when the government built Interstate I-35, taking some parts of Duffy's golf course. Things went well for Duffy, and he built another 18-hole golf course at Norman that he later sold and bought several thousand acres of land west of Guthrie.

Duffy was the architectural designer and builder of his first course he called Cedar Valley, an 18-hole course he later expanded to 36 holes with challenging trees and lakes. Duffy could be seen on his own tractor doing work on the course and even using a shovel from time to time. Duffy Martin was not lazy. As a child of the Depression, he knew what hard work was and what had to be done to survive.

Duffy later designed and built a 36-hole complex at the west city limits of Guthrie. This Cimarron National golf course has beautiful trees, lakes, rolling hills, and all the challenges of a championship course. The RV Park, holding 50 or so rolling homes on wheels, is full most all the time except in the dead of winter.

Movie actor and comedian Leslie Neilsen was parade marshal at Guthrie's '89er Celebration one year and met Duffy. It changed Neilsen's life. He became good friends with Duffy and was captivated by Duffy's fart box. After instructions and practice, he became nearly as adept as Duffy. Before his death, Neilen would make appearances on national network television shows where he would practice his expertise at farting while being interviewed live and on camera by a talk show host. Not cracking a smile or cognizant of his actions, talk show hosts and other guests would try to ignore Neilsen's sound effects. They would finally realize what was going on and burst into laughter.

Leslie Nielsen

Duffy's son, Jeff, says his dad began building the fart machines using two mustard jar lids, putting a spring between them, and covering with bicycle rubber inner tubes with a small hole. When compressed in the palm of the hand, it would make a farting sound.

Duffy made them for years by hand but now has them manufactured professionally. The Han-D-Gas gadgets are available at the clubhouse on his golf courses.

Duffy died in 2015 at age 99. He was the national PGA champion of the 90 and over golfers. He underwent a knee replacement when he was 94 years of age so he could still play golf and dance…and make people laugh with his Han-D-Gas fart machine. Google Duffy Martin for a YouTube feature that will have you laughing.

WILLIS WARREN, ANSWERING GOD'S CALL TO AFRICA

Willis Warren was a man of God. Had been since he was just a kid growing up in Lampasas, Texas and later Chouteau, Oklahoma, where he worked as a section hand for the MK&T Railroad that ran through Chouteau. It was hard work and he decided to pursue a career in the ministry. His faith soon took him to Greenville, South Carolina, in 1922. He arrived with $20 in cash and his entire earthly possessions packed in a small trunk. There he entered Holmes Bible Institute and Missionary School, established by the Pentecostal Holiness Church. Willis met fellow student Della West, a lovely young lady who was gifted at playing piano and singing gospel songs. They married soon after graduation.

Willis Warren

Willis and Della were sent to South Africa as missionaries in 1929. The objective was to bring the Gospel to the native tribes of that country. After all, the black tribal members should be exposed to the words of the Bible and know that Jesus was their Savior as well as the white folks who were to teach about God's love to all his children, black or white.

The missionary couple was trapped in South Africa when the Japanese attacked Pearl Harbor in 1941 and World War II began. Civilian travel was banned for the remainder of the war. The couple went about their business bringing the message to the natives. Willis traveled to remote regions on a bicycle. Sometimes a church-owned 1934 Ford would take them to the hinterlands, but gasoline was rationed In South Africa as well as the U.S. during the war. The gospel was taken to tribal members in their native dress where Della played, sang and taught them "Jesus loves me this I know" followed by a sermon where Willis urged them to revoke their tribal ways, become Christians, and know the love of God.

While in Africa, three children were born to Willis and Della, daughters Margaret and Bonnie were followed soon by a son, James. The five of them continued their missionary work, Willis preaching, Della singing while their white children played with the children of the tribal members. The British initially settled the region of South Africa assigned to the Warrens to spread the Gospel. Consequently the general population spoke English with a British accent. The Warren children adopted the dialect quite naturally since it was the language of the country. They still have remnants of the British accent today.

Finally WWII ended, and the missionaries could return home and see family they had not seen, Willis since 1922. Having been born in South Africa, the Warren children only knew their family roots by what they had heard from their parents. It was a joyful reunion and meeting when they arrived at the home of Willis' mother, Amanda, in Muskogee, Oklahoma. Willis had been faithful in corresponding with the family while in Africa, but the mail was slow in arrival at each place. Now they could meet the Warren children they had only heard about in letters.

Willis set about writing a book about their experiences in the foreign land. Willis' book, *Answering God's Call to Africa*, was published in 1946, and the Pentecostal Church sent him to several regions of the country to preach about his success in bringing all those "heathens" to the altar of God and Jesus Christ. While in Muskogee, Willis was invited to preach at the local Pentecostal church, where his Muskogee family was able to hear him preach for the first time. Willis Warren was a very quiet, soft-spoken man. His personality changed when he was behind the pulpit. He roamed the stage from one end to the other, Bible in hand, preaching hellfire and damnation in loud and emotional voice to nonbelievers.

Willis was the fair-haired preacher of the Pentecostals, who assigned him a resident church in South Carolina. Willis immediately started spreading the Word of God to the black population in his South Carolina town. When blacks began showing up in Willis' church to enjoy the Word and fellowship with the white parishioners, he found the wrath of the Pentecostal Church, not the wrath of God, come down on him in a hurry!

After all, those people of color are accepted into a church of the South, but it sure isn't in South Carolina! Willis became a Methodist—as a parishioner, not preacher!

(Willis Warren was my uncle, my mother's brother.)

ROSEMARY'S PETS

Rosemary Lehmann always had compassion for animals, but it was always dogs. Our first dog was a stray maroon-colored Cocker Spaniel that wandered to our apartment when we were first married. We fed "Roger" and he stayed. Friendly dog but peed all over everything when you petted him. We wondered if it was because of mistreatment by his owner or if it was just the nature of the breed. We moved to Texas shortly after, but a neighbor took Roger, faults and all.

Cathy and Baby

When we moved to Ponca City, Oklahoma, a few years later, Rosemary got a collie-mix dog from the litter of a friend's dog. She named the dog "Baby,' and it became the companion of our daughter Cathy. As Baby grew, she was like our second child. Cathy and the dog were inseparable. She watched Cathy like a babysitter. I watched from the porch one day when Cathy took a step toward the street from the curb, and Baby grabbed her by the seat of the pants and brought her back. She was with us for several years, but one day disappeared. We never knew what happened to Baby, but we were heartbroken.

Our next dog was a purebred Labrador retriever. I enjoyed duck hunting and bought the dog from a family in Kansas for $50. Princess was a wonderful dog and a wonderful companion to Cathy and Gene, who had joined the family by then. I trained Princess to retrieve ducks from the water and doves. She hated doves. The first dove she retrieved shed feathers in her mouth. From then on when retrieving a dove, Princess would pick it up by the tip of its wing. Smart dog.

We had Princess bred to a champion retriever from Tulsa. She gave us seven beautiful Lab puppies, all of which we sold or gave to friends. I kept one and named him "Old Black Joe of Bluestem." Princess developed problems from the pregnancy that could not be overcome by the vet, and we had to put her down. Our family grieved at the loss of this beautiful dog that had been a wonderful companion. I trained Joe but was never able to break him from leaving the duck blind before shots were fired.

Someone gave Cathy a Toy Collie she named "Rebel." Rebel was a pretty dog with long, silky hair but he was somewhat crazy. Certain sounds would make the dog howl. Cathy could make a moaning sound, and the dog would "sing." She took the dog when she married and left home.

Cathy and Rebel

Our next dog was a cocker-Pekingese mix we called "Pug" because of her pug nose. This was a delightful little dog. A terrapin stayed around our house for several years and wintered under the back porch step. Pug always went to the opening under the step to see of she could find the terrapin.

Gene then had a dog he called "Fred," that was a black and white spaniel mix. Fred was a good companion for Gene in his teen years, but he got in trouble with our Republican

Rosemary and Pug

neighbors who complained that Fred tore up Republican yard posters while leaving those alone of the Democrat candidates. They even brought pictorial proof, but I thought they probably put dog food on them. Fred met his demise by a automobile we were told.

Gene's next dog followed him home, a black and white English setter. He named this dog "Mollie" and took her out to the country to see if she would point quail. The dog came down on a covey, holding point beautifully. He then took her out to the country with a shotgun. Mollie trembled and shook and ran back to the truck. She was gunshy, probably from her owner who abandoned her because of the fault. Mollie remained with us after Gene went to college. She enjoyed pointing the bullfrogs on our fishpond. Mollie had to be put down when she developed cancer.

Rosemary had two heart attacks two days apart in December 1978. She was only 50 years of age. Following recovery, she developed compassion for all animals, now including cats. We had never had cats before, but now she began to accumulate them. She was given a cat she named "Doctor Watson." Then came "King Tut," followed by "Meow-Meow," "Skeezix," "Top Cat," "Mz. Spots," and "Dusty." No, she wasn't the crazy cat lady, but almost. We did have five cats at one time. While she was walking one day, Rosemary rescued Mz. Spots from a pile of concrete debris in a ravine near our house. The cats came and went as she gave them to friends, but the vet would spot her car in the drive, prepare shots and treatment, and say. "Here comes another $100 alley cat."

Muffin

We were spending more time in Texas, so Rosemary finally was able to move the last cat to a new home. We had added a new dog, a beautiful little Peekapoo (Pekingese and Poodle mix) we named "Muffin." She had white, curly hair that never shed. When she was a puppy, Rosemary would take Muffin in her purse shopping and no one ever knew she was in there. She went with us everywhere, even on the oil drilling rigs. Muffin was with us for 19 years before she died.

Rosemary and I were petless for several years after the loss of Muffin. But one spring morning I was potting some plants on the patio when I heard a faint "meow." Looking down, I spotted a little gray kitten looking up at me. Rosemary had wanted a dog but at our age and with health issues, I felt it was best we not have a pet for the well being of the animal. But I made the mistake of taking the little kitten in to show Rosemary. She said we had to keep her if no one showed up to claim it. She named it "Little Bit." She is a Russian Blue shorthair and has been with us for nearly 10 years.

Rosemary and Little Bit

Little Bit helped fill a void that was missing in Rosemary's life, but she still yearned for a dog. Little Bit, like most cats, was very aloof but at times jumped in Rosemary's lap and allowed petting. Rosemary never forgot her love for animals, making contributions to several animal welfare groups over the years.

Health issues for us both caused our children to call for us to move in with them in Ada in 2013. Our new home on Deer Creek east of the city is abundant with woods and wildlife that we enjoyed watching from the patio. Raccoons came out of the woods in the evening, and Rosemary enjoyed this show. She also loved watching as bluebirds fledged and took to wing and as wild turkeys wandered in from time to time.

Rosemary died in May 2014, but Little Bit and I remain to care for one another.

ROGER VAN DYKE
SMALL IN SIZE, BIG IN HEART

Roger Van Dyke never shied away from a challenge. Even as a schoolboy he stepped into activities that were risks to life and limb. Small in size, but stout in desire, Roger was an all-state quarterback for the Pawhuska Huskies football team. He took bruising licks from hefty opposing linemen and linebackers but bounced up quickly to execute the next play. When not playing football, he would be riding mean, cantankerous bulls in local rodeo competition. Though standing five foot five and three quarter inches tall, Roger thought he was six foot five! Gaining a scholarship to Oklahoma University, Roger found the competition at quarterback a little too stout. It was difficult to see over the behemoth linemen in Division I football, so he transferred to Connors State College at Warner, Oklahoma, where he gained all conference honors at the Division II School. Undecided about his future after college, he chanced to

meet a U.S. Navy Recruiter at a restaurant in his Pawhuska hometown. The recruiter suggested he would be a good candidate as a navy fighter pilot, so Roger signed up.

When he reported for duty in the naval aviation school, the instructors put a tape measure to Roger's height and found he lacked a quarter inch of being tall enough for the program. They finally waived his shorter stature and he began flight training. Everything went his way, and with Roger's adventurous spirit and grit, he was soon flying the Navy A-4E Jet Skyhawk fighter-bomber and doing takeoffs and landings on the tiny aircraft carrier runways. How would you like to have a rocket tied to your ass and be hurtled through the air at 350 mph and have to land on a football field? This suited Roger to a "T." It was smoother than riding a bull!

Deployed for duty in the Vietnam War in 1967, Roger was soon flying missions into enemy territory, bombing and strafing enemy targets from his USS Hancock aircraft carrier base. May 26, 1967, his squadron was engaged in dive-bombing raids on Kep Airfield near Hanoi. Enemy antiaircraft fire hit Roger's plane three times. The enemy missiles also hit the plane of his companion, Lt. Read Mecleary. After Mecleary's plane sustained major damage, forcing him to eject from the aircraft, he was captured and held prisoner of war for six years.

The antiaircraft missiles that struck Van Dyke's plane caused the hydraulic system to fail, but Van Dyke was able to pull it out of the dive and maneuver his airplane more than 70 miles over enemy territory and back to his carrier using manual controls and landing without flaps, an extremely difficult feat.

Roger Van Dyke flew 85 bombing missions over Vietnam during his service. He was awarded the Distinguished Flying Cross for his "courage, and extraordinary airmanship in face of grave personal danger" in a citation by the admiral of the Pacific Fleet,.

Following service in the military, Van Dyke enrolled in medical school at the University of Arkansas, receiving a degree in eye surgery specialty. He established a clinic outside Groton, Connecticut, where he practiced eye surgery before retirement in 2010.

The challenges of his younger days may not be as numerous, but don't mess with him. Roger Van Dyke still believes he is six foot five and bulletproof!

CARL ALBERT MAKES SPECIAL VISIT

In the 1970s the Republicans gerrymandered a large part of Oklahoma in redistricting designed to benefit their party at election times. Oklahoma 3rd District U.S. House of Representatives and Speaker of the House Carl Albert's district was gerrymandered along a slender, snaky line that ran 159 miles all the way from McAlester, his home district, to include Guthrie. This made no sense whatever, but Republicans being what they are, gained a few more Republican votes in an otherwise heavily Democrat "Little Dixie" area.

Albert and his wife, Mary, came to Guthrie for a visit to get acquainted with constituents in the new area assigned him. They had come in their own private car with no G-men or security of any kind. Albert, as Speaker, was third in line to become president of the United States. It was a much different time in the history of this country.

Speaker Carl Albert, Rosemary and Bill Lehmann

Rosemary and I were invited to be on the reception committee to take them around Guthrie where they might visit with some of the voters in the new district. Albert would not have needed a single vote in Logan County to be returned to office when election time rolled around. But being a very astute politician, he made the trip to "press the flesh" and meet the people. After all, that's why he was so popular in the first place. Albert had an excellent memory. After meeting you for the first time, he would call you by name the next time he saw you.

As the end of his Guthrie visit was nearing Rosemary told him it was a shame our son, Gene, couldn't be here to see Albert but he had to work that Saturday. Albert asked his name and was told that Gene worked at Cahill's Dairy Maid. Albert joined a line of folks awaiting service at Cahill's and finally moved up to the window where Gene was working. Gene looked up to see U.S. House Speaker Carl Albert at his window. Albert said, "Hello, Gene, your mother told me you would be disappointed in not seeing us during this visit, so I thought we would stop and see you on the way out of town." Lois Cahill relieved Gene at the window allowing them time for a short visit.

It was a very memorable day for a 15-year-old kid who couldn't even vote yet!

BILL LEHMANN

Musicians

Bill with the Country Tradition, 1996

BECOMING A "MUSICIAN"

Bought my first guitar when I was 14. Paid $5 for an f-hole, arched top Kay guitar at a Muskogee pawnshop. For another dollar I got a book on "How to play the guitar in 30 minutes." That was a week's pay as usher at the Broadway Theater.

I had been to my first country music show the night before at Muskogee's Municipal Auditorium. Roy Acuff was there and I was going to see him perform "The Wasbash Cannonball" in the flesh. Bought my $2 ticket and went in. There was Roy himself greeting everyone as they came in. "Howdy, neighbor. Glad you are here. Hope you enjoy the show," he said as we walked in. Boy, did I ever! I wanted to pick and sing like all the guys I saw in Roy's "Smoky Mountain Boys" band. I thought it would be a great life and I could just picture myself up there performing with them.

I'm ready for Nashville.

The guitar instruction book told me how to make a C, F and G chord. If the song were in G chord, there was a D that went in there. Then the book showed a hundred other chords with flats, sharps, and minors it said I would be able to make after learning the basic chords. I positioned my fingers on the frets as the book illustrated. You had to be somewhat of a contortionist to be able to get your wrist screwed around to position your fingers the way the pictures in the book showed. After 15 minutes of sour notes and muffled sounds, my fingers felt like someone and put a blowtorch to them. My fingers were on fire! My God, how can musicians stand this torture and still smile?

Reading the book further, it said to expect the fingers to be sore until calluses built up on the fingertips, and then you could glide through the frets and play like Chet Atkins! Boy, it was going to have to wait on me! I stayed with the guitar, playing in pain a little each day until finally some calluses built up and it wasn't quite as painful. I had improvised on making some of the chords to fit the way I could do them more easily and faster. They were not conventional with the book, but they worked for me and sounded okay when I did get the full sound of the chord, which wasn't often.

I kept struggling a little each day until I was playing some 3-chord songs and singing Earnest Tubb's "Walking the Floor Over You," and a Bob Wills tune or two. I wasn't ready for the stage yet, but I was getting there. I even embroidered some flowers on a couple of shirts like the country music stars wore so when Nashville called I would be ready to go in an instant! I never had anyone to play music with. The years passed. I married and still lugged my old Kay arch top guitar with every move, playing occasionally when the mood struck. I finally faced reality and knew I would never get that call from Nashville.

We moved to Pawhuska in 1959. My cousin Frank Woodard lived there. Frank had grown up in several towns in Oklahoma, but had moved to Pawhuska where he was assistant manager at Benson Lumber Company. When Frank came by for a visit one day, he spotted my old Kay guitar sitting in a corner of the room. I never had a case for it. Frank picked it up, tuned a few strings, and started playing. My God, Frank was good! He was making that old Kay sound like Chet Atkins and Merle Travis were playing it! I never knew Frank played guitar, but he was very good, played mellow finger picking style or played straight single string style. He was all over those frets and up and down the neck like a real pro.

Frank invited me to come jam with some of his friends, so I went over one night to play with them. They were completely out of my league. There was Rolland Webster, a great fiddle player. Frank played lead guitar and Ed Pradmore played rhythm guitar. Pradmore was one helluva rhythm guitar player. Every note was a different chord and you didn't need drums with Ed playing rhythm. Ed's wife, Liz was there that night and sang harmony on Merle Haggard's "I'll Break Out Again Tonight." Their harmony was so pretty it would raise the hair on the back of your neck. They sang regularly in church.

I added absolutely nothing with the guitar I had never learned to play. But I knew lots of songs, and none of them sang. I knew all the Bob Wills songs, and Rolland knew all of them on the fiddle. So I would strum along with them, (very softly to not ruin their sound), and sing some songs with them. They were kind and put up with me and kept inviting me back. It was the first time in my 35 years that I had ever played with anyone else, and I enjoyed it. But with three guitars and a fiddle—something else needed to be added. I decided to buy a bass guitar and see if I could learn it well enough to play with them and add another dimension to the sound.

Frank and I went to Tulsa one day and selected a Silvertone electric bass guitar and a piggyback bass amplifier with a 12-inch speaker, total cost a little over $100. I thumped around on it at home but couldn't wait until we got together again to jam. Ed Pradmore showed me some easy bass runs that were like bass licks on the guitar.

These came pretty easily, and I was able to add a thump-thump bass to their sound, and it wasn't too bad. The best thing was there weren't any minors, augments, sevenths, or other finger bending contortions to have to make playing bass—just one string at a time. And the strings were bigger and didn't cut into your fingers like a small gauge guitar string. I liked the bass more and more.

I kept practicing at home, placing records on the record player and thumping along with the music on the record. I liked the "walking bass" technique Doyle Holly did with the Buckaroo band. Buck Owens was the hottest thing going in country music at the time, and I was singing the Buck Owens songs and playing bass at the same time when we got together. I was far from being a good bass player but was getting by, and the bass added to the overall sound of the band. I enjoyed it.

We practiced at my house, and on most occasions we would find neighbors sitting on the sidewalk or listening at the open windows of the house. And they weren't throwing rocks! Bill Sweeden came by to hear us one night and said we were better than the bands they booked for their Roundup Club dances. He wanted us to play there one night. We decided to give it a try and booked in. They liked us and wanted us back. Someone said the band needed a name. Rolland suggested The Country Gentlemen, so that's what we became. One pundit suggested the name was only half right; we sure were country, but there wasn't a gentleman in the bunch.

Soonafter, the Roundup Club wanted us to play every two weeks on Saturday night. Rolland didn't really want to play that much, but Ed needed the money and Frank and I didn't object, so we agreed. We started off as a garage band just playing for our amusement and amazement, but others liked us and it was nice to play for a crowd. We dressed alike with white shirts, black ties and black slacks. We added a drummer, John Duncan, a high school boy. John kept a good country beat but would have been happier playing rock and roll music for the younger crowd venues.

Frank had been eyeing a new Fender Stratocaster guitar at a music store in Bartlesville. Now that we began playing to entertain others, Frank decided to buy the instrument. We went to Bartlesville one Saturday afternoon, and Frank played the guitar he wanted for quite a long time. He finally decided to buy it for a little over $300. We raced back to Pawhuska, and the two of us began playing in the den at my house. Frank's wife, Marla, spotted his car and came in to find us playing. "Where did you get that guitar?" Marla asked. Frank told her we would be playing more and he needed a better guitar. He said the money we earned playing gigs would pay for it. She turned, went out the door never saying another word, and went downtown and bought a new bedroom suite she had been eyeing for some time. She had hesitated buying it until they could afford it. But if he could afford that guitar, they could afford that bedroom suite! We needed to play a lot of gigs to pay for both! But there was no divorce.

We played for older crowds that liked to hear the two-steps, waltzes, and Western swing music. But we threw in a lot of Buck Owens and Merle Haggard songs, too. Some of the younger dancers wanted some rock and roll tunes so we learned a few, much to the dismay of Rolland, who was older, having grown up in the country music tradition. He played fiddle breakdowns, waltzes, and the Bob Wills swing music. He wasn't into any rock and roll! Occasionally a dancer would request a Schottische or polka. Rolland knew all of the old ethnic dance tunes, and we could satisfy the requests. I learned a lot of music I had never heard before by playing with Rolland.

Rolland Webster was a country gentleman if there ever was one! Rolland worked for Oklahoma Natural Gas as a maintenance man. Hundreds of ladies depended on him to start the pilot light on their water heaters when it went out or to light their furnaces in the winter. They wouldn't call the gas company—they called Rolland at home. He went gladly. That was small town America in another era!

Big news to the Country Gentlemen band came when it was announced that Buck Owens would be coming to Cain's Ballroom in Tulsa. Cain's Ballroom was the historic Mecca dance hall and show place built by Bob Wills and the Texas Playboys back in the dirty '30s. We gathered up the wives and headed for T-Town. The Buck Owens band was hotter than fire in country music at that time. They had racked up several number one hits. The place was packed that night to see Buck Owens and Don Rich.

We found a table and set up to dance a little and watch the band. Our band played several of their songs, and we were anxious to see them, because we were fans, too. The Buckaroos were dressed in all their finery. The band members were dressed in sparkling silver suits, while Buck's outfit was a shiny gold. Buck Owens and Don Rich both were playing sparkly silver twin Fender Telecaster guitars. Don Rich was Buck's all-around musician. He played lead guitar and fiddle and furnished harmony that fit Owens' voice like a glove. They played all their hits. Frank and I stood in front of the bandstand awed by the solid performance.

During a break, Buck and the band mingled with the crowd. The crowd loved them. I heard one fellow say to Buck as he passed by their table, "Hey, Buck, have a drink." Owens smiled and said "No, thanks. I might drink and play and like it, but you wouldn't!"

Our wives even had a good time that night. They got to dance a little, which was something they didn't get to do when we were playing our own gigs.

THE COUNTRY GENTLEMEN

The Pawhuska Round Up Club hosted a Cavalcade of state roundup clubs each year in July. Roundup clubs from all over the state of Oklahoma came to Pawhuska, set up camps at the fairgrounds, competed in rodeo events and other cowboy activities. A public dance was held in the fairgrounds buildings Friday and Saturday night of the Cavalcade.

The committee wanted to book our band for the events. The Country Gentlemen band had arrived with that call! The Cavalcade dances were the premier event of the year. A thousand or more people would attend the Cavalcade dances and it paid very well. They told us every time the bands took a break, fights would break out among the cowboys who might have a bit too much to drink and become a little "randy." As a band we decided we would play three straight sets without a break to try and eliminate fights. This we did. As far as I know there were no fights inside the dance as there had been in the past. But playing in a large building with only large circulating fans in an Oklahoma July is one big sauna. When we finished playing, there was not a dry thread on our shirts. Even a cardboard penny box of matches in my shirt pocket was completely saturated and none of the matches would strike.

A few people from Dexter, Kansas, were at the Cavalcade dances, liked our band and wanted to book us for a Saturday night in Dexter. The little town was 100 miles from Pawhuska, but they offered us $750 to play. We decided to accept the gig and off to Dexter, Kansas we went—the first leg of what would probably lead to our world tour. I had a 1960 Ford station wagon with a large, roomy cargo space behind the back seat. All the equipment fit in there very nicely with room for all five band members to ride in the passenger seats. Dexter, Kansas—here we come!

Our new friends in Dexter welcomed us with open arms. They had rented the community building in the small farming town and were ready to "Daintz all night." We got tuned up and started the dance at 9 p.m. The place was packed! They applauded after every number. First break everyone was patting us on the back and telling us how good we were. Everyone was having a great time and getting happier with each drink. We were scheduled to play until midnight, but at the beginning of the third and last set, they came wanting us to play an extra hour. Another $100 had been raised to sweeten the pot. We agreed to play an extra hour.

The Country Gentlemen Band: Rolland, John, Bill, Ed, and Frank.

At the beginning of the extra period, they came again adding another $100 to the pot if we would play one more hour. Damn, these Kansans liked to dance and drink! Talking it over, we decided not to accept the offer. We were all dead tired and faced at least two more hours on the return trip back to Pawhuska. Rolland taught a Sunday school class. He hadn't missed one Sunday since he started 10 years earlier. He would not miss this Sunday either. When Rolland explained to them that while we appreciated their enthusiasm and support, we must get back home because of the late hour. The mood suddenly turned ugly!

Rolland collected our money, and we started tearing equipment down and loading up for the return trip. Former happy faces turned sullen. Harsh words toward the band replaced the previous accolades. We finished loading and headed out of town. Cars followed us with honking horns, obscenities, and flying beer cans. My God! These people had become monsters! A belly full of too much whiskey can sure change people in a hurry! For the first time, I was concerned for our safety. It wasn't because we sounded bad; it was because they really WERE ready to daintz all night.

We finally left the cars and irate dancers in the rear view mirror of my '60 Ford wagon, much to the relief of all the Country Gentlemen band members. Mark Dexter, Kansas, off as a return gig!

The Country Gentlemen continued playing locally around Pawhuska, but in 1966 I was asked by my boss to transfer to Guthrie as publisher of the newspaper there. I was really torn by the thought of leaving a town and people I had grown to love—and the band. They had accepted me, teaching me and putting up with my thumping on the bass. I felt like I had finally fit into a musical group and I loved it. I wasn't ready for Nashville, but I wasn't that bad either.

I reluctantly accepted the transfer. My days as a "musician" appeared to be over. I was sad about that but looked forward to challenges that lay ahead.

MY SECOND "CAREER" IN MUSIC

Son Gene came in one day and asked me to show him some chords on the guitar. This was unusual because he had been interested in sports up to this point in his young life. He hadn't shown much interest in wanting to play an instrument, opting to play sports in Little League, then junior high. He was now a sophomore, playing basketball, but now he wanted to learn some guitar chords. He had grown up listening to the Country Gentlemen band in which I played bass. He had never expressed an interest in wanting to play, but now he did and I would show him what little I knew about guitar. I showed him some basic chords. He started practicing at home.

One evening Gene came in with two classmate friends, Kip Stratton and Victor Fey. They wanted me to show them more chords, which I did. The three practiced together a few times at our house. They were into a folk music mode while I was puree-dee country. There wasn't much I could show them about Dylan, Peter, Paul and Mary and Joan Baez. I could show them some stuff by Merle Haggard, Buck Owens, Earnest Tubb or Bob Wills. They received some pointers elsewhere, but still showed up at our house. They were sounding pretty good playing folk and soft rock songs.

High school days were over and the three friends drifted off in different directions and different colleges. I settled into my regular routine at the newspaper.

But one Sunday I received a call from Kip. A group of guys had gotten together at Harold McCallister's house for a little jam session and wanted me to join them. My equipment had been in the closet for nine years and I hadn't played a lick since moving to Guthrie. But it sounded like fun so off to Harold's house I went. Kip was sweet on McCallister's daughter, Celia, at the time. The gathering included McCallister, playing guitar, Kip on guitar, and Gene Moad, playing steel guitar. They were playing pure country so I was able to keep up with them. The session ended after a couple or three hours. I had enjoyed myself very much and it was nice to play music with a group again after being idle for several years. A few days later I received a call from Gene Moad. He told me he was playing with Bud Smith's '89er Opry stage band, but Bud had booked a dance at Blackwell. The band's regular bass player, Martin Bettes, would not play dances. Moad told Bud about me, and they wanted me to sit in. Sounded like fun, so I decided to go with them.

Gene Moad picked me up in his pickup truck. As we headed out of Guthrie, he said, "What do you think about picking up a little bottle to nurse on for the drive to Blackwell?" Sounded good to me, so we picked up a pint of Jack Daniel's. We had a couple of nips on the trip, and Gene placed the half-empty bottle under the seat of his pickup. We set up and started playing at nine o'clock.

Bud Smith was an old pro fiddle player, having played fiddle, guitar, and bass since we was a toddler. Well into his 60s, Bud was still going strong and directed the '89er Opry Show every two weeks at the American Legion Hall in Guthrie. Bud could play any song in any key—didn't matter what it was, he could play it. His technique was a little scratchy, but he could do it. Gene Moad played steel guitar very well and sang. J.C. Pope played guitar and sang, and Donald Dean played drums and sang as well. I played the bass. The band sounded pretty dang good together.

A young lady had pestered Bud several times to let her sing with the band. She was about 20, shapely and pretty. She would look good in front of any band whether she had singing talent or not. At the end of the second set, Bud told her she could open the last set and to be ready. I thought she was a little snockered, but it wasn't my call. At the beginning of the third and last set, Bud handed her the microphone after introducing her. She was going to sing Patsy Clone's "Crazy." The band kicked off the intro and she opened her mouth to sing. The first note never came. She took a nosedive off the bandstand, passed out cold. They took her to the back room, where she regained some of her composure but did not return to the bandstand. We never found out if she had singing talent, but she looked good.

Sunday morning came, and Moad's wife got in the pickup to go to church. A very religious lady, she objected to alcohol. Her nose instantly picked up the scent of Jack Daniels whiskey that lingered in the truck. Looking under the seat, she recovered the bottle, marched in the house, confronting Moad with the bottle. "Oh, that damn Bill Lehmann left that bottle in the truck," he told her. Things were a little rocky between them for a while. Moad asked me to their house to play from time to time. Things were never smooth between Moad's wife and me, but I was tolerated. I quietly accepted blame as a bad influence.

The Moad family was very talented as a group. There was Gene; Beverly, who was knockout beautiful; sons Mack and John, and the youngest, a girl named Marsha. They sang together in church and church was a big part of their lives through Beverly, who had the voice of an angel. Their voices melded perfectly. Mack, about 12 years old, played guitar and sang very well. He wanted to do more rock and roll, but Gene was keeping him country. Gene worked in construction and Beverly was a Walmart supervisor when the company was in its infancy. She traveled to other stores in her management role. I hope she bought Walmart stock. If she did she is worth millions today.

Gene Moad called me from time to time to play dances. I hadn't sought to be a member of a band on a permanent basis, but did go as a fill in, occasionally playing with Moad and Pope. J.C. Pope was a former rocker who was raised in Seminole. He located to Tulsa where he played in bands and then drifted to California and Alaska. He had come back to Oklahoma and was selling insurance in Guthrie. He played with Smith's stage band and filled in with other bands, as I was doing. Moad, J.C. and I were playing more and more together. My association and friendship with J.C. Pope would last a lifetime.

J.C. booked a dance one night at the Green Lantern, a bar next to the Blue Bell Saloon in Guthrie. The bar was notorious for being an attraction for the younger crowd where the exchange of money was made with weed and pills during the night. It was a rock and roll crowd and J.C. was in his element. He had taught me enough rock and roll licks that I could get by. I felt somewhat out of place in that environment and group of younger, longhaired musicians. Now I was the "old man" of the group. Things were going well. J.C. was belting out "Proud Mary," "Pretty Woman," and other upbeat songs by Bob Seeger and J.J. Cale.

J. C. Pope

During the break, a crowd had gathered outside in the alley to watch a pissing contest between a woman and a man. It seems the woman and her companion had entered the bar and started a conversation with some of the barflies. The companion was telling the others that his girlfriend could piss farther standing up than a man. Bets were quickly taken and they went to the alley. The bartender had a tape measure that would determine the winner. The guy who had drunk the most beer without peeing went first. He measured somewhere around six feet. The woman was next. She pulled up her skirt, hooked her high heel shoe in the bumper of a car, pushed forward and let 'er fly. She beat him by a foot and a half! It was said the pair went from town to town making the challenge in bars and collecting the winnings. Strange things happen in bars.

Back inside the bar things were getting a little rowdy. The beer, pills and weed had taken effect. All of a sudden a big fight broke out between Tattoo Dorothy and another woman. Tattoo Dorothy was known to go "both ways." She was rough and tough and looked the part with tattoos up and down her arms, on her neck and Lord knows where else. She dressed in men's clothing. Pretty soon others joined in the fracas and it erupted across the bandstand. Everyone in the band backed away while the brawlers were going at it. J.C. dropped his gold top Les Paul guitar on the floor and Tattoo Dorothy promptly left a big print of her tennis shoe on it as she chased one of the "ladies" across the bandstand. Tattoo Dorothy's footprint remained tattooed on J.C.'s guitar.

A couple of years passed and Moad started his own band and Mack was playing bass with him. A divorce happened in the Moad family, and Gene and Beverly split. Whiskey may have played a part because Gene drank when he played, and Beverly did not approve. I saw Gene Moad sometime later with a much younger woman. They looked mismatched to me besides the difference in age. She weighed at least 350 pounds and Moad weighed maybe 175. They were going to be married, he told me, and said, "I don't know what she sees in me." He must have seen beauty in youth because she was a two compared to Beverly, whom I thought was a knockout 11! This was a tragic situation happening to a formerly beautiful family.

Somebody ought to write a country song about whiskey breaking up a marriage! Oh, someone already has?

Thanks to Kip Stratton, my musical "career" came out of the closet and stayed out for many years after. It has been a fun part of my life.

MUSICIAN FRIENDS REMEMBERED

My life has been enriched with music from the time I first heard Bob Wills, Roy Acuff and Earnest Tubb as a youth. Then I added the big band sounds of Glenn Miller, Tommy Dorsey and Frank Sinatra to my favorites. Later came Hank Williams, Merle Haggard, Waylon Jennings, Chet Atkins, Dire Straits, J.J. Cale, Eric Clapton and Vince Gill. I have always been a music junkie and loved all kinds of music. Some of my best memories have been the bands and musicians I have played with.

After spending a few years in the newspaper business, son Gene came back to Guthrie to take up college studies again. He had learned to play fiddle from one of my former band mates, Rolland Webster. I called another one of my friends, J. C. Pope to come over and jam with us one night. Pope added a new dimension to the country music and fiddle breakdowns Gene had been playing. He brought the sounds of current pop and rock and roll to be added to our repertoire. J.C. then called Robert Dunn, with whom he had played in church to join us. Dunn played guitar and steel guitar. Then we invited Chuck Slack, a drummer to join us, with me on bass. We soon had an invitation to play a dance and we named the group Cimarron and moved out of my living room and into clubs and restaurants.

Cimarron was a very versatile group playing everything from Bob Wills, Buck Owens, George Strait, Roy Orbison to the Sons of the Pioneers. Gene playing the "Orange Blossom Special" on fiddle was always a crowd favorite. Our harmonies added greatly to the overall sound, especially the old cowboy favorites "Cool Water" and "Tumbling Tumbleweeds." Restauranteur Harvey Hardy kept us busy weekends playing his restaurants. The historic Blue Bell Saloon in downtown Guthrie was one of our favorite places to play. We did some shows, openings and celebration events. It was very nice for me to be able to play music with my son and the other fellows in the band. We had fun and enjoyed playing together.

Cimarron Band: Robert, Chuck, Gene, J. C., and Bill

But all good things must end it seems. After more than a year we went separate ways. Dunn left for another group, Gene joined two former classmates and they formed a trio they called the Charlatans, specializing in folk music and writing and singing their own songs. Chuck Slack, a very tasteful and talented drummer began playing full time professionally in Oklahoma City. Later Gene moved to Texas, ending our days of playing together in a band. J.C. and I played with other groups from time to time and booked our own gigs picking up other musicians.

Then I had a call from Bud Smith who headed the '89er Opry show at Kingfisher. His regular bass player had left to join another band and Bud asked me to play bass with the Opry band. I told him I would play until he could find a replacement. But I enjoyed playing with this group so much I hoped he didn't find another bass player. The '89er Opry Band was a real joy to play with. They played every two weeks at the Shafenberg Music Hall east of Kingfisher, Oklahoma.

Bud Smith headed the Opry Band. He played fiddle, guitar and bass. Name any song and he could play it on the fiddle, in any key.

Bud had a great, friendly personality and acted as master of ceremonies at Opry shows. Webb Tipton, Bethany, Oklahoma ,played lead guitar and sang. Webb was a stellar guitar player and was a member of the small, Miami Indian tribe. Gene Holt, Oklahoma City, played steel guitar and was an outstanding musician. Wes Onley played rhythm guitar and sang Eddy Arnold cover tunes and specialized in yodeling. Onley was a crowd favorite. Steve Crawford was a very good pianist and sang for the band. I also played bass and sang with Webb and Wes as a member of their Country Gentlemen group, playing gigs in and around Oklahoma City.

Joy Goodnow of the Country Tradition band called wanting me to join their group. Joy had a beautiful voice, knew hundreds of songs and was experienced at friendly banter with the crowd that made her very popular. Joy had made some studio recordings with session musicians early in her career that were of excellent quality and sound. With the proper manager, Joy was capable of a professional career on a national level, but the right breaks never came. Joy fronted bands for several years in Vermont before relocating back to Oklahoma.

Joy Goodnow of the Country Tradition

Joy's husband, Eddy Pigott played guitar, steel guitar and sang with the Country Tradition band. J.C. Pope played rhythm guitar and sang and I played bass.

Other members of the Country Tradition band were Jerry Jones, Oklahoma City, a most outstanding lead guitar player and singer. Jerry Jones has played music most all his life, starting at age 11 when his father bought him a steel guitar. Jerry soon became good enough to play in his father's band in and around Duncan and Velma-Alma. He played steel guitar until he went into the air force. While stationed in Washington D.C. he played with a group of other servicemen. One of the barracks members complained about the "whiney" sound of the steel guitar while Jerry practiced, so Jerry switched to an electric Fender Telecaster. This was a great decision. Securing a manager, the group played many gigs in Washington, D.C., Maryland and Virginia.

Jerry Jones

Returning home, Jerry resumed civilian life, starting a family and playing guitar and steel guitar in bands in central Oklahoma. He started his own television sales and repair business in Oklahoma City. He eventually became proficient in computer programming and worked for National Cash Register Company installing and servicing ATM machines across Oklahoma before retirement in 2000.

Jerry's talents and smooth voice were of such quality he could have played professionally with any band, but family obligations discouraged such a pursuit. He now records songs featuring his voice and guitar at his home recording studio in Oklahoma City.

Alan Porter of Crescent, Oklahoma, played drums. A very tasteful drummer, he kept a solid and consistent beat making it easy to perform. Alan was very witty, making comments that kept band members laughing. But when we hooked him up to a microphone so the crowd could enjoy his wit he became mute. A crushed leg in an auto accident forced his retirement from his profession as a machinist and with the band. Joy and Ed moved to Wichita Falls, Texas, in early 2000, where they now share their gospel music talents with fellow parishioners at the Cowboy Church there.

A re-formed Country Tradition group continued playing the clubs in and around Guthrie. The new group consisted of Jerry Jones, J.C. Pope, Alan Porter and me. Pope knew more than a hundred songs, but could never remember the first few words to start the song or the key he sung it. I kept a notebook to remind him. Jones, on the other hand, had all his songs organized in a notebook he opened before singing.

Later we added Dallas Dutcher on drums, Robert Dunn on guitar and Ronnie Gulliver, from Perry, Oklahoma, on steel guitar. Gulliver had played steel guitar all over the world before huge audiences with Roy Clark's band, but tired of the constant travel that prevented a normal home life with his family. Jerry Jones and Gulliver made an outstanding dimension to the variety and sound of the band. Gene Lehmann came up from Texas occasionally to play fiddle with the group. It was a damn good band if I do say so myself!

J. C. Pope, Alan Porter, Bill, and Jerry Jones

Our band had a gig in Perry, Oklahoma, September 11, 2001. It was an outdoor concert, and we needed to arrive early to set up and test equipment beforehand. We met at a Guthrie quick trip for coffee and soft drinks and to travel together for the gig some 50 miles away. Word came over a car radio that an airplane had crashed into the World Trade Center in New York City. We, like the rest of the country, thought initially the crash was probably a tragic accident. We did not know until arriving at Perry that it was the terrorist plot that would shake the world and send us into a war that is still ongoing in many Middle East places. The concert went on as scheduled, but the tone was somber from the events that kept unfolding during the evening. This was s the most memorable gig I ever played.

Rosemary's health became an issue, causing me to curtail my activities in music. The other band members drifted to other groups or retired. My second career as a "musician" ended but it had been a delightful 35-year run with some very talented individuals that became good friends.

BUD SMITH, LOGAN COUNTY'S MUSIC MAN

Bud Smith couldn't read a note of music. Wouldn't have played it if he could. His music came from a lifetime of love for music and pure soul in playing country, blues and jazz. His repertoire included hundreds of songs he could play in any key, on the fiddle or guitar. Name a song and he could sing and play it. Bud Smith was a big man, standing more than 6 feet tall and weighing in at more than 250 pounds. He had an equally big voice and an infectious laugh that would draw you to him. You knew when he was in the room.

Bud Smith

Smith was born October 25, 1916, in Lovell, Oklahoma. His given name was Rufus, a name he hated. The family soon moved to Guthrie where Bud graduated high school. He learned a trade as a heavy equipment operator for Clarence L. Boyd Company in Guthrie. The Boyd Company also sold heavy equipment such as road graders, bulldozers and other construction equipment. Bud not only learned how to run them, he could also do repairs.

He started learning music at an early age playing fiddle and guitar with old timers around the neighborhood. In the 1930s, he watched the bands that played at the Silver Lake Club on the east edge of Guthrie. The club attracted some of the best-known bands in Oklahoma at the time, and fans packed the club where they danced to the music of bands like Bob Wills and the Texas Playboys and Merle Lindsay and the Oklahoma Night Riders. He watched and learned and soon was playing dances at the Silver Lake himself with local bands. Bud built a big bass fiddle from scratch during this period and played it in the bands as well as singing, playing fiddle and guitar. The bass is now in a Crescent museum.

The music of the era was coined as country and western, but it was far more than that. Bob Wills perfected the sound of Western Swing that was a mixture of country, blues, pop and jazz. It was far more than 3-chord country. The arrangements included majors, minors, augments and riffs that brought new life to the music. Bud watched and learned as the guitar players made every note a different chord.

Bud and bass

Music was Bud Smith's life and he played in many dance bands in and around Guthrie for many years. In the 1960s he organized the '89er Opry Music show, playing every two weeks at Guthrie's American Legion Hall. The venue of the show included regular band members he recruited that played the two-hour show. Bud acted as mc and regularly invited two or three guests, many from other towns to perform. He also scheduled members of the band to sing two songs, or take a lead solo ride at each show.

In the 1970s Bud moved the '89er Opry show from Guthrie to the Shafenberg Music Hall in Kingfisher. Located a few miles east of Kingfisher, the Shafenberg facility was built by O. M. Shafenberg as a convention center for the study of reincarnation. A huge Longhorn steer and a buffalo greeted visitors to the center. They were reincarnated from Sam Houston and Sitting Bull, it was said by Shafenberg.

In the mid-70s, the bass player quit the band, and Bud called wanting me to take his place. I told Bud I would play temporarily until he could find a new bass player. Weeks passed and no bass player showed up, but by that time I enjoyed playing with the group so much that I really hoped he wouldn't find someone else. The band consisted of some stellar musicians: Bud Smith fiddle,

Gene Holt, steel guitar, Webb Tipton, lead guitar, Sam Rains, guitar, Chuck Slack, drums, Alton Scott, fiddle and steel, Wes Onley, yodeler and Steve Crawford, piano.

89er Opry Show

The Shafenberg building was outfitted with a stage, sound equipment and seating for more than a hundred. In addition, video equipment was installed and each reincarnation conference was recorded on tapes and video. The reincarnation programs attracted followers from around the world. The '89er Opry was also videotaped and available for the fans and perfomers to purchase. The kitchen served full meals to reincarnation attendees and snacks and desserts to those attending the Opry shows. The music shows were staged every other Saturday from 7 to 9 p.m. with seating usually full.

Bud delighted in having youngsters take part in the shows. At least one boy wanting to be the next Garth Brooks or girl to succeed Reba McEntire would be given their shot at becoming the next big star. The mommas would have them all gussied up in their finest dresses, boots and hats for their debut. Some had talent and some didn't, but they had their chance to shine. Male and female singers from all across central Oklahoma participated in the '89er Opry shows. Their numbers would be counted in the hundreds during the time Bud promoted the '89er Opry. Gospel music was not forgotten, and a show devoted entirely to gospel music was regularly scheduled. This brought out many church groups and individuals who specialized in gospel music. The gospel shows were always crowd favorites.

A contract disagreement with Shafenberg caused Smith to move the show to Crescent's Community Center. The venue continued in Crescent through the 1980s until Smith's health became an issue in being able to devote the necessary time to keep it going. Bud Smith's love for music never faltered. Though his activity as a promoter had been curtailed, Bud and his wife, Irma Lee, were regular visitors to Perkins, where Bud performed at the Perkins Music Show in that city. Several fans from Guthrie and Crescent also followed Bud in attending the Perkins show.

Bud on stage

Bud Smith died June 7, 2005, and was buried in Guthrie's Summit View cemetery. Perhaps a premonition preceded his death. The pastor at Bud and Irma Lee's Crescent church paid them a home visit and asked Bud to play a song on the fiddle. After the pastor left Bud placed his fiddle in the case and told Irma Lee, "That's the last time I'll play." He never took it out of the case again.

FRONTING TOMMY COLLINS

Leonard Sipes was born in Bethany, Oklahoma in 1930. He was a talented poet, played guitar and sang in his little church, was religious and attended Bible college after graduation. He also performed at venues in Oklahoma City with Wanda Jackson, an aspiring country singer who would later become famous in establishing the "Rockabilly Sound." The Jackson family moved to California about 1950 and Tommy went with them, living with them until the Jacksons soon returned to Oklahoma.

Leonard stayed in California deciding to continue to seek a career in country music. He had written several songs and was a good singer with a voice that was a little different than the rest. He impressed the record producers at Capitol Records with his songs and they signed him to a contract.

But who would buy recordings by Leonard Sipes? They changed his name to a more country and simple sounding name that would be more easily remembered. So little country boy Leonard Sipes became Tommy Collins. Tommy quickly fell in with other aspiring country music singers and songwriters with Okie backgrounds. There was Johnny Bond, Spade Cooley, Wynn Stewart, Buck Owens and Merle Haggard, Bonnie Owens, Ralph Mooney, all centered in and around Bakersfield. Country music artists in Nashville had developed an identifying sound. The minute the first notes were played on recordings by Hank Williams, Earnest Tubb, Johnny Cash, Roy Acuff or Hank Thompson you knew who it was.

The Fender Telecaster guitar had just been introduced to the West Coast and the sound was attracting more country artists. The high tinny sound was beginning to compete with the more mellow sounds of Nashville. Tommy Collins was one of the first to latch on to the new sound. His lead guitar player was Buck Owens, whose career was to blossom later. Tommy Collins recordings were becoming more popular and the little guitar riffs played on the Fender with the tinny sound was unique and quickly identified Collins as the artist. Collins songs were usually humorous, but occasionally Leonard Sipes would influence Tommy to write and record some spiritual or inspirational songs.

Tommy Collins career was beginning to take off, as well as the other artists with Okie ties. This group of artists is credited with being the founders of what became known as "The Bakersfield Sound," with that tinny upbeat, dominant Fender Telecaster sound.

But with success came temptation. Satan was tugging with Tommy to abandon his Christian teaching and yield to the wild side of life like the lyrics in Tommy's songs. Sex, whiskey and cocaine became a part of Tommy's life. It destroyed his marriage and changed his life to a dependency on drugs and alcohol. Leonard Sipes kept tugging with Tommy's mindset and finally led him away from music and back to Oklahoma where he took a little country church in western Oklahoma as pastor.

As pastor of the little church Tommy soon turned his life around as Leonard Sipes again. He walked the straight and narrow path of Christianity again, leading his flock in song and sermon. But Tommy Collins kept entering the mind of Leonard and soon influenced him to trade the pulpit for life again in front of a microphone of the musical stage and recording studio. His return to music gained him moderate success again but the influence of Satan overpowered the influence of Leonard and Tommy was back to his old ways again. Leonard secured another hold and they returned once more to Oklahoma as pastor of another small church.

But Tommy persuaded Leonard to return to California once more and this time it stuck. Time had faded his popularity but he appeared with some of his old Bakersfield friends, and wrote songs. He wrote a hit song for Merle Haggard called "The Roots Of My Raisin' Run Deep," that could have been about Collins himself. Faron Young recorded an old song of Tommy's called, "If You Ain't Loving, You Ain't Living." The song topped the charts for the second time and added to Tommy's royalty earnings that were considerable despite not having any new hits of his own. He did pen a song recorded by George Jones and Mel Tillis, titled "New Patches." That song was perhaps his last hit.

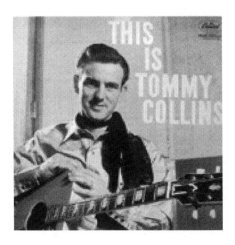

Collins later migrated to the Nashville area and was active in personal appearances with others. Haggard penned a song titled "Leonard," that was a kind of biography of Tommy's life and struggles. One line in the song told about Tommy bringing groceries to a career-struggling Haggard, "long before Muskogee (Haggard's big hit) came along." Oddly, Tommy Collins had a fan base in Germany, Holland, Norway and Switzerland. He appeared in those countries backed by local bands that loved American country music.

I had occasion to play in a band that backed Tommy Collins in the late 1980s. A friend of Collins had been injured in an oilfield accident and a money raiser had been scheduled to aid the victim. Tommy Collins had agreed to appear in a benefit show to support his friend and the Bud Smith '89er Opry band was selected to back Collins. I played bass in the band and was excited to be able to meet and back Tommy Collins, who had long been one of my favorite song writer/entertainers. A crowd of perhaps 250 people showed up for the show, a good-sized crowd for Crescent, Oklahoma.

The Opry band opened the show and did a few numbers, and then Tommy made his appearance doing some of his songs. Our guitar player, Webb Tipton did a good job in imitating the signature sound of Tommy Collins. The audience loved him and was very responsive. When we took a break, I had a chance to visit with Collins one-on-one. We went outside for a cigarette. I told him I had always liked his songs and saw a parallel with the humor in the songs of Roger Miller, whose songs were riding high on the charts at that time.

"Yes," he said to me, "Roger told me that my songs were a great influence on him and also his uncle, Sheb Wooley, who had some hit recordings with 'The Purple People Eater,' and a couple of others." During our smoke break I asked Tommy to do one of his funny songs when we went back on stage. I requested "All of The Monkeys Ain't In The Zoo," a song about crazy things people do that compare to monkeyshine antics. We went back on stage and started the song but had to quit. Tommy forgot the words. But it had been many years since he had done it, he explained.

Tommy Collins and Leonard Sipes died in Tennessee in 2000. They were 70 years of age and had colorful careers. I hope they are resting in peace with one another.

Google "Tommy Collins" to see some video clips and hear the songs of Tommy.

BOOGER RED'S

Tucked 'way back in the rolling hills of eastern Logan County's scraggly blackjack trees, cedar trees and impenetrable plum thickets was Booger Red's Bar. It was not a place you would stumble onto. You had to want to go there. The roads were of the Oklahoma red clay that churned up clouds of fine ed dust when dry and slick as snot when wet.

There was an old 1920s-something rusty red bulldozer parked near the entrance to the acreage that had been cut out of the blackjack and cedar trees. An old rusty pickup truck sat on blocks and about three goats wandered around that kept the weeds down. They were low maintenance animals and kept the snakes killed. There were chickens of all mixed-breeds and colors. They pecked away at jumping grasshoppers and bugs in the worn-down yard that held a few clumps of Bermuda grass here and there. A hog pen could be seen among the blackjacks about 50 yards in the distance.

The bar and living quarters was a small frame building that had seen much better days. 1930s-era asbestos siding was broken in many places exposing the black tarpaper insulation between the shingles and the wooden frame. There was a large plateglass window at the door to the bar entrance. A hand-lettered sign warned "Notice: Thieves will be shot! Survivors will be shot again!"

We had come on Saturday night to play music for the patrons at Booger Red's. My friend and band mate J.C. Pope had booked this gig. "Lordy, what has he got us into this time?" I thought to myself as we pulled up into the drive. It looked like it could be a bucket of blood when those hillbillies get liquored up! It would have been a good scene in *The Grapes of Wrath*, a novel about Okies of the thirties. I had played many scary places before, but this one took first prize! I was getting ready to tell J.C. to get us the hell out of there before we even unloaded equipment, but Booger Red came out the door to greet us.

"Glad to see you, boys," he said as he came out the door. "We're gonna have a rockin' good time tonight. I got the word out and we'll have a good crowd." Red was a small, but muscular man about five feet eight inches tall. His hair might have been red at one time but now the hair was grey coming out from under the baseball cap he wore. The cap was a faded red that had a St. Louis Cardinal icon on the front. Red hadn't shaved in several days and his white whiskers were stained with reddish-brown tobacco juice that had dripped on his chin when he spit, that he hadn't wiped it away.

Red reached inside the bib pocket of his well-worn overalls and pulled out a big wad of cash. He counted out four $50 bills and handed them to J.C. That was the pay for the four of us. I saw several Ben Franklin's in that roll as he placed it back in his bib. It was the first time I had played anywhere that the booker paid the band up front. We hadn't even set up. Most bookers waited until the end and then wanted to quibble about the price if the crowd wasn't good.

We walked into the bar to set up at the little upraised bandstand Red had built himself. It would be crowded with amps plus the mike stands and us four. Red had to shoo a few chickens out the door that had wandered in and were walking around on the worn wooden floor.

A pretty girl bartender smiled at us when we cane in. Red said she sang and wanted her to do a few songs with us during the night. Brenda was about 30, very pretty with shoulder-length blondish hair. Her shapely body was covered by a cotton print dress that had probably just come out of the dryer and hit a few licks with an iron to smooth out some wrinkles. She had three little ones at home but the husband would stay with them while she had her "night out" and got to sing with a real band instead of the radio. Red took care of the bar himself but called Brenda in for special occasions.

A calendar behind the bar had days that had passed marked off with an "X" by a magic marker. A Billy club rested on a shelf in easy reach if someone became a little rowdy. A few Bud Light and Coors beer signs dotted the walls. There were also a few framed pictures of Red in his younger days when he was a roughneck. There were also some Polaroids of rigs he had worked on. A framed picture of Elvis painted on black velvet hung above the beer box cooler. One spigot for draught beer was behind a small bar that seated maybe ten people.

Red himself played guitar, J.C. told me, playing solo sometimes when patrons called for him to do so. He might play a couple of numbers with us, J.C. said. Red liked country music. Didn't want "none of that rock and roll shit!" Willie, Waylon, Hank Williams, Merle Haggard, Bob Wills and George Strait, that was what Red wanted. People started coming in as we were tuning up—local folks in all sorts of dress that lived in the area on four or five acres cut out among the blackjack and cedars, friendly people, smiling and saying they were glad we had come to play.

Brenda came up and wanted to know if we knew all the chords in "Crazy," a crooked Willie Nelson song made famous by Patsy Cline. We did enough of the song that satisfied Brenda that we could back her, so she went back to pulling some "draw" beers for a couple that had just come in. I was beginning to like the atmosphere. It wasn't Carnegie Hall by any stretch, but it sure had "character." It was beginning to look like fun and some of my apprehension began to calm.

Red said most of the patrons lived in the area. Few "outsiders" wandered in unless they were lost or seeking directions to someone who lived in the region. If they came looking for trouble they would get a double dose of it from Red and his friends, he assured us. Most men worked in the oilfield or at Tinker Field in Oklahoma City. Many lived out in the sticks to get away from restrictions or crowded housing of city living. The secluded space would permit them to have some chickens, maybe a goat, and grow a little pot. And their kids could raise some sheep, goats, rabbits or other animals for FFA projects and activities at school. Most of the housing was mobile homes set back among the trees. A few manufactured homes could be seen.

We started playing the bluesy "Honky Tonk" instrumental. A few in the crowd of about 50 started dancing on the creaky, wooden floor, but most listened as they sipped their beer. Lots of applause followed each song. It was obvious they were enjoying themselves. Red brought out his blond Fender Telecaster guitar and plugged it into J.C.'s amp. He sat in a chair at the side of the bandstand because there was no more room on the tiny bandstand itself. Red put down his guitar to tend bar when Brenda wanted to sing. He never returned. Brenda came up and sang "Crazy," to the delight of her friends, ranging in age from thirty to sixty, which gave her a rousing round of applause. "She's better than them singers in Nashville," I heard one say.

When break time for the band came, everyone wanted to visit with us. A couple of guys came up to me to visit. They were very friendly and had enough to drink to want to talk—a lot about nothing. I was glad when they left me to engage others in their conversation about nothing. Booze has different effects on people. Some want to fight, some want to talk, while some want to make love. The crowd this night just wanted to have fun. So they did-and so did we.

It was nearing one o'clock. We had played a little longer than usual, but we were all having fun. Everything had gone beautifully. Brenda had come back to sing a couple of more times, including "Crazy" again, "by special request," probably hers. J.C., being a rocker, snuck in "Proud Mary," which Red probably didn't notice or didn't care by that time. J.C. ended the night with "Pretty Woman." The crowd was really into this one. Everybody was up dancing and moving their bodies to the throbbing upbeat song. He ended with "Magnolia," a slow, romantic J.J. Cale ballad that let the dancers snuggle up for close dancing that probably produced thoughts of what might happen later.

Booger Red's was a delightful place to play, and we went back several times. Red always paid us upfront out of the big roll of bills he carried in the bib pocket of his overalls.

Booger Red and his blackjack and cedar tree friends are among the parade of interesting characters that have brought fun and variety to my life.

A LESSON IN DEDICATION AND PERSEVERANCE

If ever I need a reminder of dedication and perseverance to a purpose I need look no further than to my own son, Gene Lehmann. At age 26, Gene decided he wanted to learn to play the fiddle. When he told me he wanted to learn fiddle I told him that was something her should have taken up at age six, not 26! No musical instrument is easy to play, but the fiddle? It was a most difficult instrument.

When Gene was a teenager he came to me and wanted me to show him some chords on the guitar. I had played guitar, but was not good at it. I showed him C, F and G chords, about all I knew. Gene and some of his friends gathered at our house, eager to learn to play and would practice. Gene, Kip Stratton and Victor Fey were learning to play together and were sounding pretty good playing light rock and folk songs of the day. Then came college, jobs, and they all went separate ways.

Gene married and lived in Bartlesville. He called one night saying his wife had bought him a fiddle. He complained he was unable to find a teacher to teach him to play the styles he wanted to play. He had gone to several teachers but they wanted to teach him to play by notes on sheet music, but he wanted to learn old-fashioned breakdowns and western swing styles. This is usually played by ear, feel - and soul!

I told Gene to call Rolland Webster, a friend of mine with whom I had played bass in a band we had in Pawhuska. Rolland had grown up with a fiddle and played the styles Gene wanted to learn. Rolland played all the Bob Wills tunes as well as the old square dance and traditional breakdown styles. Gene had known Rolland from listening to our band, but we had left Pawhuska when Gene was 10 years old. Gene called Rolland and then called me back a little later, very dejected, saying Rolland told him he didn't believe he could help him. I told Gene to call Roland right back and tell him he would be up to Pawhuska the next Monday for a lesson. Gene called Rolland again, and then called me saying Roland had relented and told him to come ahead.

Gene learning the fiddle

Before lessons began, Gene divorced and moved to Claremore. He drove from Claremore to Pawhuska each week for two years to receive a lesson from Rolland. Rolland soon discovered Gene's dedication to learn, even giving him one of his own fiddles and never charged Gene a dime for any of the lessons. Gene had learned to "rock the bow," play harmony notes and was becoming very good on the instrument. Finally realizing he should have finished college brought Gene back to the Guthrie nest. He enrolled at Central State University in Edmond and went to work at a Guthrie liquor store. By that time I had found a group of guys and was playing bass with a couple of bands off and on. I gathered a group together to jam and Gene was playing fiddle with us.

Gene was very good playing the Western swing and country music, but in the group was J.C. Pope, a former rock and roller who introduced Gene and the rest of us to some rock arrangements. Gene picked up some new licks with the group that broadened his style and repertoire. We decided to start a band and called it "Cimarron." We were successful in getting some gigs in and around Guthrie. Band members included, Pope, guitar and vocals, Robert Dunn, guitar, steel guitar and vocals, Gene playing fiddle and vocals, Chuck Slack on drums and me on bass.

The Cimarron band played a great variety of music from J.J. Cale's "Cocaine" to The Sons of the Pioneers old cowboy songs "Cool Water" and "Tumbling Tumbleweeds." We played the music we liked and had a great time. For dances we also played country, two-step and western swing music. We played for more than a year together, then Robert Dunn quit and Chuck Slack took a job in Oklahoma City and we disbanded our group.

Gene soon found a couple of other Guthrie players his own age and they formed a trio called "The Charlatans," with Gene on fiddle, Joel Melton, guitar and Don Kelley on bass. They wrote much of their own material and sounded very good with tight three-part harmony. They stayed active and were in good demand around Guthrie and Oklahoma City. The Charlatans did a studio recording of their original songs they distributed and sold at their gigs. Bands come and bands go and The Charlatans became history by Kelly leaving to play in a rock and roll band.

Charlatans: Don, Gene, Joel

Gene and Joel then joined a group called "Crossfire" from Oklahoma City. They played weekly at the Cimarron Steakhouse in Oklahoma City for more than two years. This group included Gene, Joel, Roger Mashore, bass, Billy Perry, banjo. Crossfire also played a large variety of music and opened shows for the likes of George Jones, Lorrie Morgan, The Whites and the Dixie Chicks, all professional road personalities and Grand Ole Opry stars.

Gene took a job as editor of the *Athens Daily Review* newspaper in 1992 and moved to Texas. He soon found a guitarist and bass player, and they had an instant meld as a group. Dave Powell on guitar and Dave Davis, bassist, with Gene formed "Wild Oats," and they became quite active around Texas. With Mike Gray on horn they recorded a studio album titled "Wild Oats." The selection of songs had great variety including some songs Gene had co-written with The Charlatans. They later added Kirk Overmoe, on keyboards, Tom Konrad, saxophone, and Richard Haynie, drums, playing many private parties around Dallas and shows in Texas. The addition of the horn and keyboards allowed Wild Oats to expand its repertoire to include many jazz and Broadway tunes.

Gene formed "Wild Oats" with Dave Powell, right, on guitar, and Dave Davis on bass. Their country band became quite active around Texas.

Gene became active in teaching music from his home. He had several guitar and fiddle students. One of his students was a beautiful young lady, Stacy Dodd, who shared the same enthusiasm as Gene in the desire to learn to play fiddle. In a couple of years, Stacy developed an interest in Texas Style Contest fiddling, something Gene had little interest in playing. He arranged to send her to a teacher in Dallas.

Gene did not charge Stacy for any of the lessons, saying it was payback to Rolland who had given him so many lessons without charge. Stacy is fiddler in a country band that performs regularly in many Texas venues.

Gene with one of his students, Stacy Dodd, now a fiddler with a country band.

Gene's two high school student friends that gathered in our living room to practice music went on to greater things. Victor Fey, with great dedication and working long hours, as a medical student at Oklahoma University, became a medical doctor, with a very successful practice in Clinton, Oklahoma. W.K. "Kip" Stratton now lives in Austin, Texas, where he has become a very successful author, penning some five books and one book of poetry. Kip follows the music industry avidly and is an authority on bands and musicians. Expect an important book soon on this subject by Kip.

Gene is now Senior Writer for the Chickasaw Nation in Ada, Oklahoma, after spending many years as editor of newspapers in Oklahoma and Texas. He still plays a damn good fiddle!

I am extremely proud of all these young men and their accomplishments.

ABOUT THE AUTHOR

Lehmann examining the first off-set copy of the Guthrie Daily Leader *in 1965.*

More than forty years as a newspaper man qualifies Bill Lehmann to be a professional observer of people. He has lived life joyously surrounding himself with people, the great and the humble, the politically powerful, and the disenfranchised, the affluent and the impoverished, alcoholics, teetotalers, historians, artists, drifters, oil drillers, poets, preachers, and musicians. His life is richer for having known all those he writes about.

As newspaper editor in several Oklahoma towns and as publisher and General Manager of the *Guthrie Daily Leader*, Lehmann used his "tons of newsprint and barrels of ink" to advance issues, both grand and meek, to touch and improve the quality of life in his communities— Laredo, Ponca City, Pawhuska, and Guthrie.

At 85, the award-winning newspaper man is retired, but he has not ceased observing people, enjoying life, and pondering the past and the future...sometimes in the company of another old friend, Jack Daniels.

Lehmann is the author of two others books, *Blood on the Bluebonnets* and *An Okie from Muskogee Recalls Growing Up in the Dirty '30s.*

ABOUT THE BOOK

Bill Lehmann, an award-winning newspaper columnist, became a newspaperman straight out of high school and went on to become general manager and publisher of several other newspapers in Oklahoma. *After the Parade* is his recollection of the newspaper business, and of characters he got to know in Laredo, Ponca City, Pawhuska, and Guthrie during his days behind the news desk.

History has always been Lehmann's passion, so the book includes history he has written of places he's lived and characters he's met or is related to, more than one of them a murderer.

After his newspaper days, he was tempted to try his hand at becoming an oil man. The book contains some stories about the oil boom and bust in Oklahoma during the 1970s and 80s. Throughout all these years and endeavors, he was also a musician, having learned to play the guitar as a teenager and sitting in on several bands throughout his life at more than a few honkytonks in Oklahoma. The book includes character sketches of several musicians he met along the way.

After the Parade is a collection of stories and character sketches, of history and mystery, covering the 1950s Oklahoma into the next century. Lehmann's sense of humor and attention to detail make this book a great read for anyone interested in Oklahoma history during the latter half of the twentieth century.